Mesopotamian Goddess Nanāja

Olga Drewnowska-Rymarz

Mesopotamian Goddess Nanāja

Wydawnictwo AGADE

Warszawa 2008

This book has been published with the financial support
of the Faculty of Oriental Studies, University of Warsaw

On the cover:
Nanāja on the *kudurru* of Melišipak

AGADE
ul. Krasińskiego 18 m. 252, 01-581 Warszawa
e-mail: m.kapelus@uw.edu.pl
www.agade.com.pl

Warszawa 2008

ISBN 978-83-87111-41-0

TABLE OF CONTENTS

PREFACE

Ancient Mesopotamian religions present the variety of local beliefs. At first, it was a worship of forces of nature, and the personification of these forces and division of their domains led to the rise of a well-populated world of gods. Thanks to the existence of local pantheons, the Mesopotamian pantheon counted hundreds of gods and goddesses. Each ancient city-state venerated a guardian deity of the town, each ruler a guardian of his dynasty or his reign, each man and woman his own guardian deity. The conquest of a city or state could mean the incorporation of the "conquered" deities into the pantheon of the victors; occasionally, efforts were made to assimilate deities with similar attributes. The invaders therefore took over the culture and beliefs of the population they had conquered. Other phenomena also took place in Ancient Mesopotamia: the coexistence of culturally different peoples, who sooner or later became assimilated, resulted in the coexistence of gods and goddesses with similar attributes. Despite the fact that certain peoples worshipping a given divinity disappeared from the eye of history, the object of their worship continued to exist and was even capable of assimilating a similar deity of the other peoples or else was itself assimilated by another god.

God lists made an appearance in the Early Dynastic period. Rather than reflect attempts at syncretism in this period, these lists demonstrate the purely Sumerian practical approach to an understanding of the world. The Assyrians and Babylonians continued this work, incorporating the lists in their canons of school education.

To study a deity one needs to understand how its ancient worshippers perceived it. The various written documents that were composed and the few surviving examples of architecture and evidence from other domains of life and art make it possible to determine the role of a given divinity and place it in the religious system.

The objective of the present study is to give a comprehensive discussion of representations of the goddess Nanāja. An analysis of the role of this goddess and the perception that the ancient inhabitants of Mesopotamia had of her will aid in a better understanding of the entire pantheon of the Sumerians, Babylonians and Assyrians. Following the example set by authors of other monographs of deities, I have analyzed cuneiform sources, which contain mentions of Nanāja, coming from many ancient cities of Mesopotamia and representing very different literary genres. To achieve a clearer picture I have refrained from chronologically dividing the material into millennia or geographically into centers where the goddess was worshipped. Instead, I have grouped together texts either of the same genre or which close thematically, reflecting specific aspects under which Nanāja was venerated.

The Introduction contains a discussion of the present state of knowledge regarding this goddess, as well as a description and characteristic of the texts in which her name appears. I have also presented the graphy of her name and theories concerning Nanāja's origins.

The first part of the study is constituted by documents attesting the worship of Nanāja: records of offerings made to the goddess, inscriptions concerning her newly erected or renovated temples, lists of temples as well as year formulas. I have also discussed priests of Nanāja, rituals dedicated to this goddess and personal names incorporating the Nanāja element, evidenced over the millennia.

The texts mentioning Nanāja discussed in successive chapters are grouped around the following themes: magic and oracles, hymns and prayers, love lyrics, lamentations, *kudurru* and letters.

Each of the chapters ends with a brief summary intended as an attempt at defining Nanāja's role in each category of documents. The study closes with an overall summary. I have also added an appendix in which I have reviewed the existence of the cult of Nanāja in territories peripheral to Mesopotamia proper.

The present book is an extended version of my doctoral thesis submitted to the Faculty of Modern Languages at Warsaw University in 1999. I am particularly grateful to Prof. Krystyna Łyczkowska who supervised my work on the dissertation. I would also like to thank Prof. Edward Lipiński, who suggested the subject and whose candid remarks were frequently instrumental in shaping my views. Special words of thanks go to my Master, Prof. Jan Braun, for his assistance and continued education over the years, not the least for teaching me to be patient, a trait no philologist can do without.

My grateful acknowledgements also go to Dr. Bram Jagersma, as well as Dr. Marek Stępień and the staff of the Faculty of Mathematics of Warsaw University for allowing me access to their database on the Ur III period.

The present study goes against today's trend of presenting entire local pantheons,[1] for it considers a single deity in a diachronic approach. Despite being slightly *passé* in this respect, it nonetheless provides a picture of the deity that can be obtained only through a thorough analysis of a variety of texts.

Nanāja is one of the few goddesses of the Ancient Near Eastern pantheon whose cult lasted into the era of the Roman imperial conquests. She bore the same name throughout this time. She did not appear until the Ur III period when she became a second embodiment of the goddess Inanna. Continuously distinguished from her in the first millennium BC, Nanāja nonetheless assimilated herself with the goddess Ištar. She took over from Ištar and her worship outlasted the fall of Babylon and spread both to the east and to the west of Mesopotamia proper.

A study of texts connected with Nanāja should help in explaining the still elusive processes of syncretism occurring between deities and the opposite phenomena when despite similarities in attributes deities retain their separate identities.

[1] W. Sallaberger, *Der kultische Kalender der Ur III-Zeit*, Berlin 1993; G. Selz, *Untersuchungen zur Götterwelt des altsumerischen Stadtstaates von Lagaš*, Philadelphia 1995; Th. Richter, *Untersuchungen zu den lokalen Panthea Süd- und Mittelbabyloniens in altbabylonischer Zeit*, AOAT 257, Münster 1999; P.-A. Beaulieu, *The Pantheon of Uruk during the Neo-Babylonian Period*, CM 23, Leiden 2003.

ABBREVIATIONS

AAN = Anthroponymie et Anthropologie de Nuzi – see E. Cassin, J. J. Glassner

AAS = *Archives administratives sumériennes* – see J.-P. Grégoire

AbB = Altbabylonische Briefe in Umschrift und Übersetzung
10 – see F. R. Kraus
12 – see W. H. van Soldt

ABIM = Altbabylonische Briefe des Iraq Museums
1 – see A. Al-Zeebari

ABL = *Assyrian and Babylonian Letters belonging to the Kouyunjik Collection of the British Museum* (Chicago 1892-1914) – see R. F. Harper

ABRT = *Assyrian and Babylonian Religious Texts*
I – see J. A. Craig

AfK = *Archiv für Keilschriftforschung* (Berlin 1924-1925)

AfO = *Archiv für Orientforschung* (Berlin 1926 ff.)

AGE = *Akkadische Götterepitheta* – see K. Tallqvist

AHw = *Akkadisches Handwörterbuch* (Wiesbaden 1959-1981) – see W. von Soden

AION = *Annali dell'Istituto Universitario Orientale de Napoli* (Napoli 1959 ff.)

AJSL = *American Journal of Semitic Languages and Literatures* (Chicago 1895-1941)

ANET Suppl. = *The Ancient Near East Supplementary Texts and Picture relating to the Old Testament* – see J. B. Pritchard

AnOr = Analecta Orientalia
7 and 19 – see N. Schneider

ANRW = *Aufstieg und Niedergang der römischen Welt*
II 18/4 – see M. Gawlikowski

AO = tablets in the collections of the Musée du Louvre (Antiquités orientales)

AOAT = Alter Orient und Altes Testament
5/1 and 5/2 = LAS – see S. Parpola
233 – see D. R. West

247 = Fs Röllig – see B. Pongratz-Leisten, H. Kühne, P. Xella (eds)
253 = Fs Römer – see M. Dietrich, O. Loretz (eds)
257 – see Th. Richter
291 – see R. da Riva

AoF = *Altorientalische Forschungen* (Berlin 1974 ff.)
ArOr = *Archív Orientální* (Praha 1929 ff.)
ARRIM = *Annual Review of the Royal Inscriptions of Mesopotamia Project* (Toronto 1983 ff.)
AS = Assyriological Studies
16 = Studies Landsberger – see H. G. Güterbock, Th. Jacobsen (eds)
27 = Studies Biggs – see M. T. Roth *et al.* (eds)

Ash. = tablets in the collections of the Ashmolean Museum, Oxford
ASJ = *Acta Sumerologica* (Hiroshima 1979 ff.)
AUCT = Andrews University Cuneiform Texts
1 and 2 – see M. Sigrist
3 – see M. Sigrist, C. Gavin

AUWE = Ausgrabungen in Uruk-Warka. Endberichte
5 and 11– see E. Gehlken
8 – see K. Kessler
23 – see A. Cavigneaux, R. M. Boehmer

BA = Beiträge zur Assyriologie und semitischen Sprachwissenschaft
5/5 – see K. D. Macmillan

BaghForsch = Baghdader Forschungen
16 – see B. Pongratz-Leisten

BaghM = *Baghdader Mitteilungen* (Berlin 1960 ff.)
BBSt = *Babylonian Boundary Stones* – see L. W. King
BE = Babylonian Expedition of the University of Pennsylvania, Series A: Cuneiform Texts
VI/2 – see A. Poebel
VIII/1 – see A. T. Clay
IX – see H. Hilprecht, A. T. Clay
X – see A. T. Clay

Bib. Mes. = Bibliotheca Mesopotamica
24 – see D. B. Weisberg
BIN = Babylonian Inscriptions in the Collection of J. B. Nies
I and III – see C. E. Keiser
II – see C. E. Keiser, J. B. Nies
BiOr = *Bibliotheca Orientalis* (Leiden 1934/44 ff.)
Birmingham = *Catalogue of Cuneiform Tablets in Birmingham City Museum, Neo-sumerian Texts from Drehem*
I – see P. J. Watson
BJRL = *Bulletin of the John Rylands Library of Manchester* (Manchester 1903 ff.)
BM = tablets in the collections of the British Museum, London
BMECCJ = *Bulletin of the Middle Eastern Culture Center in Japan*
BR = *Aus dem babylonischen Rechtsleben*
1-4 – see J. Kohler, F. E. Peiser
BRM = Babylonian Records in the Library of J. Pierpont Morgan
I, II, IV – see A. T. Clay
BSGW = Berichte der Sächsischen Akademie der Wissenschaften
58 – see H. Zimmern
BSOAS = *Bulletin of the School of Oriental and African Studies* (London 1917 ff.)
BT = Babylonische Texte
1-4, 5, 6A, 7, 8-9 – see J. N. Strassmaier
6B – see E. T. A. Evetts
BWL = *Babylonian Wisdom Literature* – see W. G. Lambert
CAD = *The Assyrian Dictionary of the Oriental Institute of the University of Chicago*
Catalogue EPHE = *Catalogue École Pratique des Hautes Études* – see J.-M. Durand
Cat. = *Catalogue of the Babylonian Tablets in the British Museum*
II – see J.-M. Durand
CBS = tablets in the collections of the University Museum of the University of Pennsylvania, Philadelphia (Catalogue of the Babylonian Section)

C.I.A. = *Corpus Inscriptionum Atticarum*

CLAM = *The Canonical Lamentations of Ancient Mesopotamia* – see M. E. Cohen

CM = Cuneiform Monographs

7 – see I. L. Finkel, M. J. Geller

19 – see A. Cavigneaux, F. N. H. Al-Rawi

23 – see P.-A. Beaulieu

CNB = *Contrats néo-babyloniens* – see G. Contenau

Copenhagen = tablets in the collections of the National Museum, Copenhagen

CRRAI = Compte rendu de la ... Rencontre Assyriologique Internationale

17 – see A. Finet (ed.)

35 – see M. de Jong Ellis (ed.)

47 – see M. Parpola, R. M. Whiting (eds)

CT = Cuneiform Texts from Babylonian Tablets in the British Museum

22 – see R. C. Thompson

25, 26, 33 – see L. W. King

35 – see A. Leeper

36 – see C. J. Gadd

49 – see D. A. Kennedy

55, 56, 57 – see T. G. Pinches

CTNMC = Cuneiform Texts in the National Museum Copenhagen – see Th. Jacobsen

DDD = *The Dictionary of Deities and Demons in the Bible* – see K. van der Toorn

EAMES = tablets in the Wilberforce Eames Babylonian Collection in the New York Public Library – see L. Oppenheim

Emar = *Emar. Recherches au pays d'Aštata*

VI/4 – see D. Arnaud

Eršemma = *Sumerian Hymnology: The Eršemma* – see M. E. Cohen

ESP = *The Earliest Semitic Pantheon. A Study of the Semitic Deities attested in Mesopotamia before Ur III* – see J. J. M. Roberts

Ešh = *'Herzberuhigungsklagen'. Die Sumerisch-akkadischen Eršahunga-Gebete* – see S. M. Maul

FAOS = Freiburger Altorientalische Studien

2 – see B. Kienast

4 – see G. J. P. McEwan

18 – see K. Volk

Fs Falkenstein = *Heidelberger Studien zum Alten Orient. Adam Falkenstein zum 17. September 1966*, Wiesbaden 1967.

Fs Mikasa – see M. Mori, H. Ogawa, M. Yoshikawa (eds)

Fs Röllig = AOAT 247 – see B. Pongratz-Leisten, H. Kühne, P. Xella (eds)

GAG = *Grundriss der akkadischen Grammatik* – see W. von Soden

GCCI = *Goucher College Cuneiform Inscriptions*

I and II – see R. P. Dougherty

HdO = Handbuch der Orientalistik

33 – see B. H. L. van Gessel

HUCA = *Hebrew Union College Annual* (Cincinnati 1924 ff.)

IB = tablets in the collections of the Pontificio Istituto Biblico, Roma

IM = tablets in the collections of the Iraq Museum, Baghdad

IRSA = *Inscriptions royales sumériennes et akkadiennes* – see E. Sollberger, J.-R. Kupper

Isin = Isin – Išan Baḫrīyāt

IV – see B. Hrouda

JAC = *Journal of Ancient Civilisations* (Changchun 1986 ff.)

JAOS = *Journal of the American Oriental Society* (New Haven – Ann Arbor 1843 ff.)

JCS = *Journal of Cuneiform Studies* (New Haven 1947 ff.)

JEOL = *Jaarbericht van het Vooraziatisch-Egyptisch Genootschap "Ex Oriente Lux"* (Leiden 1933 ff.)

JkF = *Jahrbuch für kleinasiatische Forschungen* (Heidelberg 1950 /1951 ff.)

JNES = *Journal of Near Eastern Studies* (Chicago 1942 ff.)

K = tablets in the Kouyunjik collection of the British Museum

KAJ = *Keilschrifttexte aus Assur juristischen Inhalts* – see E. Ebeling

KAR = *Keilschrifttexte aus Assur religiösen Inhalts*
I and II – see E. Ebeling
KAV = *Keilschrifttexte aus Assur verschiedenen Inhalts* – see O. Schroeder
KB = Keilinschriftlische Bibliothek
6/2 – see P. Jensen
KBo = Keilschrifftexte aus Boghazköi
XII – see H. Otten
LAS = *Letters from Assyrian Scholars to the Kings Esarhaddon and Assurbanipal* – see S. Parpola = AOAT 5
LB = tablets in the Liagre Böhl Collection, Leiden
LIMC = Lexicon Iconographicum Mythologiae Classicae
VIII/2 – see M. Gawlikowski
LKA = *Literarische Keilschrifttexte aus Assur* – see E. Ebeling
LKU = *Literarische Keilschrifttexte aus Uruk* – see A. Falkenstein
MAOG = *Mitteilungen der Altorientalischen Gesellschaft* (Leipzig 1925-1943)
Maqlû = see G. Meier
MARI = Mari, Annales de Recherches Interdisciplinaires
MDP = Mémoire de la délégation en Perse
VI and X – see V. Scheil
XXXVII – see G. Le Rider
MIO = *Mitteilungen des Instituts für Orientforschung* (Berlin 1953 ff.)
MLC = tablets in the collections of the J. Pierpont Morgan Library
MSL = Materialien zum sumerischen Lexikon
4 – see B. Landsberger
MVAG = Mitteilungen der Vorderasiatisch-Aegyptischen Gesellschaft (Berlin – Leipzig 1896 ff.)
2/II – see P. Rost
MVN = Materiali per il vocabulario neosumerico
XIII – see M. Sigrist, J. Owen, G. D. Young
XIV – see F. Yıldız, H. Waetzold, H. Renner (eds)
XVIII – see M. Molina

N.A.B.U. = *Nouvelles Assyriologiques Brèves et Utilitaires* (Paris 1987 ff.)
NBC = tablets in the Nies Babylonian Collection, Yale University
NCBT = tablets in the Newell Collection of Babylonian Tablets, Yale University
NPN = Nuzi Personal Names – see J. J. Gelb, P. M. Purves, A. A. MacRae
OBT = *Old Babylonian Tablets*
IV – see S. Greengus
OECT = Oxford Editions of Cuneiform Texts
I – see S. Langdon
IV – see P. E. van der Meer
VI – see S. Langdon
IX and X – see G. J. P. McEwan
OIP = Oriental Institute Publications
2 – see D. D. Luckenbill
43 – see Th. Jacobsen
57 – see I. J. Gelb
OLA = Orientalia Lovaniensia Analecta
40 – see A. R. George
OrChr = *Oriens Christianus* (Wiesbaden 1901 ff.)
PBS = Publication of the Babylonian Section, University Museum, University of Pennsylvania
II/1 – see A. T. Clay
VIII/2 – see E. Chiera
PDT = *Die Puzriš-Dagan Texte der Istanbuler Archäologischen Museen*
I – see M. Çig, M. Kızılyay, A. Salonen
II – see T. Gomi, F. Yıldız
PIOL = Publications de l'Institut Orientaliste de Louvain
19 – see H. Sauren
PRU = Le Palais royal d'Ugarit
IV – see F. A. Schaeffer
PSBA = Proceedings of the Society of Biblical Archaeology
PSD = The Pennsylvania Sumerian Dictionary (electronic)

PTS = tablets in the collection of the Princeton Theological Seminary
R = *The Cuneiform Inscriptions of Western Asia*
III – see G. Smith
V – see T. Pinches
RA = *Revue d'Assyriologie et d'Archéologie Orientale* (Paris 1886 ff.)
RGTC = *Répertoire géographique des textes cunéiformes*, Tübinger Atlas des Vorderen Orients. Beih.
5 – see K. Nashef
8 – see R. Zadok
RIM = *Royal Inscriptions of Mesopotamia* (*E* = *Early Periods; B* = *Babylonian Periods; A* = *Assyrian Periods*)
RIMA 3 – see A. Kirk Grayson
RIMB 2 – see G. Frame
RIME 4 – see G. Frayne
RlA = *Reallexikon der Assyriologie und vorderasiatischen Archäologie*, Berlin 1928 ff.
Rm. = tablets in the collections of the British Museum (Rassam)
Rochester – see M. Sigrist
ROM = tablets in the collections of the Royal Ontario Museum
RS = field numbers of the tablets excavated at Ras Shamra
RSO = *Rivista degli studi orientali* (Roma 1907 ff.)
SAA = State Archives of Assyria
II – see S. Parpola, K. Watanabe (eds)
III – see A. Livingstone
IV – see I. Starr (ed.)
VII – see F. M. Fales, J. N. Postgate (eds)
IX and X – see S. Parpola
SAAB = *State Achives of Assyria Bulletin* (Padova 1987 ff.)
SAAS = State Archives of Assyria Studies
XV – see P. Lapinkivi
SACT = Sumerian and Akkadian Cuneiform Texts in the Collection of the World Heritage Museum of Illinois
1 – see Sh. T. Kang
SAHG = *Sumerische und akkadische Hymnen und Gebete* – see A. Falkenstein, W. von Soden

SAKAZ = *Die sumerischen und akkadischen Königsinschriften der altbabylonischen Zeit*
I and II – see I. Kärki
SBH = *Sumerisch-babylonische Hymnen nach Thontafeln griechischer Zeit* – see G. Reisner
SCCNH = Studies on the Culture and Civilization of Nuzi and the Hurrians
6 – see M. P. Maidman
SEG = J. J. Hondius *et al.* (eds), *Supplementum Epigraphicum Graecum*
SET = *Sumerian Economic Texts from the Third Ur Dynasty* – see T. B. Jones, J. W. Snyder
Si = field numbers of the tablets excavated at Sippar
SKFZ = *Die sumerischen Königsinschriften der frühaltbabylonischen Zeit* – see I. Kärki
SLB = Studia ad tabulas cuneiformes collectas a F. M. Th. de Liagre Böhl pertinentia
1/2 – see W. F. Leemans
SLTNi = *Sumerian Literary Texts from Nippur in the Museum of the Ancient Orient at Istanbul* – see S. N. Kramer
SMS = Syro-Mesopotamian Studies
4/3 – see W. Heimpel
SNAT = *Selected Neo-Sumerian Administrative Texts from the British Museum* – see T. Gomi, S. Sato
SpTU = *Spätbabylonische Texte aus Uruk* (Berlin)
I – see H. Hunger
II and III – see E. von Weiher
S.R.A.A. = Silk Road Art and Archaeology
StOr = Studia Orientalia
STT = *The Sultantepe Tablets*
I – see O. R. Gurney, J. J. Finkelstein
II – see O. R. Gurney, P. Hulin
Studies Hallo = *The Tablet and the Scroll. Near Eastern Studies in Honor of W. W. Hallo* – see M. E. Cohen, D. C. Snell, D. B. Weisberg (eds)

Studies Sjöberg = DUMU E_2-DUB-BA-A, *Studies in Honor of A. W. Sjöberg* – see H. Behrens *et al.* (eds)
ŠL = *Šumerisches Lexikon* – see A. Deimel
Šurpu – see E. Reiner
TCL = Textes cunéiformes, Musée du Louvre
I = TC I – see F. Thureau-Dangin
II = TC II – see H. de Genouillac
V = TEO – see H. de Genouillac
X and XI – see Ch.-F. Jean
XII and XIII – see G. Contenau
TCND = *Testi cuneiformi neo-sumerici da Drehem* – see A. Archi, F. Pomponio
TCS = Texts from Cuneiform Sources
II – see R. D. Biggs
TD = *Tablettes de Dréhem* – see H. de Genouillac
TEO = *Textes économiques d'Oumma de l'époque d'Our* – see H. de Genouillac
TIM = Texts from the Iraq Museum
7 – see D. O. Edzard
TLB = Tabulae Cuneiformes a F. M. Th. de Liagre Böhl collectae
I – see W. F. Leemans
II – see J. J. van Dijk
TPTS = *Tablettes du Princeton Theological Seminary. Epoque d'Ur III* – see M. Sigrist
TRAB = *Textes réligieux assyriens et babyloniens* – see F. Martin
TRU = *Le temps des rois d'Ur* – see L. Legrain
TSBA = Transactions of the Society of Biblical Archaeology (London 1872-1886)
TUAT = Texte aus der Umwelt des Alten Testaments
II/2 – see W. Farber *et al.*
II/5 – see W. H. Ph. Römer, K. Hecker
UCLM = tablets in the collections of the R. H. Lowie Museum of Anthropology of the University of California at Berkeley

UCP = University of California Publications in Semitic Philology
    IX/2 – see H. F. Lutz
UE = Ur Excavations. Publications of the Joint Expedition of the British Museum and the Museum of the University of Pennsylvania to Mesopotamia
    X – see L. Legrain
UET = Ur Excavations, Texts
    III – see L. Legrain
    IV and V – see H. Figulla
    VI/2 – see C. J. Gadd, S. N. Kramer
    IX – see D. Loding
UIOM = tablets in the collections of the University of Illinois Oriental Museum
UM = tablets in the collections of the University Museum of the University of Pennsylvania, Philadelphia
UVB = Vorläufiger Bericht über die von der Notgemainschaft der Deutschen Wissenschaft
    IX – see A. von Nöldecke, A. Falkenstein, A. von Haller, H. Heinrich, H. J. von Lenzen
    XVIII – see H. J. von Lenzen, A. von Haller, J. J. van Dijk, E. Strommenger
VA = tablets in the collections of the Staatliche Museem zu Berlin, Vorderasiatische Abteilung
VAB = Vorderasiatische Bibliothek
    4 – see S. Langdon
VAS = VS
VAT = tablets in the collections of the Staatlische Museen, Berlin
VS = Vorderasiatische Schriftdenkmäler der Königlichen/Staatlichen Museen zu Berlin
    I – see L. Messerschmidt, A. Ungnad
    V and VI – see A. Ungnad
    X – see H. Zimmern
    XV – see O. Schroeder
    XX – see L. Jakob-Rost, H. Freydank

W = field numbers of the tablets excavated at Warka
W.B. = tablets in the collections of the Oxford Museum (Weld-Blundell Collection)
WHM = tablets in the collections of the World Heritage Museum, University of Illinois
WO = *Die Welt des Orients* (Göttingen 1947/1952 ff.)
YBC = tablets in the Babylonian Collection, Yale University Library
YBT = YOS
YNER = Yale Near Eastern Researches (New Haven – London 1967 ff.)
10 – see P.-A. Beaulieu
YOS = Yale Oriental Series, Babylonian Texts
2 – see H. F. Lutz
3 – see A. T. Clay
4 – see C. E. Keiser
5 – see E. M. Grice
6 – see R. P. Dougherty
7 – see A. Tremayne
8 – see D. E. Faust
10 – see A. Goetze
11 – see J. J. van Dijk, A. Goetze, M. I. Hussey
12 – see S. I. Feigin
13 – see J. J. Finkelstein
14 – see S. D. Simmons
17 – see D. B. Weisberg
YOS Res. = Yale Oriental Series, Researches
I – see A. T. Clay
ZA = *Zeitschrift für Assyriologie Und Vorderasiatische Archäologie* (Leipzig – Berlin 1886 ff.)
84-2-11 = tablets in the collections of the British Museum

INTRODUCTION

STATE OF RESEARCH ON THE GODDESS NANĀJA[2]

Scholarly interest in Ancient Mesopotamian divinities outdates efforts to read cuneiform writing, yet it was not until 1880, 23 years after the decipherment of the signs, that G. Hoffmann included in his study a chapter devoted to the goddess Nanāja.[3] He collated in it the then available information concerning the goddess (originating mainly from outside Mesopotamia) and presented two of her attributes as goddess of war and nature (lunar deity). In mentioning that the goddess was known from cuneiform sources (he used the transcription Nanai), particularly as a Babylonian deity, he cited H. Rawlinson's opinion on distinguishing Nanāja from Ištar. Finally, he pointed out the closeness between the Indo-European word *nana* "mother" and the name of the goddess Nanāja.

In a corpus of Neo-Babylonian royal inscriptions published in 1912, S. Langdon believed Nanāja[4] to be a by-name of Tašmētum, although he also wrote: "Eigentlich der alte sumerische Name der Göttin von Erech." A year later he was more specific:[5] "Nanā is probably a case of vowel harmony for Ninā," adding that A. H. Sayce was the first discoverer of the identity between Ninā and Nanā. He went on to explain that the goddesses Nanā and Innini are usually treated separately in Babylonian religion despite representing the same theological aspect. A. Deimel in his *Pantheon Babylonicum* (Romae 1914, par. 2264, p. 187-188) referred to Nanāja as a divinity close to Ištar. He presented the graphy of the goddess' name, the texts (then available) in which she appeared, personal names with the Nanāja component in them and the names of deities whom Nanāja accompanied. He also

---

[2] In discussing the views on the subject of the goddess Nanāja over the course of more than two centuries, I have chosen to preserve the transcription of her name presented by the different authors.

[3] G. Hoffmann, Abhandlungen für die Kunde des Morgenlandes 7, Leipzig 1880, p. 130-161.

[4] S. Langdon, *Die Neubabylonische Königsinschriften*, Leipzig 1912, p. 305.

[5] S. Langdon, *Babylonian Liturgies*, Paris 1913, p. 105.

listed the temples dedicated to the goddess. In the summary, he emphasized that Nanāja is seldom mistaken for Inanna/Ištar. He also acknowledged that Nanāja is the Sumerian name of the consort of the god AG, the Semitic counterpart of which is Tašmētum.

In commenting on the Assyrian-Babylonian pantheon written down four hundred years after Christ, P. S. Landersdorfer mentioned in 1916 a homily said in AD 521 by the Syrian bishop and poet, Jacob of Sarug.[6] The bishop included in it a list of divinities, lines 71-76 running as follows:

> "Den Assyrern gab er (Satan) an Stelle der Götter die Elemente,
> So daß sie die Wärme und die Kälte anbeteten.
> Den einen Ort verführte er durch Nisrok, des Göttern des Krieges,
> An einem anderen stellte er Nanai als Göttin auf, um ihn in die Irre zu führen.
> Babel führte er in die Irre durch die Astrologie, welche voll ist von Weissagungen,
> Und lehrte dort die Magie, welche Wunder wirkt."

Also in 1916 M. Streck published his study devoted to Aššur-bani-apli. In the index of names of deities[7] the author brought together texts connected with Nanāja and emphasized Nanāja's difference from Ištar.

Ch.-F. Jean in his *Le milieu biblique avant Jésus-Christ* dedicated a few remarks to Nanāja.[8] He was also of the opinion that the goddess was seldom mistaken for Ištar. He went on to say that according to the traditions of Uruk, Nanāja was the daughter of Anu and wife of Nabû, while Ištar from Uruk had been sired by Sîn and became Anu's consort.

---

[6] P. S. Landersdorfer, *MVAG* 21 (1916), p. 109 ff. On Jacob of Sarug and his work "Homily on the Fall of the Idols", see B. van den Hoff, *OrChr* NS 5 (1915), p. 245-247 (quoted after P. S. Landersdorfer).
[7] M. Streck, *Assurbanipal...* III, Leipzig 1916, p. 757 (Nanâ, Nanai).
[8] Ch.-F. Jean, *Le milieu biblique avant Jésus-Christ*, Part II: *La littérature*, Paris 1923, p. 578.

Writing in the same year, 1923, the Reverend Dr. W. Szczepański discussed Babylonian civilization, and made it quite obvious in the fragment mentioning Nanāja[9] that he failed to see the difference between her and Inanna/Ištar (he gave her a key role in the myth about the descent of the goddess into the underworld and described her as a goddess of fertility and love, the spring goddess *Nanaj of Uruk*).

In his 1926 publication of the excavations at Dura-Europos,[10] F. Cumont indicated that the most important temple of the town was dedicated to Artemis, known locally as Nanāja.[11] Testifying to this was a dedicatory inscription and personal names with the Nanāja element. The author went on to explain that the ancient cult of Nanāja origin-nated from Uruk and that the goddess was "assimilée de bonne heure à Ishtar," which is not a clear definition in any case. Yet in connection with the transfer of her cult to Susa he gave an annual date: "Vers l'an 2295 avant Jésus-Christ, elle fut transportée à Suse..."[12] Cumont then emphasized the similarities between Nanāja and the two female divinities, Artemis and Ištar, in effect identifying Nanāja as a goddess of fertility and war and suggesting the meaning of her name as "mother".[13] He was persuaded that the form of the name was undoubtedly a children's word, one of the terms that are common to all languages as a designation for mother. He believed that the purely Semitic form Nanaï apparently came from Nana by adding the possessive *-i*.

In his *La religion des Palmyréniens*, Paris 1931, J. G. Février discussed the deity Nanāja (p. 99-102): "Le nom de Nanâ s'explique diffi-

---

[9] W. Szczepański, *Najstarsze cywilizacje Wschodu klasycznego. Babilon*, Warszawa – Lwów 1923, p. 16.

[10] F. Cumont, *Fouilles de Doura-Europos (1922-1923)*, Paris 1926.

[11] *Ibid.*, p. 196: "Seulement elle (Artémis) n'était pas en réalité l'Artémis grecque, mais la grande divinité indigène Nanaïa." See also p. 197-199.

[12] In a footnote Cumont provided references to, among others, V. Scheil, *RA* XI (1914), p. 183, where there is no information regarding this fact. Scheil referred to an article by F. Thureau-Dangin, *RA* XI (1914), p. 96, which explained in turn that Bēlet-Uruk, Ninni or Innana and Ištar were all one and the same deity, different from Nanāja. Scheil also drew attention to texts demonstrating the distinction between Ištar and Nanāja.

[13] F. Cumont, *op. cit.*, p. 198 and note 4.

cilement par le sémitique et il est possible que les gens d'Ourouk eux-mêmes aient emprunté à un autre peuple le culte de cette déesse."

In a footnote he referred to Zimmern, who "voit dans Nanaï l'appelation sumérienne et présémitique de l'Ishtar d'Ourouk." He then invoked P. de Lagarde (among others, "Armenische Studien" (1877) n. 1592), who believed the name of the goddess to be a Touran word.

In 1935 M. Rutten published a study concerning also the texts from Uruk.[14] The author emphasized the similar scope of authority attributed to Ištar and to Nanāja, and stated that the texts either confused the two goddesses or else distinguished between them assiduously.

In his work on the epithets of divinities K. Tallqvist represented the goddess[15] (together with her family) and collected from the then available sources all the definitions and epithets attributed to her. He assumed that Nanāja was a separate goddess from Uruk, not connected with Innin and Ištar.

In a study of Ur III period deities, published in 1939, N. Schneider became the first scholar to record the absence in this period of all personal names with the Nanāja element in spite of the well documented (by offerings) existence of the cult of this goddess.[16]

After World War II, studies of the Mesopotamian pantheon were arranged in encyclopedic form in *Wörterbuch der Mythologie.* D. O. Edzard writing on the goddess Nanāja[17] emphasized the unknown origins of the goddess and stated that Nanāja cannot be merely an evolutionary form of the goddess Inanna. He also briefly presented the cult of the goddess outside Mesopotamia. G. Dossin, who presented in 1967[18] the so-called "pantheon" of the town of Mari from the Ur III period, recognized the goddess Nanāja in the deity ^{d}N i n - N a - n a - a (he used the transcription "Nanâ" or "Nanāia.") He explained that it is a term to designate Ištar, drawing from her Sume-

[14] M. Rutten, *Contrats de l'époque Séleucide conservés au Musée du Louvre,* Paris 1935. About Nanāja on p. 48.
[15] K. Tallqvist, AGE, p. 385-386: Nanâ.
[16] N. Schneider, AnOr 19, p. 42.
[17] D. O. Edzard, "Nanaja" in: H. W. Haussig (ed.), *Wörterbuch der Mythologie* 1, Stuttgart 1965, p. 108.
[18] G. Dossin, *RA* LXI (1967), p. 97-104.

rian name Inanna ("une appellation d'Ištar, tirée de son nom sumérien Inanna").

In 1976, G. Azarpay published an article on the cult of Nanāja in Transoxania,[19] where her traces are observable until the Arab conquest. The author also presented the goddess from Mesopotamia and beyond. Azarpay was convinced that the worship of Nanāja was transferred from Mesopotamia to Susa already in the 3rd millennium BC; during the reign of the Seleucids she was the chief city goddess, although not mentioned on the coins of the period (according to Azarpay, she was worshipped only by the native population of Susa). The author also postulated (p. 539-540) "that in early medieval Transoxania, as in the ancient Near East, Nanâ's cult was a syncretic one, and that her qualities were there combined with those of a local Iranian goddess."

In his catalogue of Near Eastern Venus deities, published in 1982, W. Heimpel submitted a list of available references concerning the goddess Nanāja.[20] He found that already in the oldest texts there were indications positioning Nanāja as a Venus deity right from the beginning. Heimpel also analyzed the name of the goddess and her origins, pointing to the Aramaic culture.[21]

In studying the *sattukku* offerings made in the temple of Ninurta at Nippur, M. Sigrist considered Nanāja[22] as a goddess identified with Inanna in the rule of Sîn-iqīšam (1840-1836 BC). He also drew attention to the frequent mistaking of Nanāja with a goddess called Nin-si$_4$-an-na "Red Lady of the Heavens" (also associated with Inanna).

G. Leick's dictionary of Ancient Near Eastern mythology, published in 1991,[23] distinguishes at least two figures: Nana as a Sume-

---

19 G. Azarpay, *JAOS* 96 (1976), p. 536-542.

20 W. Heimpel, SMS 4/3, p. 15-17; bibliography arranged according to chronological periods, see *ibid.*, note 36.

21 It is difficult to accept this view, recently propounded also by M. Hutter. The coming of the Arameans to Mesopotamia is placed in the end of the 2nd and not the end of the 3rd millennium BC.

22 R. M. Sigrist, *Les* sattukku *dans l'Ešumeša durant la période d'Isin et Larsa*, Malibu 1984, p. 147.

23 G. Leick, *A Dictionary of Ancient Near Eastern Mythology*, London 1991, p. 124-125.

rian deity ("She appears in women's names since the Old Akkadian period. (...) She seems to have affinities with Inanna and Baba as a goddess of fertility") and Nanaya, also a Sumerian goddess, the daughter of An and sister of Utu, "known since the Ur III period (...) she seems to have been venerated as the planet Venus." The author went on to underscore the occasional impossibility of distinguishing between the two.

A similar distinction was presented by the authors of a textbook, D. B. Miller and R. M. Shipp:[24] Nanâ (Nana) – the Sumerian goddess of love, and Nanāya – Sumerian goddess of love and sensuality, often identified with Ištar.

An illustrated dictionary of gods, demons and symbols of ancient Mesopotamia[25] explains that together with Inanna from Uruk and her own daughter Kanisurra Nanaya formed a trinity of goddesses from Uruk in the Old Babylonian period. The authors cautiously suggest that she "seems to have shared some of the sexual aspects with Inana", while in the cultic texts her name was used "to denote more than just another aspect of Inana/Ištar."

M. Hutter connected Nanāja with the nomadic tribes of Syria and their cult.[26] He suggested the theory that Nanāja was the Venus deity of the nomads of the Syrian Desert and that she could be compared in this role to Inanna, also a Venus deity, but for the settled population of the Sumerian urban communities.

To date, the most extensive study devoted to the goddess Nanāja was presented by J. G. Westenholz.[27] In an article published in 1997, the author disputed the views that saw Nanāja as a manifestation of Ištar and identified her as a Venus deity, but foremost,

---

[24] D. B. Miller, R. M. Shipp, *An Akkadian Handbook*, Winona Lake 1996, p. 60.
[25] J. Black, A. Green, *Gods, Demons and Symbols of Ancient Mesopotamia. An Illustrated Dictionary*, London 1992 (the form *Nanaja*).
[26] See M. Hutter, *Religionen in der Umwelt des Alten Testaments* I, Stuttgart – Berlin – Köln 1996, p. 48 ff.; *idem*, „Die Religion nomadisierender Gruppen vom 3. bis zum 1. Jahrtausend v. Chr.", in: P. W. Haider, M. Hutter, S. Kreuzer (eds), *Religionsgeschichte Syriens. Von der Frühzeit bis zur Gegenwart*, Stuttgart – Berlin – Köln 1996, p. 95 ff.
[27] J. G. Westenholz, CM 7, p. 57-84.

she emphasized the impossibility of explaining the name and origins of this goddess. In her work (24 pages, 2 illustrations and a catalogue of Ur III period texts mentioning Nanāja), Westenholz presented the graphy of the goddess' name, her status and relations on the list of gods, the beginnings of her cult in the Ur III period. She went on to discuss Sumerian and Akkadian literary pieces of the 2nd millennium BC, in which Nanāja appeared as a goddess of love. This is followed with analyses of her cult in the Old Babylonian period (in centers like Uruk, Ur, Nippur, Isin, Larsa, Mari, Babilon and Kiš) and as seen in texts coming from the 1st millennium BC (Uruk, Babilon, Borsippa and Ašur). The author also discussed the spreading of Nanāja's cult to the east and west of Mesopotamia in the Hellenistic period, as well as evidence of her worship in the beginnings of our era.

The item "Nanaja" in RlA[28] gives the spelling of the goddess' name, her position on the list of gods, the nature and extent of her rule, places of cult, relations with Nabû and Ištar, and, most extensively, the manifestations of her cult (temples, temple staff, offerings, ceremonies, statues), the item ends with a collection of hymns devoted to Nanāja. The bibliography contains all the important references.

M. Stol also wrote the item "Nanea" in DDD, p. 1152-1155. There he used the transcription Nanēa or Nanea (also saying that in the earlier literature on the subject the transcription of Nanâ had also been used, but that the prevailing version today is Nanay or Nanaya). He refers to her as a goddess of erotic love originating from Uruk: "She was originally (and always remained) a goddess of Uruk...". He listed 15 sources in his list of references.

In his work on the local pantheons of southern and central Babylonia in the Old Babylonian period, Th. Richter[29] could not omit Nanāja. Discussing the main cult centers (Nippur, Isin, Uruk, Larsa and Ur) and the deities worshipped therein, he presented Nanāja and her relations with the other divinities (taking into consideration lists of gods as well as texts from everyday life). He emphasized that

---

[28] M. Stol, RlA IX, p. 146-151.
[29] Th. Richter, AOAT 257.

worshipped as the daughter of Inanna/Ištar in Ur, she was referred to in Uruk as the daughter of the Lord of the Heavens, Anu, or the moon god Nanna/Sîn. Richter believed it of paramount importance to explain the origins of the goddess, for in his opinion, in Uruk and Nippur, she had been made equal to Inanna/Ištar already in the Old Babylonian period. While this is evident only in the literary texts, says Richter, it cannot be excluded that the same genealogy of the goddesses could have influenced their identification. He considered as erroneous the commonly held opinion that Nanāja was not identified with Inanna/Ištar before the 1st millennium BC. Richter also pointed out that the separateness of the two goddesses in the cultic sphere had not been studied to date.

Edited in 2003 by Beaulieu, the pantheon of Uruk during the Neo-Babylonian period shows the author's opinion: "The syncretism between Inanna/Ištar and Nanaya was a basic tenet of Babylonian theology from very early times."[30] He gathered the texts from the Eanna archive and discussed first the paraphernalia, then the ornaments, clothing, offerings, also temples, prebends, personnel, ceremonies and toponyms connected with Nanāja, second goddess after Ištar in the local hierarchy of deities of Uruk in the 1st millennium BC.[31] The presented texts are preceded with a discussion of Nanāja starting with the III Dynasty of Ur. Beaulieu states that "by the end of Kassite rule, Nanaya's position in the theological system of Babylonia had undergone substantial modification, mainly regarding her association with the god Nabû and his wife Tašmētu. (...) Nanaya thus became the wife of Nabû alongside Tašmētu, with whom she was syncretized."[32]

The last study to be mentioned is an article by C. Ambos: "Nanaja – eine ikonographische Studie zur Darstellung einer altorientalischen Göttin in hellenistisch-partischer Zeit",[33] concerning representations of the goddess mainly from territories outside Mesopotamia.

---

30 P.-A. Beaulieu, CM 23, p. 186.
31 *Ibid.*, p. 189-216.
32 *Ibid.*, p. 185-186.
33 C. Ambos, *ZA* 93/2 (2003), p. 231-272.

A review of opinions on the subject of Nanāja reveals the mysteriousness that seems to surround her. Not only is there no evidence for her origins, but the elusive issue of the syncretism of deities does not establish a clear distinction between gods, not to mention the scope of their powers. A discussion of texts devoted to Nanāja and mentioning her could be a step toward understanding her true nature. Some of the stereotypes referring to this goddess will perhaps be rejected based on such a detailed analysis and our knowledge of Nanāja will surely be broadened considerably.

CHARACTERISTIC OF THE SOURCES (chronology of the texts)

The goddess Nanāja appears in many different texts. The currently known Babylonian myths and epic stories are the sole exception, for they never mention even her name.

The lists of divinities contain the name of Nanāja beginning with the so-called Weidner list, that is, the period of Ur III. These lists, which were copied or created in different centers (Kiš, Aššur, Babilon, Nippur, Sultantepe, Mari, Emar, Niniveh) over a period of almost two millennia, contained her name in unchanged form. Naturally, the presence of a goddess's name on a list of divinities (for example, copied as a school exercise) is no evidence of the worship of Nanāja in such centers like Mari or Emar. The lack of offerings made to this goddess is decisive proof in this case.

Lists of offerings made to Nanāja are indeed the oldest manifestation of her worship. They provide the proof necessary to show that Nanāja was worshipped at least from the reign of king Šulgi, that is, from the 21st century BC. The earliest texts mentioning Nanāja originate from the 33rd year of his reign. The fact that the goddess only then started to be mentioned on the lists of offerings could have something to do with the ruler's conquests. As far as it is known, Šulgi led expeditions to Kurdistan, as well as to Elam lying in the opposite direction. It means that the cult of the goddess could have been borrowed from either of these two regions. Another possibility is a renaissance of the worship of this pre-Sumerian deity of Uruk; this will be discussed in more detail in the part of this study devoted to theories concerning the origins of the goddess.

Worship of the goddess in the times of the III Dynasty of Ur was not restricted to a variety of offerings being made to her. There were rituals and festivals held in her name. Statuettes were also cast for her, a fact confirmed in the texts. The fall of the III Dynasty of Ur did not coincide with an interruption or end of her cult. In the 20th century BC, Lipit-Eštar built for Nanāja a temple at Isin, and in the 19th century BC in Larsa, Sîn-iddinam made offerings to a variety of different deities, including Nanāja. His successors also made *sattukku* offerings to the goddess in the temple of Ninurta at Nippur.

The number of sources concerning buildings dedicated to the goddess starts to increase in the 19th century, but even so there is no direct evidence of offerings made to Nanāja for the next thousand years. The available texts reveal that figurines were cast in homage to her and were offered to her; there is also mention of her temples. Hence, it should be assumed that the offerings were made in these buildings. The term "property of the goddesses Ištar and Nanāja" appears in the economic texts of the 7th century BC and the following ages, providing evidence for the survival of the cult in terms of existing temples or chapels and observed rituals of offerings. Apart from Uruk also Sippar, Babylon and Borsippa continued to worship Nanāja.

The 19th century texts mentioning Nanāja are chiefly year formulas of the rulers of different Isin and Old Babylonian dynasties. In his year formula, Sîn-erībam (1832-1827 BC) of Uruk commemorated the casting of a figure of himself, subsequently offered to Nanāja; Irdanene (1816-1810 BC) ordered a statue of his father Anam to be offered to Nanāja.

The existence of statues of Nanāja is confirmed also in Neo-Babylonian texts. Thus, there seems to be yet another (apparent) hiatus in the evidence for the worship of Nanāja. It is lessened somewhat by surviving texts of another kind.

Statues of the goddess were set up in her temples. The oldest building inscription concerns a store called the Emeurur in Isin, constructed in the 20th century BC. Other temples were built by the 19th and 18th century rulers at Ur, Uruk, Larsa and Babylon. For a thousand years again a silence ensues in the sources on the cult buildings to Nanāja, not to be broken until the 7th century from when the next dated texts are known from Uruk and Borsippa. Yet in an inscription speaking of the restoration of the Eḫilianna, chapel of Nanāja in the Eanna complex, Aššur-aḫa-iddina attributes its construction to the Kassite king of Babylonia Nazi-Maruttaš (1323-1298 BC) and refers to Erība-Marduk, a ruler of Babylonia from a hundred years before him (769-761 BC) as its rebuilder. Accepting the content of this inscription in good faith, one is left with the knowledge that no evidence of the worship of Nanāja exists for the period between the 17th and 14th centuries and between the 13th and 8th centuries BC. Thus, the hiatus is somewhat less than originally assumed.

Documents referring to the activities of priests (of various ranks) of Nanāja also reflect a certain chronological hiatus. These texts originate successively from the 21st, 20th, 19th, 18th and 17th centuries BC, then fall silent for around fifty years before the fall of the Old Babylonian dynasty. The next sources appear with the end of the 11th century BC and continue until the end of Seleucid rule.

Another group of texts mentioning Nanāja are the rituals. The oldest is a ritual from Larsa, dated to the turn of the 19th century BC (from the times of king Rīm-Sîn), the next come from Neo-Assyrian and Late Babylonian times. The latest and most numerous ritual texts were written down in the Seleucid period.

As far as personal names containing the name of Nanāja are concerned, it is noteworthy that none come from the period of the III Dynasty of Ur. Despite documents assuring us of the existence of the cult of Nanāja already in this period, no known personal names stand in confirmation of this. In other words, the goddess could not have been very popular at the time, perhaps indicating that her worship had been imposed in Sumer. It thus seems more probable in this case that the cult was transferred from a foreign center.

Names connected with Nanāja do not appear until the Old Babylonian period and then only in a few cities (Sippar, Tell ed-Dēr, Dilbat, Kiš, Larsa, Ur and Babylon). The data from Uruk has yet to be studied, although it should be expected that the number of names of interest to us should be quite high. Even so, it is evident that in Larsa at the turn of the 19th century, during the reign of Rīm-Sîn, these names grow in number substantially.

There is no name with the Nanāja element evidenced for the Kassite period (the sole exception is a *kudurru* of the 12th century mentioning the princess Hannubat-Nanāja). For the Neo-Assyrian period the data reveals few names of this kind, but their number increases rapidly in Neo-Babylonian and Persian times. In terms of quantity, the names with the Nanāja element are comparable to those with the Inanna/Ištar element. At Uruk, however, the ratio of the names is 2:1 to Nanāja's disadvantage.

In magic spells (*Maqlû*) and purification spells (*Šurpû*), also in "releasing" spells *Namburbû*, Nanāja is merely mentioned. In first-millennium Assyria, the "hand of Nanāja" had the same power in female illnesses as the "hand of Ištar", while the goddess herself protected women from the demon Lamaštu.

A thousand years earlier she assisted in recovering male potency, as indicated by a group of texts known as the š a_3 . z i . g a spells.

Omina devoted to Nanāja are extremely rare. Only two texts of this kind are known (one is Old Babylonian, the other Kassite). Various other oath formulas clearly demonstrate the import carried by the name of this goddess.

A group of hymns devoted to Nanāja illustrate further aspects of the goddess. The oldest text, Sumerian, dates to the turn of the 21st century BC, the next text that is known is from the 19th century. An Akkadian hymn of Samsu-iluna, hence dating to the 18th century, refers to the astral aspect of the goddess. From the Old Babylonian period there is a small fragment of a hymn in which Nanāja's name appears three times.

The next texts come from the 8th and 7th centuries BC; hence there is once again a thousand-year-long hiatus in the hymnic pieces that does not mean, however, a significant break in Nanāja's cult.

Lyrical texts from the 19th and 17th centuries BC concerning ceremonies of sacred marriage mention the goddess Nanāja as a consort of either the king (next to Rīm-Sîn) or the god Mu'ati-Nabû. The Old Babylonian dialogue between lovers from Sippar shows Nanāja as the protectress of star-crossed lovers, while in the love spells from Isin she wields power over sexual desire and is capable of endowing women with it. In turn, the b a l b a l e songs composed for Nanāja present her as a model of femininity.

The 12th-century catalogue of song and hymn titles lists works addressed to Nanāja that were performed during a variety of ceremonies devoted to the goddess.

Another ritual text, also referring to the holy marriage, but recorded in the Seleucid period, presents Nanāja as the spouse of Nabû.

The next group of texts mentioning Nanāja consists of poetic works composed in the eme-sal dialect and recited by the *kalû* priests. These texts were created in the Old Babylonian period, but they are better known from copies made in Neo-Assyrian and Late Babylonian times. No b a l a g lamentations or e r š e m m a songs composed specially for Nanāja are known to date. It seems that in these works she appears only as a synonym of Inanna/Ištar. A similar impression can be drawn from a reading of š u i l l a pieces, and the epithets assigned to Nanāja are frequently reproduced. None of the e r š a h u n g a prayers were specially attributed to Nanāja, although she does appear as a divinity mediating between people and other gods.

From the 12th century BC there are as many as four *kudurru* acts mentioning Nanāja. One of these is further illustrated by an act of endowment by the goddess, where she is represented in relief carving. The next documents originate from the 9th and 8th centuries BC. Especially the last mentioned text provides numerous epithets and designations of the goddess.

A similar time gap appears in letters and other documents of daily life. From the Old Babylonian period there are merely four texts mentioning the goddess. From Neo-Babylonian times there are two texts. Many more letters mentioning Nanāja have come down to us from the Neo-Assyrian period.

The above-presented different literary genres, in which the name of Nanāja appears, are mutually complementary in testifying to the continuity of the cult of the goddess. The biggest time gap – seven hundred years (from the end of the Old Babylonian dynasty to the start of the 9th century BC) – appears in the lists of offerings, ritual texts, letters and hymns to the goddess. Sources about statues offered to the goddess and the activities of the priests of this cult also fall silent during this period. Perhaps one should also classify here the building inscriptions, disregarding the one in which Aššur-aḫa-iddina mentions as a founder of Nanāja's temple a Kassite king of the turn of the 14th century BC. Additionally, there are numerous *kudurru* documents mentioning Nanāja going back to the Kassite period. No personal names containing the Nanāja element are known from this period, although a princess from one of the *kudurru* inscriptions bears a name with Nanāja in it.

As far as lyrical texts are concerned, they, too, are known from the Isin-Larsa, Old Babylonian and Neo-Assyrian periods.

Thus, the absence of evidence for the worship of Nanāja occurs between the end of the Old Babylonian period and the 14th century BC (with one indirect mention) and then once again between the end of the 12th century BC and the middle of the 9th. The first gap corresponds to the destruction of Babylon in 1595 by the Hittites, followed by Kassite rule in Babylonia. The stability of their position and their taking over of tradition becomes evident with regard to the worship of Nanāja only two centuries later in *kudurru* documents (typical of the period), but one can hardly deny that the number of these documents – as also the status of the goddess – is high. These two centuries are referred to as the "dark ages" because of the small number of sources.

The fall of the Kassites in 1157 BC did not bring about a break in the cult of Nanāja. A ruler from the Isin dynasty, who seized power in Babylonia, Nabû-kudurri-uṣur (1124-1103 BC) called Nanāja the goddess of the land of Namar. The next decline in sources between the end of the 12th century and the middle of the 9th should be put down to the general chaos in Babylonia and the attacks by the nomadic Sutu tribes and Arameans. A *kudurru* act from the reign of Marduk-zākir-šumi (mid 9th century BC) confirms the connection between the goddess and Nabû. A document from Borsippa written a hundred years later shows Nanāja as the benefactor of various possessions for the priest of the temple of Eanna, thus it accords her a high position in the Uruk pantheon. A Sumerian-Akkadian hymn to Nanāja, known both in Assyria and Babylonia, confirms her equal status with Ištar.

Other texts representing different genres also confirm the cult of Nanāja in Babylonian and Assyrian territory. Progressing aramaisation did not hinder the expansion of her cult; on the contrary, the worship of Nanāja spread well beyond the borders of Mesopotamia.

THE NAME OF NANĀJA (ITS TRANSCIPTION AND READING)

Personal names in the Ancient Near East are most often theophoric, referring to the form of the worshipped deity. On this basis it is possible to judge the origins of the bearer of a name. In other words, the name of a deity in a personal name indicates the individual's affiliation to a given tribe – followers of this divinity.

The case is different for god's names. The meaning of the name of a god could be connected with his domain (e.g. An, Ki, Enlil, Enki-Ea, Aššur) or not necessarily at all. Generally speaking, it may be said that names represented ideographically relate to the older, Sumerian deities and in later periods to the Akkadian divinities identified with them, although this rule cannot be applied uncritically. The name of the goddess Nanāja in the available sources always appears in syllabic notation: ^{d}Na-na-a or (much more seldom) ^{d}Na-na-a-a.[34] As-

[34] I know of only one case of the transcription ^{d}na-na (Neo-Assyrian text from Dūr-Katlimmu), see K. Radner, *Die neusumerischen Texte aus Tell Šeḫ Hamad*, Berlin 2002, no. 32; nonetheless the transcription occurring in personal names is ^{d}na-na-a, see *ibid.*, p. 233 ff. I also know of no other record of the

suming that in principle the names of Sumerian deities were recorded with ideograms, the absence of such an ideogram in the case of Nanāja could be taken as evidence for the non-Sumerian origins of the goddess. Therefore, it seems only natural to make the connection between the name of Nanāja and the Semitic tongue of the Akkadians. Yet only the ending *-āj* (*-āy*), which is characteristic chiefly of Akkadian nominal forms and hypocoristic constructions created from foreign words,[35] could point to the Akkadian origins of the goddess. Even so, it is impossible to determine the meaning of the name in view of the root *nan-* which is not known in Akkadian.

One should recall what J. J. M. Roberts observed[36], that the ending *-a* was typical of many ancient Semitic deity names (e.g. Anda, Ab(b)a, Ay(y)a, Erra, Mamma, Nanna). On the other hand, in his *Assyrische Grammatik*, Berlin 1906, F. Delitzsch came to consider the ending *-a-a* as a form of notation for *-â*, *-âi* and *-a'* (§ 13).

An unpublished commentary to Weidner's list of divinities (BM 62741) provides the following analysis of the name of the goddess: [^{d}N] a . n a . a : NA : *na-bu-u*$_2$: A : *ši-i* [*šap*]-*lu-u*$_2$.[37] According to CAD, this should be understood as follows: "Nanâ (can be analyzed as) NA "to call" and A, feminine, suffix".[38] Hence, the name of the

---

goddess' name without the dingir determinative, see D. Schwemer, *ZA* 94/1 (2004), p. 59-79 (an Akkadian text from Hattuša), discussed on p. 98-99.

35 GAG, § 56p; for these in personal names, see H. Ranke, *Early Babylonian Personal Names*, Philadelphia 1905, p. 13; J. J. Stamm, *Die Akkadische Namengebung*, Leipzig 1939, p. 113 and K. Tallqvist, *Neubabylonische Namenbuch*, Helsingfors 1905, p. XXXII.

36 J. J. Roberts, ESP, p. 80 note 117.

37 A fragment of this text is cited, s.v. *šaplu* in CAD Š/1 477a 2. suffixed (sum. grammatical element) BM 62741, 13 (comm. to Weidner God List, courtesy W. G. Lambert). See also CAD Q 23b *qabû* 1a lex.: [A//*q*]*a-bu-u*$_2$ (in an explanation of parts of the name ^{d}Na-na-a) BM 62741, 14 (comm. to god list, courtesy W. G. Lambert).

38 This interpretation is also accepted by J. A. Black, *Sumerian Grammar in Babylonian Theory*, Rome 1984, p. 80. P.-A. Beaulieu, CM 23, p. 182, states: "This is an artificial Sumerian etymology of the name of the goddess, typical of late Babylonian hermeneutics, and with the apparent purpose of providing a philological etiology of the close relation between Nabû and

goddess would mean "The one who keeps on calling" or "The Calling [One]"[39] (assuming that the repeating of the root signifies an intensification of the action).

Nanāja also occurs in a variety of Hittite texts. In a story about Appu, the cattle breeder, the goddess is connected with the city of Kiššina (Kiš perhaps?) (KUB 24.8 IV 17), and her cult in Malitaškurija is referred to in a big single-column tablet KUB 48.105 (l. 42').[40] The text VAT 7461, obv. 19' speaks of Nanāja, who was offered two houses with 20 people in the city of Daškurija.[41] Also known are personal names with the goddess's name as a component, but these facts hardly constitute the basis for thinking that Nanāja originated from the territory of Asia Minor. The subject will be treated once again when considering theories on the origins of Nanāja.

The above-mentioned actions did not lead to an univocal explanation of the origins of the name of the goddess Nanāja. There are two possibilities assuming she was not Sumerian in origins: either her worship was taken over from the Proto-Euphratean substrate or else she was borrowed from another peoples. In either case the syllabic notation in recording her name could have served to denote her foreign origins. She was perceived as a separate deity, although she revealed ties with Inanna. Were the separate domains of the two so close that the worshipper adoring Inanna had the certainty that he was addressing Nanāja, too? It is difficult to decide the case today when all we have are some preserved cuneiform sources to help.

The name of the goddess has yet to be transcribed to the satisfaction of the various scholars. The earliest form of transcription is Nanâ (*inter alia*, A. Deimel, M. Streck, Ch.-F. Jean, M. Rutten, Th. Bauer).

Nanaya. Unless one sees Nanaya as a hypocoristic form of Inanna, the name appears to be neither Sumerian nor Akkadian."

39 See AHw 699b, s.v. *nabû* II = na_3.

40 See mentions of Nanāja in: V. Haas, *Geschichte der hethitischen Religion*, Leiden 1994, p. 397, 542, 565 and B. H. L. van Gessel, HdO 33, p. 324-325.

41 [*INA* ^{UR}]^{U}*Da-aš-ku-ri-ja A-NA* ^{d}*Na-na-ia* 2 E_2^{TUM} *ŠA*$_3$ 20 NA[M.RA]. This town may be connected with Taškul/rija, see RGTC 6, p. 410.

Scholars like C. F. Lehmann[42] and F. Delitzsch[43] attempted to explain the form of the transcription. Later authors also used the notation Nanâ (K. Tallqvist, E. Ebeling, A. Falkenstein), although in 1968 E. C. Kingsbury was using the form Nana'a. Other scholars did not standardize the spelling. R. D. Biggs was inclined to use the transcription Nanaya,[44] J. Black and A. Green did the same,[45] but M.-J. Seux,[46] E. Reiner,[47] W. W. Hallo[48] and M. E. Cohen[49] followed the customary form of Nanâ. On the contrary, B. R. Foster[50] preferred Nanay, while W. G. Lambert,[51] who used to use the transcription Nanai, turned to Nanāya in the end.[52] E. Matsushima's studies also reveal a slight change of notation from Nanaia[53] to Nanaja.[54] In his PhD dissertation on the deities of Mari, I. Nakata[55] used the form Na(n)nā/Na(n)nāya. The authors of *Texte aus der Umwelt des Altes Testament*, as also A. Livingstone[56] and M. Hutter in their most re-

---

42 C. F. Lehmann, *Šamaššumukin, König von Babylonien*, Leipzig 1892, p. 140.
43 F. Delitzsch, *Assyrische Grammatik*, Berlin 1906, § 13.
44 R. D. Biggs, TCS II, p. 20: "In view of the Greek and Aramaic transcriptions of the name (...) and such OB writings as ᵈNa-na-a-a ABIM 1, 27, 9, the transcription should be Nanāya instead of the conventional Nanâ."
45 J. Black, A. Green, *Gods, Demons and Symbols of Ancient Mesopotamia*, London 1992, p. 134.
46 M.-J. Seux, *Hymnes et prières aux dieux de Babylonie et d'Assyrie*, Paris 1976.
47 E. Reiner, *JNES* 33/2 (1974), p. 221-236.
48 W. W. Hallo, *BiOr* 23, 5/6 (1966), p. 239-247.
49 M. E. Cohen, *Sumerian Hymnology: The Eršemma*, Cincinnati 1981 and *idem*, *CLAM*.
50 B. R. Foster, *Before the Muses*, Berthesda 1993.
51 W. G. Lambert, *MIO* XII/2 (1966), p. 48-51.
52 W. G. Lambert, *AoF* 24 (1997), p. 158-162.
53 E. Matsushima, *Orient* XVI (1980), p. 133-148.
54 E. Matsushima, *ASJ* 10 (1988), p. 95-128.
55 I. Nakata, *Deities in the Mari Texts: Complete Inventory of all the Information on the Deities found in the published Old Babylonian Cuneiform Texts from Mari and Analytical and Comparative Evaluation thereof with regard to the Official and Popular Pantheons of Mari*, Columbia Univ. Ph. D. 1974, p. 371.
56 A. Livingstone, SAA III.

cent works[57] write the name of the goddess as Nanaja, while other authors of *Religionsgeschichte Syriens* (P. W. Haider and W. Pratscher) use first Nannaia and then Nanai. In reference to D. O. Edzard (item "Nanāja" in *Wörterbuch der Mythologie*, p. 108), A. W. Sjöberg[58] is consistent in making use of the transcription Nanāja. In his article in RlA IX, M. Stol professes the notation Nanāja, also C. Ambos,[59] while P.-A. Beaulieu[60] prefers Nanaya.

The form used in the present study is Nanāja, recognizing the Aramaic form of the name *nn'/nny*[61] with the added Semitic ending *-āja*. It should be noted that in Greek the name of the goddess was transcribed as *Nanaia/Nanai*.

HYPOTHESES ON THE ORIGINS OF THE GODDESS NANĀJA

The absence of an ideographic notation of the name of Nanāja and her relatively late appearance in the lists of offerings from the period of the III Dynasty of Ur are a contraindication to her Sumerian pedigree. Neither does her name appear to be Akkadian in origin (I have pointed out already the distinguishable Akkadian ending *-āj*, while the root *nan-* remains unidentified).

In 1991, in a private conversation with the present author, Prof. Karlheinz Deller suggested that the Elamite root *nan*(*n*)- (signifying "day/morning")[62] would indicate an Elamite origin. I have been unable to find any further data in confirmation of this theory.

I have already mentioned the possibility of the cult of Nanāja being borrowed sometime in the reign of Šulgi (2094-2047 BC). Starting with the 24th year of his rule, this king sent military expeditions against territories to the north and northeast of Ur. After long fighting he conquered the town of Simurrum in the north and Susa,

---

57 See above, note 26.

58 A. W. Sjöberg, *JCS* 29/1 (1977), p. 16-27.

59 C. Ambos, *ZA* 93/2 (2003), p. 231-272.

60 P.-A. Beaulieu, CM 23, p. 182 and *passim*.

61 2 Mac. 1, 13, 15.

62 W. Hinz, H. Koch, *Elamisches Wörterbuch* II, Berlin 1987 s.v. *nan* and R. Zadok, *The Elamite Onomasticon*, Napoli 1984, p. 30.

where he erected a temple to Inšušinak, the highest divinity of the Elamites. There is no proof, however, that Šulgi actually transferred the cult of Nanāja to Sumerian territory.

W. Heimpel pointed out the concurrence of the growing importance of the Aramaic factor in the population of Babylonia and the increased popularity of Nanāja's cult. Her worship developed later concurrently with the culture of the Arameans. Heimpel therefore suggested that the goddess could have been of Aramaic pedigree, explaining thus the form of her name (*-ay* is a feminine ending).[63] The issue of time coherence is fundamental to this theory, as in the end of the third millennium BC when Nanāja first appears in Sumerian texts there is yet no evidence of Arameans. Heimpel also believes that the closeness between Nanāja and Inanna/Ištar with regard to their domain can be facilely explained. In view of their ethnic separateness, the worship of two Venus deities in one temple could have been admitted in the mind of their followers.

M. Hutter's research indicates that the nomadic tribes of Syria in the end of the third millennium BC worshipped a Venus deity as the chief divinity in their pantheon.[64] The fact that Nanāja does not appear in the texts before the 21st century BC might be an indication that she was incorporated into the Sumerian pantheon by assimilation, corresponding to the actual assimilation of the nomadic, pre-Aramaic tribes (assumed here to be the Amorites). By the same, she

---

63 W. Heimpel, SMS 4/3, p. 17 note 42, where he writes: "The name Nanay is not Akkadian or Sumerian. It does not seem to be Amorite either. (...) Nanay could well be an Aramaic name where *-ay* is an old feminine ending (T. Nöldeke, *Syrische Grammatik*, 83)."

R. Zadok cautiously suggests a presumed Aramaic origin. In his analysis of the feminine personal name ^{fd}*Na-na-a-ta-ḫu-ša*$_3$, occurring in the texts from the archives of Murašû, R. Zadok puts forward a guarded conjecture as to the Aramaic origins of the goddess (*N.A.B.U.* 1998/2, p. 59): "But here the form is presumably Aramaic (in view of the theophorous element)..."

64 M. Hutter, „Die Religion nomadisierender Gruppen vom 3. bis zum 1. Jahrtausend v. Chr.", in: P. W. Haider, M. Hutter, S. Kreuzer (eds), *Religionsgeschichte Syriens. Von der Frühzeit bis zum Gegenwart*, Stuttgart 1996, especially p. 95-96.

became a reflection of an already existing deity, Inanna, who was worshipped under two forms, that is, the morning and the evening stars. Unwilling to repeat roles already filled by Inanna, she occupied a position next to her, taking over some of her aspects or improving herself in them.

Prof. Edward Lipiński turned my attention to the fact that the pre-Sumerian origins of the goddess are not to be excluded. Her name, which is constructed through a simple reduplication of the root *na-* and the ending *-a* (possibly *-a-a*), could have referred to the town of Uruk inhabited by the Proto-Euphrateans, that is, a population preceding the appearance of the Sumerians.

Choosing one of the above theories in assumption of its correctness is extremely difficult. Two of them, however, should be foregone: Deller's and Heimpel's. The absence of the goddess's name from Old Elamite texts would rather point to Nanāja's different genealogy. The "Aramaic" pedigree of the goddess should also be rejected, as we could hardly speak of anything but pre-Aramaic tribes in the 21st century BC (in keeping with Hutter's theory). A theory with considerable potential is that which would see Nanāja as a Venus deity worshipped by the Syrian nomads becoming assimilated in the end of the third millennium BC on territories occupied by king Šulgi (assuming naturally that Nanāja reveals ties with the Venus planet). A look at the evidence – lists of offerings, year formulas and building inscriptions – demonstrates the growing importance of her cult, leading us to admit that she enjoyed a quick rise in popularity (it is difficult to set the time limits for this phenomenon in view of the dearth of written sources). The absence of personal names in the period of the III Dynasty of Ur and a very slow increase in Old Babylonian times would contradict this idea to some extent.

The pre-Sumerian pedigree of Nanāja seems just as possible, although the lack of an ideogram of her name is even more surprising in this case (had the Sumerians taken over her cult in Uruk, why had they not created an ideogram to write down her name?). But the most surprising factor is the absence of her name as a theophoric element in the names of worshippers (it would have to be assumed that she continued to have worshippers at Uruk). The growing number of chapels and sanctuaries erected for Nanāja, as well as the involvement of the kings of the III Dynasty of Ur in her worship, as revealed by the texts, paint a different picture. This duality speaks rather in favor of the imposition of a cult which was accepted by the population only with passing time. It would thus appear that temples and priests of the goddess's cult existed without worshippers and this is hardly an acceptable solution. I should think that for now the discrepancy between the official and local cult is unlikely to be explained to everyone's satisfaction.[65]

[65] While the division into *personal*, *official* and *local* religion seems to be the best, research has demonstrated an interrelation between personal religion and the religion of the family, clan, consequently the place where the individual lives. The currently accepted division into official and family religion, the latter including the worship of local deities and individual and distinct personal worship, is much simpler, but it carries certain interpretative inconveniences.

CHAPTER I
NANĀJA'S PLACE ON THE GOD LISTS

Lists giving the names of gods reflect the pantheon of the times. The presence of a name on the list is not necessarily tantamount with the vitality of the deity's cult, but the place on the list (defined as a given god's group or section) is testimony to the relations with other divinities.

The first list to give Nanāja's name is the Weidner God List,[66] originating from the Ur III period. The goddess's absence from earlier god lists (from Fara and Abu Ṣalabikh) could be indicative of a non-Sumerian origin for Nanāja. In Weidner's division, the goddess's name appears in Inanna's group, *AfK* 2 (1924-1925), p. 11, col. I 20 ^{d}N a - n a - a - a: [^{d}N a - n] a - a, straight after the name of Dumuzi (col. I 18) and N i n š u b u r : I l a b r a t (col. I 19).

A single-column copy of the list (OECT IV 135-149), coming from Kiš and dated to the Old Babylonian period, gives the name of the goddess as ^{d}N a - [n a - a] (col. I 20), also after the appellations of Dumuzi and Ninšubur.

A Late Assyrian version of the list from Aššur,[67] places Nanāja's name in identical position.

The Old Babylonian[68] list from Nippur puts Nanāja in Inanna's section (122 col. II 23: ^{d}N a - n a - a), just in front of Ṣarpanītum; (123 rev. col. III 16: ^{d}N a - n a - a - a).[69]

---

66 I have chosen to follow the classification after W. G. Lambert, *Götterlisten*, in: RlA III, p. 473 ff.

67 O. Schroeder, *ZA* 33 (1921), p. 123-147.

68 SLT II, 122-124. According to Ch.-F. Jean, *RA* XXVIII (1931), p. 179-194, SLT 122 is said to have been compiled in the Isin-Larsa period.

69 Th. Richter, AOAT 257, p. 248-249 on the arrangement of the list: „Diese Liste verdient insbesondere aufgrund der tatsache Beachtung, dass die Göttinnen Nanaja und Zarpanītum in unmittelbarem Anschluss an eine Inana/Ištar-Gestalt auftreten. Fraglich ist, ob mit Nanaja ein neuer Abschnitt beginnt, ob sie in dieser Liste als Gestalt der Inana/Ištar aufgefasst oder zu ihrem Kreis gerechnet wurde. Die unklare Struktur der NGL (= Nippur

Genouillac's Old Babylonian[70] list also includes Nanāja in the god Dumuzi's group (p. 103, VI 34: ^{d}N a - n a - a).

Also an Old Babylonian list of gods, from Isin[71], gives the name of Nanāja (B I 10') in the damaged part but nearly after Enki's group.

The compilers of the Emesal list, composed between 1400 and 900 BC included Nanāja's name after a section devoted to the gods Dumuzi and Inanna, between that of the goddess Ninsianna referred to as INANNA.MUL (MSL IV, tablet I 89) and the god Latarak (I 91); the notation is as follows: [^{d}G a š a n - z i l_2 - z i l_2] : ^{d}N i n - z i l_2 - z i l_2 : ^{d}N a - n a - a.

Neo-Assyrian and Neo-Babylonian tablets discovered in the Babylonian temple *Nabû ša ḫarê* yielded some 25 fragments of a single-column list of the gods Anum,[72] which counts over 240 names. Nanāja appears on this list directly after the appellations of Inanna and Dumuzi, written as ^{d}N a - n a - a (l. 20), only in the following texts: 79.B.1/ 67i; 79.B.1/ 223; 79.B.1/ 147; 79.B.1/ 235+ vi'; 79.B.1/ 171 rev. II.

The Late Assyrian list from Sultantepe (STT II, 376-382) gives the name of the goddess, which appears after the Dumuzi-Inanna group, between the divinities ^{d}ME.ME.TUM and ^{d}NIN.AMA.KAL.LA (STT II, 376 VI 2). In STT II, 382 Nanāja occurs in col. IV 11'.

The God List with Commentary, discovered in the library of Assurbanipal, preserved fragmentarily, explains the name of the goddess as follows (CT 25, 49, rev. 7): ^{d}N i n . z i l_2 . z i l_2[73] : ^{d}N a - n a - a *mārat* (DUMU.SAL) [...]. Nanāja's name appears after the

---

Götter Liste) lässt hier keinen sicheren Schluss zu; es lassen sich lediglich Indizien aufführen."

[70] H. Genouillac, *RA* XX (1923), p. 89-106. The author dates the text to either the Ur III or the Isin period.

[71] C. Wilcke, *Die Inschriftenfunde der 7. und 8. Kampagnen (1983 und 1984)*, in: B. Hrouda (ed.), ISIN-IŠAN BAḪRĪYĀT III, *Die Ergebnisse der Ausgrabungen 1983-1984*, München 1987, p. 93-98.

[72] See A. Cavigneaux, *Texts from Babylon. Textes scolaires du Temple de Nabû ša ḫarê*, vol. I, Baghdad 1981, p. 79-99.

[73] The sign zil_2 in CT 25 is read as TAG. Hence, the name here was read as: ^{d}NIN.TAG.TAG.

name of the lunar deity Sîn and before that of the god of the underworld Nergal.

The goddess Nanāja is present also on a short list[74] among the deities worshipped in the Esagila temple in Babylon next to her consort Nabû.

In the Mari "pantheon" from the Ur III period[75] (it is in reality a list of offerings, hence the quotation marks) Nanāja is represented as ^{d}N i n - N a - n a - a (the determiner "Lady" was added to the name), in the section of deities originating from Uruk (beside Dumuzi and Ninšubur, and straight after the goddess N i n - b i - ṣ i l$_2$ - l a$_2$, immediately before the goddess Nidaba). In other texts from Mari, the appellation N a - a n - n i appears preceded or not by the determinative of a divine name,[76] but in view of the different notation, I have refrained from considering it as the name of a divinity identical with Nanāja.

---

74 III R pl. 66, rev., col. V 1-21.

75 D. O. Edzard, in: CRRAI 15, p. 70; G. Dossin, *RA* LXI (1967), p. 97-104 (T. 142, l. 23); J.-M. Durand, *RA* LXXIV (1980), p. 174-176; W. G. Lambert, MARI 4, p. 525-539 (notation: $^{d.nin}$n a - n a - a). See also G. Dossin, in: A. Parrot (ed.), *Studia Mariana*, Leiden 1950, p. 41-50, l. 14.

76 I. Nakata, *Deities in the Mari Texts: Complete Inventory of all the Information on the Deities found in the published Old Babylonian Cuneiform Texts from Mari and Analytical and Comparative Evaluation thereof with regard to the Official and Popular Pantheons of Mari*, Columbia Univ., Ph. D. 1974, p. 371-374. The author records the forms N a - a n - n a, N a - n a, ^{d}N a - n a, N a - a n - ni, ^{d}N a - [a] n - n i, ^{d}N a - n i. He also cites a hypothesis put forward by J. J. Roberts (ESP, p. 46) regarding the connection between Nanni the goddess and the mountain Na-an-ni. A mountain called N a - n a - a had existed somewhere between Ugarit and Mukiš (Suppiluliuma's letter in PRU IV, p. 13 – RS 17, 340, 6').
In RlA VIII (s.v. *Mondgott*, p. 361), M. Krebernik presented his theory regarding the name of Nan(n$^{?}$)um, which sounds very much like Nanna. Among the personal names from Umma there is U r - ^{d}N a - n u - u m (BE VI/2, 13, seal), which Krebernik believes to draw from Nanāja (he cites personal names from Mari in support of his hypothesis). J. J. Roberts (*op. cit.*, p. 45) also gives two Old Semitic names: Pu-Nanna and Šu-Nanna, which he links with the goddess Nanni from Mari.

Also the god list discovered at Emar[77] mentions the name of the goddess recorded as follows: ᵈN a - n a - a : N a - n a - j a.[78] The names of the divinities mentioned here are combined in pairs (opening the list is Enlil with his consort Ninlil); other names of the gods that are used are also recorded (l. 22'-23': ᵈEnki, ᵈEa). Tašmetum is assigned to Nabû. Unfortunately, damage to the text has rendered the name of the deity assigned to Nanāja unreadable.

The three-column vocabulary (the so-called *Silbenvokabular A*), which is widely known from Mesopotamia and represents a syllabic syllabary (*Silbenalphabet A*) with two added columns in Akkadian (b and c), also mentions Nanāja among the names of deities.[79] In column b, one observes the tendency to group items in semantic groups or pairs. Column c either repeats the words or groups them according to the same principles as in column b. However, the names of divinities are much more frequent in column c. The goddess Nanāja is defined as follows (l. 71): n i n - e z e n : ᵈ[*na-na-a*] : *ma-nu-*[*u*]*m*. The absence of a determinative preceding the item in column c precludes the interpretation of this name as that of a divinity, but column a probably gives an epithet unknown outside of this text – "Lady of the Feast" (l. 31: [a] - p a p : *ra-bu-tum* : ᵈn i n - e z e n).

Document CBS 6060 lists trees, plants, animals, various objects and materials to which divinities are assigned (it might be said that the deities are made equal with the listed objects). Ištar (likewise the Ištar from Uruk, Agade and Babylon) has stones equaled to her, while Nanāja has a herb assigned to her (l. 36): [ᵍⁱ]ˢ*ziqqu* (GI.DUG$_3$.GA) : ᵈNa-na-a.[80]

---

[77] D. Arnaud, Emar VI/4, no. 539 (Msk 741651 i, Msk 74165 j).

[78] *Op. cit.*, p. 34, l. 13'.

[79] E. Sollberger, AS 16, p. 23, rev. III 71; see also p. 37 (double-column vocabulary from Ugarit).

[80] A. Livingstone, *Mystical and Mythological Explanatory Works of Assyrian and Babylonian Scholars*, Oxford 1986, p. 178, l. 36. See CAD 129a, ziqqu D ("an aromatic herb") u$_2$. d u g$_3$. g a = *ziqqu* = *la-ar-d*[*u*] "nard" Hg. D 225.

The goddess's place on the god lists and the appellations used to designate Nanāja in a variety of literary sources provide the grounds for conclusions regarding her family relations. These will be discussed in the next two subchapters.

The god lists that give Nanāja's name link the goddess repeatedly with Dumuzi-Inanna's section. This explicit positioning reveals that theologians tended to perceive the two goddesses in very similar terms. Keeping in mind Inanna's principal functions, one should surmise that Nanāja was also a goddess of fertility and growth.

The Emesal list as well as the god list with commentary mentioned above (which undoubtedly came into existence before the 7th century BC) record the Sumerian equivalent of the name of the goddess – "Lady of the Ornaments/Ornamentation" or "Lady (who) is very good." The Emesal list (even assuming its composition in the middle of the second millennium BC) is later than the first known testimonies to Nanāja's worship. Therefore, the attribution of a Sumerian (dialectal?) equivalent was of a secondary nature, even if it drew upon the appearance of the statues of this goddess.[81]

I.1 NANĀJA'S FAMILY ACCORDING TO THE GOD LISTS

In the Weidner list Nanāja is connected with Inanna's group. The so-called theological arrangement of the list confirms the very early association between Inanna and Nanāja, dating back to at least the early second millennium BC, if not the end of the third millennium. Was this relation imposed by the Sumerian priests? Or was it intrinsic in view of the similarity between the two goddesses? It is impossible to settle the issue today. Dumuzi's name (which appears above Nanāja's name on the list) further confirms the idea that we are dealing with Inanna's double. Recorded immediately under Nanāja's name is the designation of another goddess, ^{d}B i_2 - z i l - l a_2[82] (NE.NUN.LAL),

[81] The number of ornaments attributed to Nanāja during the Neo-Babylonian period in Uruk matches those of Ištar, see P.-A. Beaulieu, CM 23, p. 187.
[82] E. von Weiher, SpTU III, no. 108, l. 21, reads the name as ^{d}Ne-sil_2-la.

who often occurs next to Nanāja in administrative texts (concerning offerings) from the Ur III period and the "pantheon" from Mari of Ur III date as well. The next name is ^{d}K a - n i - s u r - r a. A Late Assyrian double-column version (KAV 63) of the same god list from Aššur lets one suppose that Kanisurra[83] was the name of a daughter of Nanāja. The meaning and origins of her name are equally unclear. She is known from the Maqlû series (V 59 ff.) as *bēlet kaššapāti* "Lady of Spells"; Anam built a temple to her as the "Lady of the Iturungal canal." Next to the goddess ^{d}G a z - b a b - b a, she is designated as a daughter of the Ezida temple in Borsippa.

The goddess Gazbaba[84] (also recorded as ^{d}G a z - b a - a - a), who is a sister to Kanisurra, would thus be Nanāja's other daughter. The form ^{d}GAZ.BA.A occurs in Hittite texts as well.[85] Neither goddess has a clear role to play. It should be noted that both are also recognized as the daughters of Nabû.

Both Old Babylonian lists – the one from Nippur and the Genouillac list – link Nanāja with the group of Inanna-Dumuzi, the pair of lovers. According to Th. Richter,[86] the Genouillac list contains: "eine kleine Nanaja-Sektion an die sich die Namen Lugalbanda und Ninsuna auschliessen" (col. VI 38-39). Directly after the name of Nanāja there comes (col. VI, l. 35-37): ^{d}Z i l_2 - z i l_2,[87] ^{d}I n - n i n - š a_6 - g a, and ^{d}M u_6 - a - t i.

The Emesal list also makes a connection between the name of the goddess and the section of Inanna and Dumuzi. In the Emesal dialect, the name signifies: "Lady of the Ornaments/Ornamentation" or "Lady (who) is very good", its counterpart in the Emegi does the same (^{d}N i n

---

83 See D. O. Edzard, "Kanissura", in: RlA V, p. 389; J. Black, A. Green, *Gods, Demons and Symbols of Ancient Mesopotamia*, London 1992, p. 134 believe Uṣur-amāssa to be the Akkadian counterpart of this goddess.

84 See E. Weidner, "Gazbaba", in: RlA III, p. 153.

85 This is a form used to designate the goddess Huwaššanna from Hupišna, see B. H. L. van Gessel, HdO 33, Part II, p. 632-634.

86 Th. Richter, AOAT 257, p. 258.

87 See ŠL 126, 52: $ZIL_2.ZIL_2$, b) *zu'unu* "schmücken"; PSD: zil_2(TAG) 1. "(to be) good", 2. "(to be) beneficent."

- z i l_2 - z i l_2, written as NIN.TAG.TAG), and only the third column (which is presumed to give the name in Akkadian) presents the version of the name that was in use at the time.

Another two texts apparently give the Sumerian equivalents of Nanāja's name. The god list with commentary is the first (K 1451 in CT 25, 49); according to the colophon, it is an Assyrian copy of an older original coming from Babylon. It gives the following (rev. 7-8): [d]N i n - z i l_2 - z i l_2 : [d]*Na-na-a mārat* (DUMU.SAL) x x x *ša₂ man-za-as-su ša₂-qu-u be-let tak-ne₂-e*[*-ti*][88] "goddess Nin-zil_2-zil_2 : goddess Nanāja, daughter (...), whose place is high, Lady of Loving Care/Behavior." As the lunar deity Sîn appears in the line above, Nanāja should presumably be identified as his daughter.[89]

The other text is a bilingual prayer to the temple (Rm. 97 in OECT VI 27), which refers to Ninzilzil/Nanāja as follows: "Lady who imparts the final shape on rites" and "the one who like a great dragon goggles at the enemy."

The texts from the *Nabû ša ḫarê* temple also confirm the relation between Nanāja and the Inanna-Dumuzi group. Nabû and Tašmētum occur far below (l. 66-68). The group of Inanna names appears separately (starting with l. 157).

Nanāja's ties with Inanna is thus very distinct in the god lists and is to be traced from the Ur III period to Neo-Babylonian and Neo-Assyrian tablets. The first to finger Nabû as Nanāja's consort is the god list of the Esagila temple and Babylon, but this text obviously reflects a later period in the development of Mesopotamian beliefs.

The Genouillac list brings other appellations, possibly no more than epithets, after the name of Nanāja: "Lady of the Ornaments" or "Lady (who) is very good" and "Sweet/benign Inanna." The next is Mu'ati, a deity identified with Nanāja's spouse, Nabû, god of writing.

---

88 The title *bēlet taknē* is also a designation of the goddess Bau, see KAR 109, 22.

89 See W 19900, 1 = UVB XVIII, pl. 28c. This text leads us to think that Sîn sired both Istar and Nanāja.

He appears next to Nanāja in a lyrical piece from the turn of the eighteenth century BC, which will be discussed further later on.

Two goddesses of ill defined function, Kanisurra and Gazbaba, appear as daughters of Nanāja (and also the god Nabû).

I.2 NANĀJA'S FAMILY AFTER OTHER DOCUMENTS

In other documents Nanāja is referred to as a daughter of An. The first text to designate her so dates from the reign of Rīm-Sîn (1822-1763 BC), that is, from the turn of the nineteenth century BC; the next is Samsu-iluna's hymn from the eighteenth century BC (1749-1712 BC).

According to texts from the Neo-Assyrian period, the moon god Sîn was her father and the sun god Šamaš her brother. Nabû was made her spouse, hence she became a daughter-in-law to Marduk. What is surprising is that in such a configuration she would have to be a sister to Ištar, yet this epithet never appears. For a long time she remained in the shadow of the great Inanna/Ištar, was her reflection, "a ward", as Samsu-iluna's hymn puts it. Few texts actually use the explicit term "daughter of Inanna." The first is the Sumerian votive inscription of Lipit-Eštar (1934-1924 BC),[90] which referred to Nanāja as d u m u k i - a g_2 ^{d}I n a n n a, that is, "beloved child of Inanna." In a first millennium BC recension of a *balag* song,[91] written for Inanna/Ištar, one reads: ^{d}N a - n a - a d u m u - s a g - z u "Nanāja, your firstborn." A bilingual oath formula (K 3179+) calls upon Nanāja DUMU.MI_2.SAG$^{!}$ ^{d}I n n i n - n a - k e_2 : *mārti reštiti ša*$_2$ ^{d}*Ištar*, that is, the firstborn daughter of Ištar. Naturally, it cannot be excluded that these are no more than epithets assigned to Nanāja in order to confirm the closeness between the two goddesses.

A *kudurru* text from Borsippa, written in the middle of the eight century BC, again refers to Nanāja as the firstborn of Anu, beloved of Marduk, sister of Šamaš and spouse of Nabû.

---

90 M. Civil, *N.A.B.U.* 1997/3, no. 98.
91 M. E. Cohen, *CLAM*, p. 651, l. 7.

The texts of joy and sorrow written in the eme-sal dialect bring to the fore a different set of familial relations. In these texts Nanāja is designated the "firstborn of the god Uraš", identified with Ninurta and also Nabû. The god of writing considered as Nanāja's spouse had another legal wife, Tašmētum.[92] Her name is purely Semitic ("Listening") and she appeared as Nabû's wife starting with the Old Babylonian period. In both Weidner's and Genouillac's god lists the two divinities are included in the Marduk group; in the Neo-Babylonian period Nanāja also joined his divine court.

In Neo-Babylonian and Neo-Assyrian times the *hieros gamos* or sacred marriage ceremony took place between Nabû and Tašmētum (according to Assyrian documents) or Nabû and Nanāja (according to Babylonian works). In some texts the two goddesses occur side by side (e.g. ABL 119, ABL 120, ABL 23), confirming by the same their autonomy.

Text K 1354 composed in the middle of the ninth century BC, most likely a cult song[93] in which the evoking voice could be either Ištar or Nanāja, or possibly a deity personifying the two goddesses (because of the relations with the cities mentioned in the song), led A. R. George to conclude that Nanāja was Nabû's lover,[94] much better known than his rightful spouse Tašmētum.

Apart from a spouse or lover, Nanāja also had daughters (who were also Nabû's offspring). Testifying to this is a calendar of ritual feasts from the Seleucid period.[95] It contains, among others, the sacred marriage ritual between Nanāja and Nabû, and records in col. IV 45: [*mārāte Ezid*]*a* ^{d}*Gaz-ba-ba u* ^{d}*Ka-ni-sur-ra me-rat* ^{d}*Na-na-a* "[daughters of (the temple of) the Ezid]a – Gazbaba and Kanisurra – daughters of Nanāja."

---

92 See K. Tallqvist, AGE, p. 470 and E. Matsushima, *Orient* XVI (1980), p. 133-148.

93 A. R. George, *SAAB* 1 (1987), p. 38: "Rather, K 1354 is considered a song for use in the cult." C. Bezold (*Catalogue...*, p. 273) thinks it to be a "list of temples."

94 The SAA series indexes Nanāja as a goddess of love, Nabû's concubine or spouse.

95 G. Reisner, SBH VIII, VAT 662.

Thus, depending on the religious circle (and the ethnicity of the author of a text), Nanāja has different fathers: the god of the heavens An, the lunar god Nanna/Sîn and the god of the city of Dilbat – Uraš. Her mother or guardian is always seemingly only Inanna/Ištar. It is difficult to settle the regularity of her marriage to Nabû who also had another wife. Applying our modern principles to the world of the ancient Mesopotamian gods, it could be said that Nanāja's children with Nabû – the daughters Gazbaba and Kanisurra – were recognized as the couple's legal issue.

CHAPTER II
THE CULT OF NANĀJA

Assuming that cult is the material representation of the ideas and beliefs surrounding a deity[96] and accepting what J. G. Westenholz said that, "cult is a set of rituals comprising the worship of one deity,"[97] it is essential to present a variety of cuneiform texts in order to be able to render the worship of Nanāja. A key source lies in the lists of offerings made as material proof of cult, the related votive gifts and texts speaking of temples, chapels, statues, robes etc. The worship of Nanāja depended on priests as well as common people, and her popularity over the millennia is expressed in the number of personal names containing her name. The rituals devoted to the goddess and other deities, discussed in this chapter, render the official cult and are a reflection of her role in the pantheon.

II.1 OFFERINGS

The Drehem tablets provide rich material on the offerings made to Nanāja.[98] Lambs were the most frequent offering (1 s i l a_4 ^{d}N a - n a - a).[99] Textual evidence confirms this form of offering, made in various months, starting in the 44th regnal year of Šulgi (2094-2047 BC) and continuing until the second year of the rule of Ibbi-Sîn (2028-2004 BC). Fattened sheep (u d u n i g a ^{d}N a - n a - a)[100] were also very often dedicated as offerings. He-goats (m a $š_2$ ^{d}N a -

[96] M. G. Hall, *Moon-god*, p. 250.
[97] J. G. Westenholz, in: CRRAI 35, p. 298.
[98] Dr. Bram Jagersma of Leiden University has kindly shared with me his collection of transliterations of all the available Drehem texts. Among the texts connected with Nanāja, those from the reign of Šulgi are preponderant with the earliest being dated to the 33rd or 32nd year according to the current count. See also N. Schneider, AnOr 19, p. 42. Through the kind offices of Dr. Marek Stępień of The University of Warsaw, I also had access to a computer database containing economic texts from the Ur III period, prepared specifically for his teaching needs at the Faculty of Mathematics, Computer Science and Mechanics of The University of Warsaw.
[99] Only once was an offering made of eight lambs: PDT 1, 342 [IS 2].
[100] The oldest text known to the present author: TCND 178 = TCS 223 [Š 36].

n a - a),[101] kids (^{munus}a š$_2$ - g a r$_3$ ^{d}N a - n a - a) and bulls (g u$_4$ n i g a ^{d}N a - n a - a) were seldom given as offerings.[102] Occasionally, different animals were offered together. Texts also mention offerings made to Inanna and Nanāja (the sequence in which the goddesses are mentioned is always the same) in different months and on the occasion of various feasts (e.g. a$_2$ - k i - t i š u - n u m u n "(feast) a$_2$ - ki - ti (of the season) of sowing", celebrated in the seventh month at Ur.)[103] Regular s a$_2$ - d u$_{11}$ offerings and other irregular ones were made to Nanāja on the first and second day of the month at Uruk.[104] During a feast in the middle of the third month at Uruk, a couple of sheep were given in offering to Nanāja.[105] Nanāja also took part in the *nabrium* feast, which came at the turn of the eight month.[106] It is also known that the bark of An was used to carry offerings for Inanna and Nanāja.[107] Night offerings are evidenced (a n - b a r$_x$ and a$_2$ - g i$_6$ - b a - a), as well as evening offerings (a$_2$ - u$_4$ - t e - n a) and morning offerings (a$_2$ - g u$_2$ - z i - g a), made to Nanāja from the reign of Šulgi to that of Ibbi-Sîn, that is, throughout the 21st century BC.

During the Ur III period in Uruk and Ur, the texts mention cumulatively offerings made to the goddesses Inanna, Nanāja, Bēlat-

---

[101] The oldest text known to the present author: MVN XVIII 56 = AnOr 7, 56 [Š 35].

[102] A kid in offering was noted for the first time in the 35th year of Šulgi and is the oldest of the confirmed offerings (MVN XVIII 56 = AnOr 7, 56 and PDT 2, 998).

[103] P. J. Watson, *Birmingham* I 68 [Š 47 vii 5]. Another designation appearing in the texts: š a$_3$ a$_2$ - k i - t i "(offering) for (the feast of) *akītu*."

[104] T. Gomi, BJRL 64, no. 66. The tablet MAH 19352 (M. Sigrist, in: Studies Sjöberg, p. 500) speaks of the journey to Ur of king Ibbi-Sîn who was crowned in Nippur; this trip by boat was interrupted at Uruk where offerings were made to Nanāja and Ninsun among others.

[105] PIOL 19, 357 [AS 9].

[106] TCND 178, 4 = TCS 223 [Š 36].

[107] MVN XVIII 62 = AnOr 7, 62 [Š 37, i t u a$_2$ - k i - t i] and W. M. Nesbit, Drehem 12 [Š 45 xi 25].

tirraban, Bēlat-suḫnir, Anunītum and Ulmašītum,[108] but also the others (TRU 282). W. G. Lambert identified the pair Anunītum and Ulmašītum as Ištar of Babylon and the Ištar of Akkad.[109] The pair Bēlat-tirraban and Bēlat-suḫnir is adopted from the Semitic pantheon.[110] The ritual devoted to these goddesses was called g i - r a - n u m_2 (the term is a form of the Akkad. *girrānu*, which is rendered in the lexical lists as e r_2 "wailing, lamentation"). At Uruk the lamentations for Nanāja fell in the sixth month (PDT 2, 998 and AnOr 7, 55 – both texts dated to the 35th regnal year of Šulgi). It should be emphasized yet again that this is the earliest date connected with the cult of Nanāja.

The same goddesses are the addressees of offerings made in the "place of disappearance" – n i_3 - k i - z a h_3. Offerings to Nanāja are evidenced at Uruk in the first[111] and fifth[112] months. Offerings made in the "place of disappearance" confirm Nanāja's affiliation to the sphere of Dumuzi who left the world of the living periodically; perhaps this aspect of the cult should be considered as a form of worship of deceased rulers. A. Cavigneaux and F. N. H. Al-Rawi (CM 19, p. 9 note 31) write: "On peut imaginer — à titre d'hypothèse — que Nanāya, dont le nom semble être un hypocoristique, représente à l'origine un

[108] M. E. Cohen, *The Cultic Calendars of the Ancient Near East*, Bethesda 1993, p. 136-140.
[109] W. G. Lambert, in: Studies Sjöberg, p. 324.
[110] Th. Jacobsen believes the elements of the names of these goddesses to be the names of towns, possibly from the Kirkuk region, see Th. Jacobsen, OIP 43, p. 143. See also B. Lewis, E. R. Jewell, *ASJ* 4 (1982) p. 55-56 (text no. 1 – A 14643 [Š 29?] and M. Sigrist, *Drehem*, Bethesda 1992, p. 237, where the author writes that Suḫnir and Tirraban are names of cities in the Kirkuk region; Sigrist is of the opinion that the cult of these two goddesses was introduced no later than the 32nd year of Šulgi, after he had conquered the city of Simurrum.
[111] These are n i_3 - k i - z a h_3 offerings to gain entry to the *giparu* building, n i_3 - k i - z a h_3 evening offerings for Nanāja, morning offerings to gain entry to the temple, to gain entry to the *giparu* and for Nanāja – J.-M. Durand, *Catalogue EPHE*, 289; AnOr 7, 87 = MVN XVIII 87 [Š 47].
[112] Th. Jacobsen, *Copenhagen* 9 [Š 37]. See also texts AnOr 7, 58 = MVN XVIII 15 and 60 [Š 36], and AnOr 7, 62 = MVN XVIII 62 [Š 37].

surnom de Ninirigala. Pour l'association de Nanāya au culte funéraire des rois d'Uruk on remarquera que des statues d'Anam, de Sîn-erībam sont introduites dans le temple de cette déesse par leurs successeurs," (discussed in detail in part 2 of this chapter).[113]

The text TCL II 5482, which raises interpretative difficulties, is presumed to be evidence for making offerings to Nanāja also in private dwellings (col. II 7 and 19). On the other hand, however, the document provides a very detailed list of divinities for whom the offerings are intended (the offering s i s k u r$_2$ e$_2$ - g a l and others included), and the high number inclines one to doubt as to whether a house chapel could have contained all of them.

Usually offerings to Nanāja were combined with offerings made to other deities, e.g. (AnOr 7, 56 = MVN XVIII 56 [Š 35], l. 1-9): 1 s i l a$_4$ / e š$_3$ - š e$_3$ / 1 m a š$_2$ k a g i$_6$ - p a r$_3$ - r a / 1 m a š$_2$ ^{d}N a - n a - a / š a$_3$ U n u g^{ki} - g a / ... / 2 u d u g i - r a - n u m$_2$ / e$_2$ ^{d}B e - l a - a t - s u ḫ - n i r / u$_3$ ^{d}B e - l a - a t - t i r$_3$ - r a - b a - a n "1 lamb / for the temple, / 1 kid for entry to the *giparu*, / 1 kid for Nanāja / at Uruk, /.../, 2 sheep (for the ritual of) *girrānu* / for the temple of the goddesses Bēlat-suḫnir / and Bēlat-tirraban." This can testify not only to the proximity of the chapels, but can also be proof of a similarity in the origins of these goddesses.[114]

---

[113] On the links between the cult of Dumuzi and that of the dead, see M. Cohen, *The Cultic Calendars of the Ancient Near East*, Bethesda 1993, p. 476-481; J.-P. Grégoire, AAS, commentary to text no. 152; J. G. Westenholz, in: CM 7, p. 62 note 42 (n i g$_2$ - k i - z a h of Nanāja).

[114] About the archive of Šulgi-sīmti, Šulgi's l u k u r, see M. Sigrist, *Drehem*, Bethesda 1992, p. 222 ff. Sigrist writes (on p. 246): "Le but de la fondation de Šulgi-simti semble avoir été de pouvoir à un culte lunaire et funéraire à Uruk. A Ur par contre se déroulaient des cultes provenant d'un fonds akkadien et sémitique pour des divinités venant de Diyala." In all likelihood, Šulgi-sīmti originated from the region of Kirkuk. Moreover, the š a b r a of Nanāja's temple paid b a l a together with the e n s i s of Ešnunna and Išim-Šulgi (LB 3073 = RSO 9, 472; P 368; LB unnumbered [AS 4]; TD 26 [AS 4]) or with e n s i of Šuruppak (YOS 4, 56).

Other than animal offerings Nanāja was worshipped by pouring libations (k a š - d e$_2$ - a ^{d}N a - n a - a).[115] There exist categories of offerings defined as ^{d}N a - n a - a š a$_3$ e$_2$ - g a l - l a "(for) the goddess Nanāja (made) in the palace,"[116] ^{d}N a - n a - a š a$_3$ U n u g^{ki} - g a "(for) the goddess Nanāja (made) in Uruk" and simply e$_2$ ^{d}N a - n a - a "(for) the temple of Nanāja".[117] There exists also a text (AUCT 3, 508) that testifies to libations of beer being offered to the goddess by a woman[118]: k i[119] ^{d}N a - n a - a k a š i n - n a - n i - d e$_2$ - a.

The phrase s i s k u r$_2$ ^{d}N a - n a - a and a - r u - a ^{d}N a - na - a[120] also occurs. The texts indicate that offerings were made in various places, e.g. CTNMC 9 mentions animals offered in Nanāja's "place of disappearance" and in the temple of Nanāja. The text MVN XVIII 58 = AnOr 7, 58 demonstrates that offerings for the "place of disappearance" were made in the palace (n i$_3$ - k i - z a h$_3$ ^{d}N a - n a - a š a$_3$ e$_2$ - g a l - l a).

H. Sauren's[121] research has shown that in the Neo-Sumerian period offerings to Nanāja followed a defined rhythm, that of the appearance

---

[115] PDT 1, 582 [Š 45], MVN XVIII 60 [Š 36], MVN XIII 102 [Š 41] – in the palace; also see AUCT 3, 508, YBC 15415; AnOr 7, 60 [Š 36] – at Ur.

[116] This interpretation has been proposed by P. J. Watson, *Birmingham* I 111, l. 6-8: 1 g u$_4$ n i g a ^{d}N a - n a - a / s i s k u r$_2$ š a$_3$ e$_2$ - g a l / l u g a l k u$_4$ - r a "1 fattened bull (for) Nanāja / – offering in the palace – / brought by the king" [ŠS 9]; see also AnOr 7, 61 = MVN XVIII 61 [Š 37]; AnOr 7, 58 = MVN XVIII 58 [Š 36]; SET 88, obv. [IS 2]; YOS 12, 92 [Si 3]; see W. Sallaberger, *Der Kultische Kalender der Ur III-Zeit*, Berlin 1993, table no. 75.

M. Sigrist, *Drehem*, Bethesda 1992, p. 189 admits to not understanding the sense of this expression owing to the lack of clarity as to the role of the ruler in this act of worship. See also R. F. G. Sweet, *ARRIM* 1 (1983), p. 25-26 (XXIV. H 36c l. 9' with translation "when the king entered (the temple)."

[117] MVN XVIII 56 = AnOr 7, 56 [Š 35], L. Legrain, TRU 275 [Š 41]; PIOL 19 80 = EAMES F6 [AS 9]; AnOr 7, 62 [Š 37].

[118] J. G. Westenholz, CM 7, p. 64, poses the question: "Could these libations be related to rites after rising from childbirth?"

[119] According to B. Jagersma, it is "u$_4$" not "ki."

[120] MVN XIV 415 l. 2 [ŠS 3]; D. I. Owen, G. D. Young, *JCS* 23 (1970), p. 112, no. 14 l. 2; W. W. Hallo, *JCS* 14/3 (1960), p. 114, no. 22 (NCBT 1413) rev. col. V 3 (a - r u - a).

[121] H. Sauren, in: CRRAI 17, p. 24-25.

and disappearance of the planet Venus (it would stand in confirmation of the idea that she was a Venus deity). At the same time, there exist other texts that confirm offerings being made to the goddess during the new moon (e š$_3$ - e š$_3$ u$_4$ - s a - k a r: MVN XVIII 62 = AnOr 7, 62; PDT 2, 1272) and the full moon (e š$_3$ - e š$_3$ u$_4$ - 15: M. Sigrist, *Rochester* 13).

Uruk king Šulgi's spouse, Šulgi-sīmti practiced actively in the city cults. Her archives have yielded some of the texts concerning offerings made to Nanāja.[122]

The coming of an ethnically different population group and foremost a change of ruling dynasty had no effect on the kind of offerings made to Nanāja. Texts concerning the distribution of breeding stock from the reign of Sîn-iddinam[123] of Larsa (1849-1843 BC) confirm an offering of one sheep for the temple of Nanāja (1 g a n a m e$_2$ ^{d}N a - n a - a - a). In his studies, A. Goetze[124] has demonstrated that the group of deities whose temples are mentioned most often during this period includes: Šamaš, Adad, Inanna, Nanāja and Nerīgal. The Sun god usually received three rams while the other deities had to be satisfied with one each. The goddesses were offered female animals, the gods male ones.

The variety of offerings made to Nanāja is confirmed by a seven-day ritual worshipping different gods of Larsa,[125] dating most likely from the second year of Rīm-Sîn (1822-1763 BC). On the nineteenth day of the month Nanāja received offerings not only of roasted or live animals, but also bread made from a variety of flours, beer, oil, butter, slave girls and diverse jewelry. A feast with a libation terminated her holiday.

The text TCL X 100, from the 45th year of Rīm-Sîn, speaks of corn intended for storage (*ana takmisi*) for the goddesses Inanna and

---

[122] See W. Sallaberger, *Der Kultische Kalender der Ur III-Zeit* 1, Berlin 1993, p. 219 ff. and tables nos. 62c, 67, 71, 74, 75.
[123] See A. Goetze, *JCS* 4 (1950), p. 90; UIOM nos. 2019, 2021, 2022, 2031, 2026; YBC nos. 4974, 5606, 8728, 10249 and others.
[124] *Op. cit.*
[125] E. C. Kingsbury, *HUCA* 34 (1963), p. 1-34; l. 541-626 are devoted to Nanāja.

Nanāja of Uruk (l. 24-27) and for Inanna and Nanāja of Larsa (l. 31-33). Textual evidence from the 58th year of Rīm-Sîn's reign confirms deliveries of silver to the Uruk temples of Inanna, Nanāja and her daughter, Kanisurra (BM 23373; the name of the latter goddess could be read as ^{d}K i r$_4$ - z a l - s u r - r a.)[126]

A text from Uruk (W 20472, 104)[127], dated to the rule of Anam (1821-1817 BC), reports an offering in Nanāja's temple consisting of four (gur) *a-na ma-ak-ki-im* / *u*$_3$ *pi-ri-ik-ki-im* (l. 9-10) "for the *makkum* offering and for the lion symbol", this still remaining unclear.[128] In the times of this king regular s a$_2$ - d u$_{11}$ offerings were made to AN-^{d}INANNA-^{d}*Na-na-a* (W 20472, 72 and W 20472, 80)[129] and n i d b a offerings to AN-^{d}INANNA *u*$_3$ ^{d}*Na-na-a* (W 20472, 105).[130]

In the Isin-Larsa period, texts that were lists of *sattukku* offerings (that is, s a$_2$ - d u$_{11}$) made in the Ešumeša temple of Ninurta in Nippur also record the name of the goddess. It appears on five-column tablets after the name of the god Ningišzida and the goddess Ninsianna (often regarded as an aspect of the warrior Inanna).[131]

No texts recording offerings to Nanāja survive from a period one thousand years long. In no way should this be construed as a break

---

126 See J.-M. Durand, Cat. II, index of divinities (^{d}K i r$_4$ - z a l - s u r - r a or ^{d}K i r i$_4$ - z a l - s u r - r a.)

127 Sh. Sanati-Müller, *BaghM* 21 (1990), no. 142, p. 202-203 notes 4 and 5. A text W 20472, 123 = Sh. Sanati-Müller, *BaghM* 21 (1990), no. 89, p. 138, also from the 31st year of Anam, speaks of the throne of Nanāja being covered with silver.

128 See K. van der Toorn, *Family religion*, p. 73 note 33.

129 Sh. Sanati-Müller, *BaghM* 22 (1991), no. 154, p. 316, l. 2 and no. 155, p. 317-318, l. 2, in Sh. Sanati-Müller's translation: *regelmäßige Leistung für An, Inanna, Nanâ.* There is obviously no mention here of AN-^{d}INANNA, but of separately existing deities An and Inanna. Also Nanāja has been treated as a separate divinity. Th. Richter, AOAT 257, p. 236 is of the same opinion. See below note 240.

130 Sh. Sanati-Müller, *BaghM* 23 (1992), no. 166, p. 126, l. 9.

131 R. M. Sigrist, *Les* sattukku *dans l'Ešumeša durant la période d'Isin et Larsa*, Malibu 1984, p. 147.

in the cult or even a momentary “waning”, for there are other sources to belie this.

Proof of offerings being made to Nanāja is provided by an inscription of the Assyrian ruler Šulmānu-ašaridu, who reigned in 858-824 BC. He was the inspirator of the famous bronze gates of Balawat, richly adorned with relief decoration and accompanied by a text testifying to the glorious achievements of the king. The inscription mentions, among others, offerings made by the king in various Babylonian temples. He also brought offerings to the Ezida temple in Borsippa to worship its lord and lady, the god Nabû and goddess Nanāja.[132]

Numerous economic texts from the times of Nabû-nāṣir (747-734 BC) record mentions of wool from sheep belonging to Nanāja (BRM I 21).

The ruler of Assyria at this time, Tukultī-apil-Ešarra (744-727 BC) made offerings to ten different deities, including Nanāja, at the temple of Ḫursagkalama (presumably in Kiš)[133] (l. 15-16): *a-na Aš-šur* ^{d}*Še-ru-'u*$_{2}$*-a Bēl*(EN) ^{d}*Zēr-bāni-ti*(NUMUN.DU$_{3}$.TI) ^{d}*Nabû*(AG) ^{d}*Taš-me-tum* ^{d}*Na-na-a / Be-let-Bābili*(KA$_{2}$.DINGIR.RA)^{ki} ^{d}*Nergal* (U.GUR) ^{d}*La-az niqê*(UDU.SISKUR)^{meš} *ebbūti*(KU$_{3}$)^{meš} *i-na Ḫur-sag-kalam-ma*^{ki} *aq-qi*$_{2}$.

It is evident that the deities were meant to be listed here in married pairs (Aššur – Šerua, Bēl – Ṣarpanītum, Nabû – Tašmētum, Nergal – Laṣ). Nanāja was assigned to Bēlet-Bābili, who is Ištar. Contemporary literary texts support the conviction that the two goddesses were perceived as equals in this time.

In mentioning his decision to send troops against a rebellion in southern Babylonia, Sîn-aḫḫē-erība (705-681 BC) reports that the army reached as far as Uruk.[134] The ruler mentions the deities Šamaš of Larsa, the Lady from Uruk, Nanāja, Uṣur-amāssa, Bēlet-balāṭi, Kurunnam, Kaššitu and Nergal as inhabiting this city.

---

132 TSBA VII, p. 89 ff.; D. D. Luckenbill, *Ancient Records of Assyria and Babylonia*, vol. I, no. 624; RIMA 3, Shalmaneser III, A.O. 102.5, col. VI, l. 1b-5a.

133 P. Rost, *Die Keilschrifttexte Tiglat-Pilesers III*, Bd. II, Leipzig 1853, Pl. XXXII and XXXIII; D. D. Luckenbill, *op. cit.*, no. 784.

134 OIP II, p. 87, l. 31-33.

The poorly preserved tablet from Uruk (VAT 14519 = RIMB 2 B.6.31.1001) probably refers to Aššur-aḫa-iddina (680-669 BC); it concerns a rededication of animals (the scattered herds) of Ištar and Nanāja.

The document AO 6793[135] from the reign of Šamaš-šuma-ukīn (668-648 BC) informs of some land estates being given to Ištar and Nanāja (or rather their temples in Uruk) (l. 5-6: *šiddu*(UŠ) *elû*(AN.TA) *u šaplû*(KI.TA) *ultu Sippar*(ZIMBIR)^{ki} / *adi* ^{al}*Sūrānu išaddad*) in the intention of the king's life. In this text Nanāja is referred to always as *ra'mat* ^{d}*Nabû u* ^{d}*Marduk* "beloved of Nabû and Marduk" (l. 15-16).

Texts dated to the reigns of three rulers: Nabû-kudurri-uṣur (604-562 BC), Nabû-na'īd (556-539 BC) and Cambyses (538-532 BC) bring the phrases: NIG$_2$.GA ^{d}GAŠAN-*ša*-UNUG.KI *u* ^{d}*Na-na-a*, NIG$_2$.GA ^{d}INNIN-UNUG.KI *u* ^{d}*Na-na-a*, NIG$_2$.GA ^{d}15 *u* ^{d}*Na-na-a*, NIG$_2$.GA ^{d}*Iš-tar u* ^{d}*Na-na-a*.[136] This is proof of offerings being made to the goddesses Ištar (designated as the Lady-of-Uruk or Inanna-of-Uruk) and Nanāja in Uruk in the 7th and 6th centuries BC. These offerings were made in each of the twelve months of the year.

The first of these kings, having beautified the Ezida temple in Borsippa and "introduced (Nabû and Nanāja) to the seat of delight", established a daily offering to this couple, consisting of fattened animals, fish, fowl, honey, butter, milk, oil, beer, wine and other gifts.[137] The

---

135 RIMB 2 B.6.33.2001 – inscription of Sîn-šarra-uṣur, a governor of Ur during the time of Šamaš-šarra-ukīn. See also G. Frame, *N.A.B.U.* 2004/3, no. 69.

136 R. H. Sack, *Cuneiform Documents from the Chaldean and Persian Periods*, London 1994: nos. 76, 84, 85, 86, 88, 90, 91, 94, 96, 99, 101. See also E. Gehlken, *Uruk. Spätbabylonische Wirtschaftstexte aus dem Eanna-Archiv*, Teil I (AUWE 5), Mainz 1990: nos. 27, 43, 70, 73 (only Nanāja), 75 (only Nanāja), 77 (only Nanāja), 78 (Ištar, Nanāja, Bēlet-ša-Rēš), 79 (only Nanāja), 80, 81 (only Nanāja), documents concerning temple estates – nos. 130, 131, 133. Also H. Freydank, *Spätbabylonische Wirtschaftstexte aus Uruk*, Berlin 1971, gives 42 texts connected with offerings for Nanāja (see p. 13-16).

137 E. Unger, *Babylon*, Berlin 1970, p. 282, col. I 1-13. See also P.-A. Beaulieu, *N.A.B.U.* 1991/3, no. 79.

phrase "property (of the temple of) Ištar and Nanāja" confirms the idea of there being a joint temple for the two goddesses. The goddesses were further entitled to one *zakītu*[138], an incomparably small number compared to the 50 Puqudeians offered to the temple of Ištar and Nanāja around a hundred years earlier by Šarru-kīn II and Sîn-aḫḫē-erība.[139]

Nabû-na'īd in turn undertook to reorganize the Eanna temple already in the first year of his reign. He reinstated the *maššartu* offering to the divinities worshipped in this temple (PTS 2097),[140] including Nanāja (gifts of various kinds of grain and dates).

Thanks to P.-A. Bealieu's study *The Pantheon of Uruk during the Neo-Babylonian Period*, based on the archives of the temple of Eanna as the chief source of material, we have become well aware of Nanāja's position in the Neo-Babylonian pantheon of Uruk. Lists of offerings have permitted the author to establish a hierarchy of Uruk deities: Ištar and Nanāja stand at the head of the pantheon. Their worship was practiced in association with the seats of appropriately Bēl and Nabû. The word *šubtu* "seat" (in YBC 9135 there is *kakku* "symbol") refers to a small altar, on which the symbols of these gods rested.

Deities worshipped at the temple of Eanna formed a pentad: Ištar-of-Uruk, Nanāja, Bēltu-ša-Rēš, Uṣur-amāssa, Urkajītu. The first three of the goddesses are often referred to as the "Goddesses of Eanna" or with the collective term "Eanna."[141] Ištar occurs under the name of Lady-of-Uruk (Bēltu-ša-Uruk) with the epithet *bēlet Uruk*, while Nanāja as Queen-of-Uruk" (*šarrat Uruk*).

Sacrificial animals offered to Nanāja encompassed ox (*alpu*), sheep (*immeru*), goose (*kurkû*), fish (*nūnu*), duck (*paspasu*), lamb (*puḫādu*) and turtledove (*sukanninu*). As unprocessed food and drink we have: Telmun dates (*asnû*), emmer (*kunāšu*), flour (*qēmu*),

---

[138] AO 6827, 15.
[139] BIN II 132 = NBC 1219.
[140] See G. Frame, *ZA* 81/1 (1991), p. 37 ff.
[141] See P.-A. Beaulieu, CM 23, p. 74 and S. Zawadzki, *BiOr* LXII/3-4 (2005), p. 296 who is convinced that ^{d}GAŠAN.MEŠ in Uruk was instead of *mārāt* (DUMU.MI$_2$.MEŠ) *E$_2$-an-na*, the term known from literary tetxs.

dates (*suluppū*), salt (*ṭabtu*) and barley (*uṭṭa/etu*). As processed food and drink for Nanāja, the following are evidenced: bread (*akalu*), *mersu*-cake and beer (*šikaru*).

Quoting Beaulieu:[142] "(...) Ištar and Nanaya each received approximately twice the number of animals offered to any of the other deities on a daily basis for the *ginû* offerings."

As far as we know, the conquest of Babylonia by Cyrus did not cause any substantial changes in the state system. The temples continued to be cult centers. The continuity of Nanāja's worship within the city of Uruk is confirmed by a Babylonian contract[143] with Aramean legend. The text was written in Uruk, in the sixth year of Cyrus the Great, and concerns a loan from the temple treasury (the phrase NIG$_2$.GA ^{d}*Bēlet*(GAŠAN)-*ša-Uruk*(UNUG)^{ki} *u* ^{d}*Na-na-a* was used: "property of Bēlet-ša-Uruk and Nanāja"; rev. l. 2. only Bēlet-ša-Uruk).

A list of gods worshipped in the Neo-Babylonian Sippar was compiled on the grounds of texts concerning the distribution of animals and robes in the city (CT 55-57).[144] It includes Nanāja of Dūr-Kurigalzu (*ša* KUR.TI^{ki}).

Texts from the Seleucid period originating from Uruk included, apart from rituals to Anu and Ištar, a hundred-line list of daily offerings made in the temple of Anu[145] (AO 6451). To judge by the colophon, the tablet belonged to a set of ritual texts the originals of which had been collected by Nabû-apla-uṣur (625-605 BC), and were rediscovered 300 years later in Elam by a priest-copyist living in the reigns of Seleucos and Antiochus. The list includes offerings to Anu, the god's spouse Antu, the goddesses Ištar and Nanāja, as well as other divinities designated with the phrase "divinities residing in Uruk" or "deities residing in the temples of Rēš, Irigal, Ešarra and Baramaḫ." "Occasionally, Ištar and Nanāja are referred to indirectly as divinities of Uruk (l. 41) or deities of the temples of Anu and Antu (l. 63, 68, 71).

---

142 P.-A. Beaulieu, *op. cit.* p. 101.
143 V. Scheil, *RA* XI (1914), p. 183-187.
144 See F. Joannès, *RA* LXXXVI/2 (1992), p. 159-184; R. da Riva, AOAT 291, p. 278.
145 TUAT II/2, p. 227-232.

The calendar of offerings made in Babylon in the months of *araḫsamna*, *kislīmu* and *ṭebētu*[146] informs of offerings made, among others, to Nanāja on the 25th day of the month of *kislīmu* (November/December) in two temples (l. 47-48): *i-na* ^{iti}*kislīmu*(GAN) *ūmu*(UD)-25-KAM *ša*$_2$ ^{d}*Lugal-Marad-da* / *ša*$_2$ ^{d}*Na-na-a* e$_2$. u r$_5$. š a$_3$. b a *ša*$_2$ ^{d}*Na-na-a* e$_2$. m e . u r$_4$. u r$_4$. In the sixth year of the reign of Cambyses offerings were brought to Nanāja and Sûtîti in Borsippa.[147] The latter is believed to be a goddess of the tribe of Aramaic nomads, the Sûtû; she bore the cognomen of *bukur Ištar* "firstborn of Ištar." Sûtîti had been known in Borsippa since at least the middle of the 8th century BC as the texts from the 8th regnal year of Nabû-šuma-iškun (760-748 BC) mentions her *šangû* priest and the *ērib bīti* priest (VAS I 36 iv 2,9).

The latest offerings[148] are from 502/1 BC – for Nabû and Nanāja in Borsippa.

Offerings made to a deity constitute irrefutable proof of the existence of an official cult. The texts present a variety of gifts brought to Nanāja. It should be kept in mind that there is a time gap in the textual evidence, covering practically a millennium (between the 20th and 9th century BC), during which time not one of the rulers of Mesopotamia even mentions having made offerings to the goddess Nanāja.

The pair of goddesses – Bēlat-suḫnir and Bēlat-tirraban – mentioned next to Nanāja in the Neo-Sumerian offering texts merits attention. As discussed above, W. G. Lambert considered them to be of Semitic origin, while M. Sigrist referred the origins of their cult to no later than the 32nd regnal year of Šulgi. According to text A 14643[149] the formal worship of these goddesses was established already in the 29th year of Šulgi. Thus, it cannot be excluded that Nanāja could al-

---

146 A. T. Clay, BRM IV, New Haven 1923, no. 25 (MLC 2608) = G. Reisner, SBH VII, p. 144 (VAT 398); see E. Unger, *Babylon*, p. 260.
147 VS VI 113.
148 See R. Zadok, *N.A.B.U.* 2002/3, no. 65 and *idem*, *N.A.B.U.* 2003/2, no. 33.
149 B. Lewis, E. R. Jewell, *ASJ* 4 (1982), p. 53-68.

so be considered as a deity whose worship was brought to the land of Sumer from the north, together with the cult of goddesses of an undoubtedly Semitic prototype.

II.2 VOTIVE GIFTS
STATUES AND STATUETTES
YEAR FORMULAS
TEXTS CONCERNING ROBES AND ORNAMENTS

Votive offerings accompanied the variety of offerings described above. There are six texts evincing the existence of copper figurines of the goddess Nanāja in the times of the Ur III Dynasty[150]. In his *Le travail du métal au pays de Sumer au temps de la III Dynastie d'Ur* (Paris 1960), H. Limet stated that these statuettes (about 12 cm high) were cast of copper[151] and coated in silver, leaving some parts, like the eyes, mouth and arms to be inlaid with gold. Five of the texts provide an exact date: for UET III 525, 529, 538 it is the 11th year of the king of Ur Ibbi-Sîn (2028-2004 BC), for UET III 509 it is the 15th year and for UET IX 569 it is the 16th year of the same king. The summary in text UET III 740, undated, speaks of a total of five silver-coated bronze statuettes of Nanāja.

Further information on statues and statuettes devoted to Nanāja comes from the year formulas of the reigns of rulers of the Isin and Old Babylonian dynasties.

Enlil-bāni (1860-1837 BC) offered a golden statue to the goddess[152] (mu ^{d}En-lil$_2$-ba-ni lugal-e alan ku$_3$-sig$_{17}$ ^{d}Na-na-a-a-ra mu-na-dim$_2$). Also the next ruler of the Isin dynasty, Zambīja (1836-1834 BC), offered Inanna and Nanāja five golden statuettes, a fact that was also noted as the most important event of the

[150] UET III nos 509, 525, 529, 538, 740 and UET IX 569.

[151] H. Limet, *op. cit.*, p. 129 and 152. See also A. Spycket, *Les statues de culte dans les textes mésopotamiens des origines à la Ire dynastie de Babylone*, Paris 1968, p. 69.

[152] See M. Sigrist, *Isin Year Names*, Berrien Springs 1988, p. 34.

year (m u ^{d}Z a - a m - b i - i a l u g a l a l a n k u$_3$ - s i g$_{17}$ 5 - b i ^{d}I n a n n a u$_3$ ^{d}N a - n a - a - r a m u - n e$_2$ - d i m).[153]

The second ruler of the Old Babylonian dynasty, Sūmû-la-El (1880-1845 BC) offered statues[154] to Inanna and Nanāja in the 26th year of his reign (m u a l a n ^{d}I n a n n a u$_3$ ^{d}N a - n a - a m u - u n - d i m$_2$ - m a).

Ruler of Uruk Sîn-erībam (1832-1827 BC) ordered a golden statue to be cast[155] (of himself) to be offered to Nanāja (m u a l a n k u$_3$ - s i g$_{17}$ ^{d}S î n - e - r i - b a - a m l u g a l ^{d}N a - n a - a - r a m u - n a - a n - d i m$_2$). And in the times of Irdanene (1816-1810 BC) the king's offering of a golden statue of his father Anam to the temple of Nanāja was deemed a momentous action (m u a l a n k u$_3$ - s i g$_{17}$ A n - a m$_3$ a d - d a - n a e$_2$ - ^{d}N a - n a - a - š e$_3$ i - n i - i n - k u$_4$ - r e - e n).[156] To judge by the number of preserved clay tablets dated to different months and days, there must have been a sizable number of these statuettes in the temples.

Surviving sources concerning statues offered to Nanāja fall silent until Neo-Assyrian times.

From a fortunately preserved letter (LAS 1, no. 277) we learn of the renovation of a statue of Nanāja carried out in the reign of king Aššur-aḫa-iddina (681-669 BC). His son Aššur-bāni-apli (668-627

---

[153] *Op. cit.*, p. 35 (A). See A (b): m u ^{d}Z a - a m - b i - i a l u g a l - e ^{giš}a l a m k u$_3$ - s i g$_{17}$ 4 - b i ^{d}I n a n n a - r a m u - n a - d i m$_2$, leading one to surmise that Nanāja received only one statuette.

[154] See RlA II, p. 165, A.40. Despite the absence of the dative ending -r a, it may be supposed that statues were offered to each of the goddesses and differed perhaps in some characteristic attributes of the deities. It cannot be excluded that it was only one statue and that it was offered in the joint temple of the two goddesses.

[155] A. Falkenstein, *BaghM* 2 (1963), no. 2, p. 9 (W 20038, 23 and others).

[156] *Ibid.*, p. 8 (no. 1) and p. 15 (no. 33) – W 20472, 93 and others. See also Sh. Sanati-Müller, *BaghM* 21 (1990), no. 150, p. 211, l. 4'-6' (W 20472, 152): i t u ^{giš}a p i n - d u$_8$ - a u$_4$ - 5 - k a m m u a l a m - k u$_3$ - s i g$_{17}$ A n - a m$_3$ a d - d a - n i e$_2$ - ^{d}*Na-na-a-* r a i - n i - i n - t u - r e - e n and *eadem*, *BaghM* 20 (1989), no. 123, p. 177 – W 20472, 112; *eadem*, *BaghM* 22 (1991), p. 324 and 329; *eadem*, *BaghM* 23 (1992), p. 160-161.

BC) occupied himself with fetching back another statue of Nanāja from Susa to Uruk (presumably one taken away much earlier by the Elamites).[157] Aššur-bāni-apli also dedicated to Nanāja of Uruk a golden bowl *makkasu* (K 1364).

Proof of the transporting of a statue of Nanāja (together with one of Bēlet-ša-Uruk) from Babylon to Uruk is the letter YOS 3, 86.[158] According to Beaulieu,[159] this had place in the first year of Cyrus who, having conquered Babylon, ordered the return of statues of Nanāja and the Lady-of-Uruk to Uruk.

From Old Babylonian Uruk (the palace of Sîn-kašid) comes an unpublished text impressed on a cylinder (W 20475). It had originally consisted of about 1000 lines. It mentions the inventory of Nanāja, including gold and silver objects and ornaments, inlaid with precious jewels. We have also the information about the throne of Nanāja (W 20472, 123 = *BaghM* 21, 138, no. 89, l. 1-4) and about the star on the gate of the temple (W 20472, 152 = *BaghM* 21, 191, no. 135, l. 8-10).

The text K 8247 + K 13182 (F. M. Fales, J. N. Postgate, SAA VII, 60), which is a list of possessions belonging to the deities of Agade sent to Elam, recalls 12 sheckels of gold added to the gold from the old rings of Nanāja with the sole purpose of making new ones (l. 8-9: 12 GIN$_2$ *ina* UGU! O! *ša$_2$-bir* KUG!.GI! / *la-bi-ru-tu$_2$ ša* ^{d}*Na*-[*na*]-[*a*].)[160]

---

157 On the subject of the statues of Nanāja in the reign of the mentioned rulers, see further p. 59-60.

158 See chapter VIII, p. 151.

159 P.-A. Beaulieu, *The Reign of Nabonidus*, New Haven – London 1989, p. 232.

160 This leads to an interesting question: Were the statues of divinities once taken away by the Elamites preserved and decorated by the Assyrian kings? Perhaps the text concerns a period just before the return of the statues to Uruk; Aššur-bāni-apli must have brought into the Eanna temple a statue that was appropriately prepared. P.-A. Beaulieu states (CM 23, p. 198): "In the 7th century the Assyrian imperial authorities sponsored repair work on the cult statues of Uruk as part of their effort to reverse the repressive measures of Sennacherib."

The Neo-Babylonian texts mention oil used to clean the jewelry of Nanāja (GCCI I 141), the silver (GCCI I 251) and stones (GCCI II 45; VAS 20, 19) needed to repair this jewelry, even an instrument belonging to the goddess (GCCI II 25). They also record a variety of ornaments that were given to the jewelers for repairs (BIN II 126; YOS 6, 216; AUWE 11, 162) or cleaning (YOS 6, 117), the quantity of alum[161] for treating a kid's skin belonging to Nanāja (BIN II 128) and robes assigned to Nanāja (YOS 7, 183) as well as textiles intended for sewing a curtain (GCCI II 381).

In his *The Pantheon of Uruk during the Neo-Babylonian Period*, on p. 189-208, P.-A. Beaulieu presented systematically fragments of texts concerning Nanāja's cultic paraphernalia. The following demonstration of the variety of these temple furnishings and the statue of the goddess is based on his presentation (classification from pages 6-25[162]):

I. Cultic paraphernalia:

1. Components of the shrine and cella: *gidlû* "door curtain", *šiddu* "dividing curtain", *šubtu* "altar, cultic socle, cultic seat", *tallu* "balustrade", *zaratu* "tent."
2. Furniture: *kankannu* "potstand", *kišukku* "grate", *paššūru* "offering table", *pišannu* "chest."
3. Cultic vessels: *dannu* "vat", kallu "bowl", *mê-qātī* "water bassin", *šappu*-container", *taphu* "kettle."
4. Textiles: *kitinnû* "linen towel."

II. Ornaments:

1. Headdress: *agû* "tiara", *kulūlu* "crown."
2. Ornaments of headdress: *ajaru pānû* "frontal rosette (for the crown and tiara)", *gappu* "quill, feather (for the tiara)", *sāmtu* "carnelian bead (for the crown)."

161 On the *aban gabî* (IM.SAHAR.NA_4.KUR.RA), see A. Degraeve, *Akkadica* 99-100 (1996), p. 28.

162 Beaulieu's classification has been modified to an extent to suit Nanāja cultic paraphernalia. It should be kept in mind that she was also considered as a member of the group of "Goddesses."

3. Breast ornaments: *irtu* "breast ornament", *irat ḫurāṣi* "breast ornament of gold", *irat ḫurāṣi ebbi* "breast ornament of pure gold", *irtu ša uskāri* "crescent-shaped breastplate", *irtu ša birīt qātī* "breast ornament set between the hands", *irat ḫurāṣi ša birīt qātī* "breast ornament of gold set between the hands", *irtu ša apsasî* "breastplate with a representation of a sphinx", *irat ḫurāṣi ša apsasî* "breastplate of gold with a representation of a sphinx", *irat ḫurāṣi ša nēsi* "breastplate of gold with a representation of a lion", *irat ḫurāṣi ṣeḫertu ša ṣēri tēbî* "small breastplate of gold with a representation of a rising snake."
4. Jewelry:
   a/ Necklaces, chains, rings and pins: *dudittu* "fibula", *ḫarḫaru* "chain", *inṣabtu/anṣabtu* "ring, earring", *kišādu* "necklace", *qudāšu* "ring", *semeru* "bracelet", *unqu* "finger-ring."
   b/ Jewels: *arzallu*-piece of jewelry, *ajaru* "rosette", *ajaru ša tamlê* "inlaid rosette", *diglu* "gem", *e/irimmatu* "egg-shaped ornament", *inbu* "fruit-shaped ornament", *kilīlu* "circlet", *kumāru* "frame, framed ornament", *maknaktu* "seal", *ṣipru* "ornamental trim", *šamšu* "sun-disk ornament", *šanduppu*-ornament, *tarkīsu*-ornament.
5. Articles of beauty: *muš/lṭu* "comb", *mušālu* "cosmetic jar", *muttabiltu*-recipient, perhaps for cosmetics, *nāmaru* "mirror."
6. Figurines: *iṣṣūru* "bird", *pazūzu* "Pazūzu head."
7. Door-locking mechanisms: *ḫandūḫu*-part of a lock, *ḫargullu* "lock", *pingu* "knob", *sanḫu* "ring."
8. Beads and stones:
   a/ According to substance, color, or appearance:
   aban ḫurāṣi "gold bead", *abnu* "stone, bead", *arzallu*-stone, *ašgikû* "turqouise", *muššaru*-stone, *pappardilû* "banded

agate", *saggilmud*-stone, *sāmtu* "carnelian", *tarkīsu*-stone or bead, *uqnû* "lapis lazuli", *zakukû* "glass."

b/ According to shape:

binītu "fish-roe-shaped beads", *īnu* "eye-stone", *kunukku* "cylinder-seal-shaped bead", *nurmû* "pomegranate-shaped bead", *t/dubk/qātu*-stone or bead, *tukpītu* "kidney-shaped bead", *zēr qiššê* "melon-seed-shaped bead."

III. Clothing

1. Articles of clothing: *adīlu* "tassel(?)", *eru* "headband", *guḫalṣu* "scarf, braids", *ḫullānu* "blanket, wrap", *ḫuṣannu* "sash, belt", *kusītu*-garment, *lubāru kulūlu* "head scarf", *muṣīptu*-garment, *naḫlaptu* "wrap, outer garment", *naṣbatu*-garment, *paršīgu* "turban", *ṣabû* "dyed garment", *ṣibtu*-garment, *šalḫu*-cloth.
2. Materials and dyes: *argamannu* "red purple wool", *miḫṣu* "woven cloth, fabric", *tabarru* "red-colored wool", *takiltu* "blue covered wool."
3. Qualities: *da'mu* "dark colored (fabric)", *peṣû* "pale, bright, white colored (fabric)."

We have attested the clothing ceremonies of different gods, including Nanāja (PTS 2783; NBC 4769; YOS 17, 305; PTS 3257) and sacred meals for Nanāja (TCL XIII 221; YOS 17, 166).

From the 6th century, the reign of Amēl-Marduk, comes a tablet discovered at Uruk[163] listing the various jewelry products belonging to Bēlet-ša-Uruk and Nanāja. These objects were intended for repairs or cleaning. Listed among jewelry are 86 golden rosettes and *tenšû* ornaments from the *kusītu* robes of the goddesses (l. 3-4: 86 *a-a-ri* KU_3.GI u_3 *te-en-ši-i* KU_3.GI / $ša_2$ UGU *ku-si-*tu_4 $ša_2$ ^{d}*Na-na-a*). L. 8-9 refer to the same ornaments, but a much larger quantity (1300). At the very end of the text we are informed of total ornaments belonging

[163] NBC 4577, R. H. Sack, *ZA* 69/1 (1979), p. 42-43 and P.-A. Beaulieu, CM 23, p. 157 with note 189.

to Nanāja (l. 12-14: [PAP 1]412 / *a-a-ri* KU_3.GI *u te-en-še-e* / *ša*$_2$ ^{d}*Na-na-a*). Other texts (e.g. YBC 3441) prove that a very large number of rosettes and ornaments *tenšû* belonged to Nanāja.

From the same period comes text NBC 4504[164] which mentions sending ornaments of the *kusītu* robes of goddesses Bēlet-ša-Uruk and Nanāja packed in a basket.

The text YOS 6, 117, discussed earlier, dating from the reign of Nabû-na'īd (556-539 BC), speaks of cleaning the golden elements of the *kusītu* robe of Nanāja (there is mention of 706 golden rosettes and 706 golden *tenšû* ornaments).

Concerned about the disappearance of the *kusītu* robe of Nanāja brought from the Ezida temple to "the city of the goddess Bēltija", the son of Nabû-na'īd wrote letters (proof is to be found in the letters of a priest from the Eanna temple: YOS 6, 71 + dupl. YOS 6, 72).[165] We also learn from the letter that the robes of Nanāja were sent from the Eanna temple to the town of Bēltija twice in the reigns of previous rulers: Nabû-kudurri-uṣur and Nergal-šarra-uṣur. The means of transport then was a ship called *elippu ša kusīti.*

The archives of the temple of Bīt Rēš have yielded a text (NCBT 1244)[166] dated to the 59th regnal year of Antioch II (260-246 BC). It is an inventory of materials (GADA/*kitû*) that made up the wardrobe of Anu, Antu and Nanāja. Chiefly represented are decorative materials used to cover the statues, as well as curtains, table-spreads and veils. The function of some of these textiles remains unclear.

Votive inscriptions are represented by the text of a l u k u r priestess whose name was Nanāja-ibsa,[167] a concubine of Būr-Sîn, ruler of Isin (1895-1874 BC). Her title is unclear: l u k u r - k i - a g$_2$ - k a s k a l

---

[164] R. H. Sack, *op. cit.*, p. 44.
[165] See L. Oppenheim, *JNES* 8 (1949), p. 179-180; E. Matsushima, *ASJ* 17 (1995), p. 242 and *eadem,* in: H.I.H. Prince Takahito Mikasa (ed.), *Cult and Ritual in the Ancient Near East,* Wiesbaden 1992, p. 12-14; also *eadem*, *Orient* XXX-XXXI (1995), p. 173-175 and P.-A. Beaulieu, CM 23, p. 200. The letter is also discussed below, in chapter VIII, p. 150-151.
[166] P.-A. Beaulieu, *RA* LXXXIII (1989), p. 69-74.
[167] TLB II 17; IRSA 178-179, 7c; I. Kärki, StOr 49, Būr-Sîn 3; RIME 4 1.7.3.

- l a - k a - n e₂ "his beloved l u k u r (priestess) of the journey."[168] Nanāja is her mistress and Būr-Sîn is the beloved of both Inanna and Nanāja. The priestess offered Nanāja an agate plaque in the intention of the king's life and her own life; the plaque was placed on the statue (literally, on the body) of the goddess. This 20-line Sumerian text ends with a curse formula threatening with Nanāja's evil curse anyone who dared destroy the offering (ᵈN a - n a - a ... a š₂ - g i g - g a h e₂ - e n - d a b).

The discussed texts evince the existence of both small statuettes placed as votive offerings in the temples of Nanāja and big statues of the goddess. How characteristic these statues were, allowing them to be distinguished from statues of Inanna/Ištar and other goddesses, it is difficult to say. In the case of the last-mentioned inscription, a copy of which in the form of a plaque was found on the statue of the goddess, identification proved facile for anyone knowledgeable in the art of reading. It should be remembered, however, that most people then were illiterate. Also the robes and ornaments of statues of Nanāja and of Inanna/Ištar do not seem to have differed from one another.

Rulers of the Isin dynasty are especially proud to emphasize in their year formulas that they had offered Nanāja (and Inanna as well) gold statuettes. A king of Uruk of the 19th century BC tells of offering the goddess statues of himself (Sîn-erībam) or of his father (Irdanene).

The gap in the sources concerning statues of Nanāja (again lasting for about a thousand years) cannot be construed as meaning a break in the cult. Under Assyrian rule in Babylonia (especially in the reign of Aššur-aḫa-iddina and Aššur-bāni-apli), the cult of Nanāja – to judge by various texts – seems to have played a momentous role for

[168] Another l u k u r priestess is Šulgi-sīmti, "the beloved mistress of king Šulgi." From her archives we have texts concerning offerings made to the deities of Ur and Uruk. On the meaning of the term l u k u r, see G. Leick, *Sex and Eroticism in Mesopotamian Literature*, London – New York 1994, p. 147-149.

the governing king. Equally so, based on preserved materials, we should consider the Neo-Babylonian and Seleucid periods as a time of flourishing development for the cult of Nanāja.

II.3 PLACES OF WORSHIP OF NANĀJA NAMES OF TERRITORIES CONNECTED WITH NANĀJA

Places of worship are evinced foremost by preserved inscriptions concerning the dedication or renovation of temples of Nanāja, year formulas mentioning her name in connection with a new building and lists of temples. I have also considered names of localities and urban territories connected with Nanāja and appearing in the texts.

The temples mentioned here have not been identified in the archaeological record with the exception of e_2 - e $š_3$ - g a l (read also as e_2 - i r i - g a l), which A. Falkenstein has identified as the temple of Ištar in Uruk. Nanāja was worshipped there under the Seleucids.

Texts from Drehem permit conclusions concerning the presence of e_2 ^{d}Nanāja (*RSO* 230; PIOL 19, 80 = Eames F6; TRU 275 – only the latest dated to the 41st year of Šulgi) where offerings were made to the goddess.

The oldest text mentioning a temple of Nanāja is an inscription of the ruler of Isin, Lipit-Eštar (1934-1924 BC),[169] where Nanāja is referred to for the first time and directly as a daughter of Inanna (col. I 1-2 ^{d}N a - n a - a / d u m u k i - a g_2 ^{d}I n a n n a). For Nanāja, his mistress (n i n - ĝ u_{10} - r a, l. 3) Lipit-Eštar built the temple e_2 - m e - u r_4 - u r_4 "on the day that justice was introduced into the land of Sumer and Akkad" (col. II, l. 17-24). The name of the temple may be translated as "House which gathers (the divine powers of) *me*,"[170] indicating irrefutably that Nanāja was taking over Innana's prerogatives. The Emeurur is referred to as e_2 - š u t u m_x (GI.NA.AB.TUM) / k i - a g_2 - g a_2 - n i / š a_3 - I_3 - s i - i n^{ki} - n a - k a (col. II 3-6) "her be-

[169] G. Pettinato, AOAT 253, p. 267-279.
[170] See A. R. George, *Temples*, no. 793, who adds that it was likely a part of the Eanna complex in Uruk.

loved home š u t u m[171] in Isin." The inscription also likely comes from Isin[172]. Texts from this city confirm the existence of e_2 ^{d}I n a n n a u_3 ^{d}N a - n a - a.[173]

At Ur, a temple to Nanāja was erected by the king of Larsa Sūmû-El (1894-1866 BC). The document dated to the early years of the 19th century BC (IM 22874)[174], known from a dozen or so copies, tells of the construction of the temple e_2 - i t u / i t i - d a[175] "House of the month," which was "her beloved temple" or depending on the copy "her temple of the joyful heart." Nanāja is called n i n h i - l i (-a) š u - d u_7 "Lady of perfect attractiveness."[176] Apart from her own temple, she also had a chapel at the Ekišnugal, the complex of Nanna/Sîn, as indicated by texts.[177]

In the middle of the 19th century BC, at Uruk, the king Sîn-kāšid (c. 1865/60-1833 BC) built for his mistress Nanāja a presumably

---

171 G. Pettinato, *op. cit.*, p. 275 translates: "Il tempio 'Eme'urur', il 'santuario' suo prediletto, in Isin, ..." RIME 4 translates e_2 - š u t u m as "storehouse", which would mean that the king was boasting about building a storehouse. Texts from Umma (MVN XIII 697, 4; MVN XIII 705, 3; MVN XIII 875, 2; SNAT 330, 8; TPTS 1, 298, 4; PIOL 19, 356, 6 + seal l. 6) originating from the times of Šulgi and Amar-Su'en, clearly demonstrate that it is a place for storing foodstuffs intended as offerings). CAD Š/3 412a s.v. *šutummu* (*šatummu*) gives: 1. "storehouse", 2. "treasury" (exemplified among others by *ZA* 75 (1985) 200, 45, love spells from Isin prepared by C. Wilcke: *kīma Ištar ina parakkim wašbat, kīma Nanâ ina šu-tu-mi-im wašbat*. According to the translation, however, the word here has the meaning *Heiligtum* "temple.")
The Emeurur temple constructed for Nanāja would then be a storehouse serving presumably to hold foodstuffs intended for offerings.

172 In *N.A.B.U.* 1997/3, no. 98, M. Civil published an inscription of Lipit-Eštar, which was a duplicate of the one discussed here, but he read the name of the temple erroneously; for the correction, see *N.A.B.U.* 1998/2, no. 57.

173 Isin IV 126 (IB 1778 9).

174 RIME 4 2.7.2.

175 See A. R. George, *Temples*, no. 540. M. E. Cohen translated the name as "House of the Moon" in: *The Cultic Calendars of the Ancient Near East*, Bethesda 1993, p. 180.

176 See *kuzbu* /h i. l i CAD K 614a "attractiveness."

177 H. H. Figulla, W. J. Martin, UET V 789 II 11'.

oval structure i b (VA 10962 = W 4152).[178] This oval chapel was said to stand in the goddess's "House of the joyful heart" e_2 - [š a_3] - h u l_2 - l a.[179] Here the goddess is designated with the title n i n - h i - l i - s u_3 "Lady full of charm" ("Lady decorated with charm.")

An analysis of documents[180] referring to Nanāja discovered in the palace of Sîn-kāšid in Uruk leads one to presume that a chapel of Nanāja called e_2 ^{d}N a - n a - a was found there, presumably as part of another temple. The texts demonstrate that this chapel was still in existence in the reign of Anam, king of Uruk (1821-1817 BC).

The short-reigned king of Uruk Sîn-gāmil (1826-1824 BC) built a temple e_2 - m e - u r_4 - u r_4 (IM 33476) for his mistress and – as the text says – the beloved daughter of An.[181] This temple was also known as e_2 - l a - l a - k a - n i – her house of abundance.[182] Whether it was a separate temple dedicated to Nanāja will presumably remain moot.

This particular place of Nanāja's worship – e_2 - m e - u r_4 - u r_4 – was renovated by Anam (1821-1817 BC). We know of this fact from a Sumerian hymn commemorating this king (W 20477).[183] A throne in the temple of Nanāja was also refurbished in his reign, as indicated by the text W 20472, 123 (l. 1-4): 6 m a - n a k u_3 - s i g_{17} - l u h - h a / [*š*]*a i-na* ^{gi}p i s a n n i_3 - š u l u g a l / ni_3 e_2 - ^{d}*Na-na-a a-na* ^{giš}g u - z a g a r_3 - b a ^{giš}e s i / *uḫ₂-ḫu-zi-iz in-na-ad-nu* "6 mines of pure gold, / which (are) from the box, at the king's disposal, / prop-

---

[178] RIME 4 4.1.6.

[179] See A. R. George, *Temples*, nos. 1018 and 455, since I. Kärki (SKFZ, p. 97 and SAKAZ 1, p. 183 – Sînkāšid 9) reads the name of the temple as e_2 - h e_2 - g a l_2 - l a.

[180] E.g. W 20472, 104 and 123 (Anam), W 20472, 125 (Irdanene), and also the formula of year 1 of Irdanene preserved in many texts (see above p. 46 and note 156).

[181] RIME 4 4.3.1.

[182] The epithet of the temple could be translated also as "her house of riches." See RIME 4 4.3.1 where the author translates: "[house] of delight", although one can hardly deny that riches can be the source of delight.

[183] See A. Falkenstein, *BaghM* 2 (1963), p. 80-82 and pl. 13 (photo).

erty of the temple of Nanāja, to line the throne with a cap of *ušû* tree were issued."

From the turn of the 19th century BC comes a bronze foundation canephore (VA 3025)[184] and three stone foundation tablets reporting on the construction of a temple of Nanāja by Kudur-mabuk and his son Rīm-Sîn, ruler of Larsa (1822-1763 BC). This temple also bore the designation e$_2$ - š a$_3$ - h u l$_2$ - l a "House of the joyful heart", but was situated most likely in Larsa,[185] beside the temple of Inanna of the same name.

Nanāja is identified as follows (l. 2 - 4): n i n h i - l i š e - e r - k a - a n - d i / n a m - s a$_6$ - g a - n i g a l d i r i / d u m u z i - l e A n g a l - la "Lady who is decorated with charm, / whose sweetness is great, / pleasant[186] daughter of the great god An." The kings built "her beloved seat" in the intention of their lives. Nanāja, n i n ^{d}l a m m a - k e$_4$ "Lady of the guardian deities", was to beseech An and Innana for the kingdom of joy, a good reign for them and guardian deities l a m m a that were assigned to them (that is, to Kudur-mabuk and Rīm-Sîn).

Thus, the goddess is shown here as an intermediary between the kings and the grand deities.

Administrative texts from the reign of Rīm-Sîn (YOS 5, 171; 172; 194), mentioning offerings made in this period, refer to her as e$_2$ ^{d}I n a n n a u$_3$ ^{d}N a - n a - a. It would signify that the "House of the joyful heart" was a joint temple of the two goddesses. It cannot be excluded, however, that two temples had existed separately.[187]

---

[184] RIME 4 2.14.3 and TUAT II/5, p. 747-750; see also L. Marti, *N.A.B.U.* 2002/1, no. 25.

[185] See *op. cit.* and A. R. George, *Temples*, no. 1018. The text of a contract BE VIII/1, no. 108, from the 6th year of Darius I, notes the presence of Nanāja in the temple of Ehuršaba in Babylon (l. 9-10: *ina* ^{iti}*šabāti*(ZIZ) *ina Bābili*(TIN.TIR)^{ki} *pa-ni* ^{d}*Na-na-a* E$_2$.HUR.ŠA$_3$.BA). J. Renger (in: Fs Falkenstein, p. 157) situates the temple in Ur.

[186] I have adopted z i - l e for z i l$_2$. See remark by J. G. Westenholz, CM 7, p. 69: "The z i - l e calls to mind the Sumerian goddess B i - z e/z i l - l a."

[187] Text UCLMA 9-1845, published by A. J. Marchant, *Old Babylonian Tablets from Larsa in the Lowie Museum of Anthropology*, Diss. Univ. of Cali-

The next temple of Nanāja was e_2 - t u r_3 - k a l a m - m a[188] "House, cattle-pen of the land", which Hammurabi (1792-1750 BC) rebuilt in the 34th year of his reign. This temple standing in Babylon was dedicated also to Anu and Inanna, both Uruk divinities; this was noted in a year formula which has survived in a few versions.[189]

One text from Old Babylonian Nêrebtum (OBT IV, no. 234, 4) testify existing of e_2 ^{d}Nanāja (written e_2 ^{d}Na-na-a-a).

For the next thousand years the texts fall silent, yet it should not be construed that a renaissance of the cult came afterwards; rather, it should be assumed that the goddess continued to be worshipped throughout this period, as other sources seem to indicate.

The next texts to mention temples of Nanāja are dated therefore to the 7th century BC. Aššur-aḫa-iddina (680-669 BC), ruler of Assyria, left a few inscriptions (found in Uruk) addressed to this goddess. The first of these[190] says that he rebuilt e_2 - h i - l i - a n - n a[191] "House of heavenly charm" (this name seems more appropriate although one cannot exclude the translation "House of the charm of An.") It was a chapel to Nanāja erected in the Eanna complex in Uruk, which Aššur-aḫa-iddina reconstructed, too. According to the king, the Ehilianna was built by Nazi-Maruttaš, king of Babylon (1307-1282 BC) (l. 12), and later renovated by Erība-Marduk, also a king of Babylon (c. 765 BC) (l. 13); hence, this architectural development should fall in the second half of the 2nd and the first half of the 1st millennium BC. This lets us believe in the enduring character of the worship of Nanāja at least in the Uruk sanctuary.

---

fornia, Berkeley 1990, pl. 189-190 mentions e_2 ^{d}N a - n a - a - a, which was supposed to be closed because of the moving of the (statue of the) goddess (presumably Nanāja). The decision was taken, according to the document, by the i š i b and g u d u priests (presumably also priests of Nanāja).

[188] A. R. George, *Temples*, no. 1117 and J. A. Black, *ASJ* 7 (1985), p. 63.

[189] D. Charpin, *RA* LXXIV (1980), p. 93.

[190] R. Borger, *Die Inschriften Asarhaddons Königs von Assyrien*, Graz 1956, Uruk D; RIMB 2 6.31.18.

[191] A. R. George, *Temples*, no. 459.

Aššur-aḫa-iddina referred to Nanāja as queen of Uruk (*šarrat Uruk*) and Great Lady (*bēlet rabîti*), naturally also his Mistress. The Ehilianna was called *bīt papaḫ* ᵈ*Nanāja* (l. 11) – a chapel of the cult of the goddess Nanāja. The ruler had taken Nanāja "by the hands" and *ana qerbīšu ušērib* šubat *darat ušarme* (l. 17), meaning he had brought her statue inside the temple and had placed it in her seat since time immemorial.

In gratitude for this act, the goddess was to plead for the king in front of Nabû, Aššur-aḫa-iddina's Lord (l. 18-20). She was also to annihilate anyone who dared destroy the inscription along with his descendants (l. 21-23).

The second of Aššur-aḫa-iddina's texts,[192] also known from a number of copies, was of a similar content but more elaborate (25 lines); it brings some details concerning Nanāja.

In the first lines already we read (l. 1-5): *ana* ᵈ*Nanāja pusumti ilāti ša kuzbu u ulṣu za'nat lulê malâtu / bukurti* ᵈ*Anim šitrāḫti ša ina napḫar bēlēti šurbâtu danūssa / ḫīrat* ᵈ*Muṣibsa tizqārti sekrat na'itti narāmti rubûtīšu / iltum rēmēnîtum alikat rēṣi šarri paliḫīša mušalbirat palêšu / ašibat Eḫilianna ša qereb Eanna šarrat Uruk*ᵏⁱ *bēlti rabîti bēltīšu* "for the goddess Nanāja, bethroted (among) the goddesses, who is adorned with charm and delight, full of splendor, / (for) the proudest firstborn of Anu, who is superior in might to all the goddesses (lit. Ladies), / (for) the illustrious spouse of the god Muṣibsa, worshipped *sekretu* priestess(?), his princely beloved, / (for) the gracious goddess, assisting the king, (who) worships her, prolonging his reign, / (for the one) residing in (the temple of) the Eḫilianna, which (is) inside the Eanna, (for) the queen of Uruk, the great lady, his mistress" Aššur-aḫa-iddina rebuilt her chapel.[193] As in the pre-

[192] R. Borger, *Die Inschriften Asarhaddons Königs von Assyrien*, Graz 1956, Uruk C; RIMB 2 6.31.17.

[193] Once again we are faced with the problem of the interpretation of the sign e_2 = *bītu*(*m*). Differentiating between a temple, which is a separate religious structure, and a chapel, which is a place or niche dedicated to one divinity, is occasionally very difficult. I have assumed that when a place of worship belongs to an entire complex (e.g. Eanna), then we should speak of a chapel (e.g. Ehilianna); but when we are dealing with a single structure

vious text, there follows a fragment about introducing the statue of the goddess into "her immemorial seat." The king further offered *niqê tašriḫti*, meaning splendid offerings and reinforced specially the doors of the chapel (*ušparziḫ šigarša* – l. 15). Nanāja, *bēltum ṣirtum* "noble lady", having joyfully taken up residence in her chapel was then supposed to intercede for the king with her spouse, Nabû (earlier designated as Muṣibsa). She is asked to prolong the king's life, give satisfaction from a long and fruitful (also as far as offspring is concerned) life and ensure *ṭub šērê u ḫud libbi* "health (for) the body and delight (for) the heart" (l. 18). Next the king addresses Nanāja in a few fine words: "Set the foundations of my royal throne as strong as a rock! Make my reign as firm as the heavens and earth!" (l. 19).

The piece terminates with a request addressed to Nanāja, the greatest lady, who is supposed to be merciless for those who would destroy the inscription and their descendants.

Nanāja is mentioned in a letter[194] addressed to Aššur-aḫa-iddina. The text speaks of restoring statues of the goddess of Uruk (including Nanāja and Uṣur-amāssa[195]) most likely in Assyria (671 BC). That Nanāja's statue was adorned with gold already during the life of the king is evinced by a source referring to the first year of the reign of his son Aššur-bāni-apli. During the ceremony of greeting the statue of Marduk in Babylon (in 668 BC) both the goddesses from Uruk[196] – Nanāja and Uṣur-amāssa – were present.

The existence of this renovated statue did not stop Aššur-bāni-apli from revindicating another old statue. This heir to the throne of Assyria (668-626 BC), in his text K 1364 (CT 35, pl. 48), spoke of sending an envoy to the king of Elam *šut alak* *ᵈNanāja ultu qereb* *ᵘʳᵘSušān ana Urukᵏⁱ* (rev. l. 7) "in the matter of the return (lit. road) of (the sta-

(eg. Ešahula), then it should be designated as a temple (although this hardly settles the issue of the size of these structures).

194 LAS 1, no. 277. See chapter VIII below, p. 149-150.

195 The name of Uṣur-amāssa had been considered by some scholars as a cognomen of Nanāja (BIN II, p. 48).

196 K 3050 + K 2694, l. 12-13.

tue) of the goddess Nanāja from Susa to Uruk." The actual return of the statue of the goddess was recorded in the annals of this king (V R col. VI, l. 107-124),[197] where Aššur-bāni-apli wrote that before 1635 years[198] (or 1535 years)[199] the goddess Nanāja "became angry and went to live in the land of Elam, a place not intended for her" (*ta-as-bu-šu*$_2$ / *tal-li-ku tu-ši-bu* / *qe-re-eb* ^{uru}ELAM.MA^{ki} *a-šar la si-ma-ti-ša*$_2$, col. VI, l. 107-109). This statement obviously refers to the looting of the temple and abducting the statue of the goddess by the Elamites.[200] Aššur-bāni-apli introduced the statue (meaning the goddess) ceremoniously into the Eanna temple, the Ehiliana chapel to be more precise (Akkad. *bīt kuzbî šamê* "House of heavenly charm.")

In his work on imperialism and religion in Assyria, Judah and Israel in the 8th and 7th centuries BC, M. Cogan[201] mentioned two or three statues of other goddesses being returned together with that of Nanāja; these could have been Uṣur-amāssa, Arkajītu and perhaps Ištar of Uruk.[202] The names of these goddesses are sometimes taken to be cognomens of Nanāja, although in the Neo-Assyrian period they appear separately. Even so, Cogan rightly remarks that "this does not preclude the possibility that at some earlier date various manifestations of Nana may have become separated and hyposta-

---

197 See list of duplicates of the prism in: R. Borger, *Beiträge zum Inschriftenwerk Assurbanipals*, Wiesbaden 1996, p. 57.

198 K 3101a, rev. l. 10; K 2628 l. 4.

199 Perhaps the date 1535 is a simple scribal error – see E. Nassouhi, *MAOG* III/1-2 (1927), p. 34-35.

200 See P. Rost, *MVAG* 2 (1897), p. 20-21 note 1, where the author attributes the looting of the statue to king Kutir-naḫḫunti (12th century BC). See M. Streck, *Assurbanipal...* III, Leipzig 1916, p. 757 (item Nanan, Nanai): "Die dortige von den Elamiten um 2285 v. Chr. weggeschleppte Statue der Göttin wurde von Assurbanipal wieder aus Suza zurückgeführt; (...)." The Elamites are likely to have stolen statues of Nanāja twice: around 2300-2200 BC and in the 12th century BC.

201 M. Cogan, *Imperialism and Religion: Assyria, Judah and Israel in the eight and seventh Centuries B.C.E.*, Missoula 1974, p. 14, note 34.

202 See damaged Rm 589, rev. III 6-10, where the following are mentioned in sequence: ^{d}*Uṣur-amāssa*, ^{d}*Ištar Agade*, ^{d}*Nanāja*, ^{d}*Anunītum*.

tized."[203] What happened to the previous statue that had also stood in the Eanna remains unresolved.

The preserved fragment of text K 2524 also concerns the return of a statue of Nanāja from Elam to Uruk. The reigning Aššur-bāni-apli states the following (l. 9): ^{d}*Nanāja ana šūrubi Uruk*^{ki} *uṭib alak-ša ana qereb Eanna* "in order to introduce the (statue of) the goddess Nanāja to Uruk, I have made the way to (the temple of) the Eanna beautiful." A bit above the cited line there is an unclear description (l. 3): ^{d}*Nanāja ina dāme nišē* ^{d}*Uṣur-amāssa* ^{d}*Arkajītu ukabbasū* ^{lu_2}*pagar qurādi* "the goddess Nanāja in human blood, the goddesses Uṣur-amāssa and Arkajītu trample the body of the hero."[204] This is the only "bloody" mention of Nanāja. Presumably the surviving fragment was part of a hymn to Nanāja or the divinities of Uruk, because the piece ends with the king asking for his kingdom to be blessed, his throne strengthened and his power extended (rev. l. 9-10).

About seventy years after the death of Aššur-bāni-apli, Nabû-na'id of Babylonia (556-539 BC) also attested his building activities in the texts.[205] In rebuilding the town of Ubassa,[206] situated between Babylon and Borsippa, he renovated the temple there: *ša* ^{uru}*U*$_2$*-ba-as-si bīrit*(DAL.BA.AN.NA) *Bābili* (KA$_2$.DINGIR.RA)^{ki} *u Bar*$_2$*-sipa*^{ki} / *i-na kup-ri*(ESIR$_2$.UD.DU.A) *u*$_3$ *a-gur-ru re-e-ši-šu u*$_2$*-ul-li-ma* / ^{d}*Na-na-a* ^{d}*Ištar šu-ur*$_2$*-bi-tum u*$_2$*-še-ri-bu ki-iṣ-ṣu-uš-šu* "(temple) in Ubassa, (standing) between Babylon and Borsippa, / I erected its top of bitumen and fired brick and / I introduced the goddess Nanāja – superior to Ištar (again) into her sanctuary." Nanāja here is referred to with the title *Ištar šurbītum* – "great /

---

203 M. Cogan, *op. cit.*, p. 14 note 34.
204 See Th. Bauer, *Das Inschriftenwerk Assurbanipals*, II, Leipzig 1933, p. 74: "[...] Nanâ (trieft) vom Blute der Menschen, Uṣur-amatsa (und) Arka'ātu treten die Leichen der Krieger nieder."
205 See CT 36, pl. XXI-XXIII. Concerning Nanāja: col. II, l. 5-7 (pl. XXII). For a copy, see E. Dhorme, *RA* XI (1914), p. 105-117.
206 P.-A. Beaulieu, YNER 10, p. 26 uses the name *Ubaṣṣi* and dates the event to between the 3rd and 7th regnal year of the king.

superior to Ištar" or simply "the most exalted Ištar", while the name of her temple was not given at all.[207]

Adding distinction to his rebuilding of the Ezida temple in Borsippa,[208] Nabû-kudurri-uṣur (604-562 BC) did not fail to write that it was he who caused Nabû and Nanāja to come and reside in this seat of delight of the heart (col. II, l. 23-25: ^{d}*Na-bi-um* u_3 ^{d}*Na-na-a / ina ḫi-da-a-ti* u_3 *ri-ša-a-ti / šu-bat ṭu-ub li-ib-bi* qe_2*-er-ba-šu* u_2*-še-ši-ib*). He also established daily offerings to this couple[209] and reinstated the previous offerings and rituals for Nanāja[210]: *simāti rēštâti / pilludê qudmūti / ša* ^{d}*Nanāja Uruk*^{ki} *bēlet Uruk*^{ki} *elletim / utēr ašrussun.*

The cult of Nanāja was present in other temples as well.

The biggest of these in the times of the Seleucids was e_2 - e $š_3$ - g a l[211] "House, great sanctuary" – the temple of Ištar in Uruk, shared with Nanāja.

Another temple existing in Late Babylonian times was the e_2 - h i - l i - d i r i - g a[212] "House of great charm", known from the list of chapels in Uruk; it was situated in k a_2 - u_6 - d e, that is, in the gate of oracles (*šu-bat* ^{d}*Na-na-a* $ša_2$ *bāb*(KA_2) U_6.DE *ina bīt*(E_2) *te-ret*[213] – SpTU I 136, l. 7' – W 22282a).

From Babylon (Tintir = Babylon, tablet IV, 30) there is known the temple e_2 - m e - u r_4 - u r_4[214] "House which gathers (the divine powers of) *me*" (designated as *bīt* ^{d}*Na-na-a* lib_3*-ba* TE.E^{ki} – "temple

---

[207] A. R. George, *Temples*, no. 1361. See E. Unger, *Babylon*, Berlin 1970, p. 92.
[208] VAB 4, p. 90 ff.; see E. Unger, *Babylon*, Berlin 1970, p. 282.
[209] VAB 4, p. 92, l. 26-35.
[210] *Ibid.*, l. 50-53.
[211] A. R. George, *Temples*, no. 270. A. Falkenstein, *Topographie von Uruk I*, Leipzig 1941, p. 30 ff. reads the name as i r i - g a l.
[212] A. R. George, *Temples*, no. 460.
[213] The chapel *bīt têret* of the Eanna temple is mentioned in the ritual of the month of Dumuzi – LKU 51, obv. 22: ^{d}*Na-na-a i-teb-bi-ma a-na bīt te-ret ir-ru-ub-ma il-lak-ku* [...].
[214] A. R. George, *Temples*, no. 794.

of Nanāja at TE.E")[215] and e$_2$ - u r$_5$ - š a$_3$ - b a[216] (tablet II, 9") "House, oracle[217] of the heart" (referred to as "the seat of Nanāja" – *šu-bat* ^{d}*Na-na-a*).

At Borsippa there existed yet another temple, e$_2$ - u r$_5$ - š a$_3$ - b a (sufficiently important to have an entire district called after it – *erṣeti*$^{ti}_{3}$ E$_2$.UR$_5$.ŠA$_3$.BA *ša qe*$_2$*-re-eb Bar*$_2$*-sipa*^{ki}),[218] while the complex dedicated to Nabû, the Ezida, incorporated a chapel[219] dedicated to Nanāja.

A text from Uruk[220] concerning king Nabû-šuma-iškun (760-748 BC) describes how this king *ina* MU.3.KAM ^{d}*Na-na-a* E$_2$.ZI.DA / *ra-'i-[m]at* ^{d}*Nabû a-na bīt*(E$_2$) *mu-um-mu u*$_2$*-še-rib-ma* "in the 3rd year (of his reign) the goddess Nanāja from (the temple of) the Ezida / – beloved of Nabû, ordered to enter the *bīt mummu*"[221] (col. II 7-8). Other deplorable acts by this king, his offenses against sanctity and religious festivals were also described.

The chapel of Nanāja at Aššur, in the e$_2$ - š a r$_2$ - r a temple, bore the name š a$_3$ - g a - a[222] "(House) inside" (which could perhaps be understood as designating an inside temple).

---

215 A. R. George, *Topographical Texts*, p. 131 says that according to the Tintir list TE.E^{ki} was a district of cult centers dedicated only to Igigi, Anunnaki and Nanāja.

216 A. R. George, *Temples*, no. 1196.

217 The sign u r$_5$ was used in the meaning u r$_4$.

218 VS V 96, 1-2.

219 A. R. George, *Topographical Texts*, 219. According to E. Matsushima (*Orient* XXX-XXXI, 1995, p. 175) the temple of Ezida could have existed in Uruk or in the vicinity of the town.

220 W 22660/0, E. von Weiher, *BaghM* 15 (1984), p. 197-224, pl. 22 and 23; *idem*, SpTU III, no. 58. For a re-edition of the text, see S. W. Cole, *ZA* 84/2 (1994), p. 227 ff., who writes: "In the third year, he again had Nanāy of Ezida, the lover of Nabû, enter the repair shop." RIMB 2 B.6.14.1. translates as follows: "Further, in the third year he brought (the statue of) the goddess Nanāja of Ezida, the beloved of the god Nabû, into the temple's sacred workshop."

221 See AHw 672a 4b) *bīt m.* 'etwa Tempel-Bildhauerwerkstätte', CAD M 198a 'work-shop (used to make and repair ritual objects).'

222 A. R. George, *Temples*, no. 1015.

A list of gates discovered at Aššur (VAT 9999) informs of the existence of *bāb*(KA$_2$) ^{d}*Na-na-a* (KAV 134, IV 4-7). There was also a "gate of Nanāja and Uṣur-amāssa."[223] It should be emphasized that a gate attested in the sources, called KA$_2$.HI.LI.SU (BWL 60, 90), should be assigned to Nanāja in view of the name, although nowhere in the literature is it explicitly so attributed.

A locality called Dûr-Nanāja in Assyria is evidenced in Assyrian trade documents.[224]

According to the Synchronistic History, Šamši-Adad V in his fifth campaign against Babylonia (815-812 BC) deported from Dēr (the border town) the goddess Nanāja among many other gods:[225] Anu-rabû, Nanāja, Šarrat-Dēri, Mār-bīti-ša-pān-bīti, Mār-bīti-ša-birīt-nāri, Burruqu, Gula, Urkītu, Šukānija, Nēr-e-tagmil, and Šakkud-ša-Bubē. This lets us presume that, if anything, Nanāja was worshipped at Dēr. Offerings to Nanāja from Dūr-Kurigalzu were evidenced for the early Neo-Babylonian period in the temple of Ebabbar in Sippar.[226]

Sîn-šarra-uṣur who administered Ur offered[227] in the intention of the good health of the reigning Šamaš-šuma-ukīn (668-648 BC) a plot of land lying between the Euphrates[228] and the town of Sūrānu. The goddesses to whom the land has been offered are mentioned twice in the text: in l. 1 only Ištar, in l. 7 – Ištar and Nanāja. In the attached curse formula, Nanāja is called the beloved of Nabû and Marduk. She is asked to speak ill continuously before Nabû of the man who would dare change the boundaries of this plot of land.

In the times of Nabû-na'īd, and later as well, Uruk also had a waterfront and canal of Nanāja, located presumably in the neighborhood

---

223 GCCI II, 214:3-4.
224 See RIA II, s.v. Dûr-Nanâ.
225 S. W. Holloway, *Aššur is King! Aššur is King! Religion in the Exercise of Power in the Neo-Assyrian Empire*, Leiden 2002, p. 129 note 180.
226 See R. da Riva, AOAT 291, p. 278.
227 RIMB 2 B.6.33.2001. It is possible that both the preserved sources originate from Uruk or from Ur. I have already mentioned this text (AO 6793) in II.1, p. 40.
228 The text, l. 5-6: UŠ AN.TA *u* KI.TA *ul-tu* ZIMBIR.KI / *a-di* URU *Su-ra-nu i-šad-da-ad*.

of her temple ($^{\bar{a}l}$*kār* ^{d}*Nanāja* – YOS 6, 107, 16 and YOS 7, 101, 15; $^{t\bar{a}mirtu}$*kār* ^{d}*Nanāja* – YOS 7, 116, 20; $^{n\bar{a}r}$*kār* ^{d}*Nanāja* – YOS 6, 101, 19; $^{n\bar{a}r}$*ḫarri ša* ^{d}*Nanāja* – YOS 17, 348, 11 ff.) The designation *kār* ^{d}*Nanāja šīḫu ša* ^{d}*Bēlet-ša-Uruk*^{ki} is also encountered (CNB 23, 19 and CNB 68, 22). Attested near Uruk are the localities: *Dimtu-ša-Nanāja (*Di-in-du ša*$_2$ ^{d}*Na-na-a*),[229] Til-Nanāja (DU$_6$-^{d}*Na-na-a*).[230] Tillē-ša-Nanāja (DU$_6$^{meš} *ša*$_2$ ^{d}*Na-na-a*),[231] as well as *Bīt-Nanāja-ēreš* and two hydronyms **Ḫarru-ša-Nanāja*[232] and *Nāru-ša-Nanāja*.[233]

A text from the Eanna archives in Uruk (1982.A.1798)[234], dated to the 11th year of the reign of Nabû-apla-uṣur (625-605 BC), constitutes an act of (the temple of) Ištar and Nanāja being taken into captivity. Some of the men mentioned in this act bear names with the Nanāja element: Nanāja-karābī and Nanāja-uṣalla.

Text TCL XIII 221 mentions the food storerrom (*bīt kannāni*) of the Lady-of-Uruk, Nanāja, Bēltu-ša-Rēš and Uṣur-amāssa.

The texts demonstrate that buildings dedicated to Nanāja were found throughout Mesopotamia. The cities of Isin, Ur, Uruk, Larsa, Babylon, Borsippa and Aššur are important cult centers. Nippur, a regional capital of Sumer, is not mentioned among them (even though the sources inform of offerings being made to Nanāja in the temple of Ninurta). To judge by the superior number of temples to Nanāja in Uruk, this city should be considered as her place of origin, the center where the inception of her cult in Ancient Mesopotamia occurred.

Nanāja is designated as a daughter of Inanna only in the text of king Lipit-Eštar, originating from the 20th century BC. In later sources she is referred to as the firstborn of Anu. Texts from the first millennium BC link her with the god Nabû.

---

229 RGTC 8, p. 119.
230 RGTC 8, p. 312.
231 RGTC 8, p. 311.
232 See V. Scheil, *RA* XXIV/1 (1927), p. 38, l. 2-3: KI^{tim} ^{id_2}*Ḫar-ri ša*$_2$ ^{d}*Na-na-a ša qe*$_2$*-reb* UNUG^{ki}.
233 RGTC 8, p. 357-358 and 392.
234 M. Jursa, *Iraq* LIX (1997), 1.

She is perceived as beautiful and charming. Once she acts as an intermediary between the ruler and the great gods (or possibly her spouse), at other times she is imbued with the power to annihilate.

The issue of separate sanctuaries existing for the cult of Nanāja, especially where temples of the same name to Ištar exist, is difficult to resolve. Joint offerings made on occasion to these goddesses lead one to surmise that the term e_2 ^{d}N a - n a - a could mean no more than a chapel inside a temple dedicated to Inanna/Ištar. This in turn leads one to conclude that all the places of worship of Nanāja were foremost dedicated to the worship of Inanna. This conviction is grounded in the apparently overlapping scope of authority assigned to these two goddesses. Therefore, it should be assumed that at least some of the temples of Nanāja functioned simultaneously as places of worship dedicated to Inanna/Ištar.

II.4 THE PRIESTHOOD OF NANĀJA

The existence of temples dedicated to Nanāja naturally required a clergy to exist to serve the goddess. The first proof of priests serving Nanāja comes from the Ur III period, just like the record of offerings made to the goddess. However, there are very few positions of priests of the cult of Nanāja attested in the sources.

In the Drehem archives š a b r a ^{d}N a - n a - a[235] – temple administrators are mentioned 11 times in the texts. Only seven of the documents are dated (Š 43, Š 47, AS 2, 3 times for AS 4 and AS 5), but the personal names of the administrators are repeated and consequently, it should be surmised that only three persons are involved. Of course, the fact that this administrators bear Sumerian names is not tanta-

[235] SACT 1, 189, col. V 9 (L u_2 - b a l a - s a_6 - g a) [no date]; M. Sigrist, *Rochester*, no. 12, 18 (L u_2 - b a l a - s a_6 - g a) [Š 43]; AUCT 1, 339, l. 2 (L u_2 - b a l a - s a_6 - g a) [Š 47]; TCL V 31= AO 6041 III 17 = *JCS* 17, 1, 1 (no name) [AS 2]; TD 26 = PD 1330, l. 6' (D u d u) [no date, probably AS 4]; YOS 4, 56, l. 9 (no name) [no date]; SAT 2, 795, rev. l. 1-2 (D u d u) [AS 4]; SAT 2, 797, l. 5 (D u d u) [AS 4]; BIN III 339, rev. l. 1 (D u d u) [AS 4]; G. Haayer, *JEOL* 26 (1979-1980) 51, 12, l. 4-5 (D u d u) [AS 5]; LB 3073 = RSO 9, 472, rev. l. 4 (N i n - l i l_2 - e) [no date].

mount to their being Sumerians. It should be emphasized that the š a b r a of Nanāja mentioned in four texts (*RSO* 9, 472 = LB 3073, TD 26 = PD 1330, M. Sigrist, *Rochester*, no. 12 and probably YOS 4, 56) takes part in the tax system, bringing appropriate b a l a values. They form a separate tax unit, occurring frequently next to e n s i and s a n g a from other towns. In the text AO 6041 (TCL V 31 = *JCS* 17, 1, 1 [AS 2]), he delivers workers e r e n_2 for harvest time.

Another priestly position attested in Drehem is g u d u_4/*pašīšum;* this priest is attested for the 43st and 47th year of Šulgi's rule (2094-2047 BC).[236]

J. Renger's study[237] of the sources on priests and priestesses from the Old Babylonian period continues to be a fundamental work for research on the priesthood. New texts have broadened our knowledge of the topic. In 1986, in a work devoted to the clergy in Ur, D. Charpin[238] gathered the material concerning priests of Nanāja from Kiš,[239] identifying in the process three separate offices:

- s a n g a/*šangû* – from the 11th, 21st and 23rd regnal year of Ammī-ditāna (1683-1647 BC) and from the «i» year of Abī-ešuh (1711-1684 BC);
- g a l a - m a h/*kalamaḫum* – from the 31st year of Ammī-ditāna;
- *erīb-bītim* – from the 31st and 35th year of Ammī-ditāna.

Two other Uruk goddesses apart from Nanāja are recorded in the texts from this period from Kiš: Ištar of Uruk (written: ^{d}Inanna-

236 BIN III, 493; L. Legrain, TRU 113: 2-3.
237 J. Renger, *ZA* 58 (1967), p. 110-198 and *idem*, *ZA* 59 (1969), p. 104-230. Also to be taken into consideration is J. Renger's "Götternamen in der Altbabylonischen Zeit", in: *Heidelberger Studien zum Alten Orient*, Wiesbaden 1967, p. 137-172.
238 D. Charpin, *Le clergé d'Ur au siècle d'Hammurabi*, Paris 1986.
239 *Ibid.*, p. 410-415. For the number of texts, see R. Pientka, *Die spätaltbabylonische Zeit. Abiešuh bis Samsuditana*, Marburg 1998, p. 329 ff.

UNUG.KI, AN-^{d}INANNA-UNUG.KI or AN-^{d}INANNA,[240]) whose worship engaged more priests, and Nanāja's daughter, the goddess Kanisurra, who had only s a n g a priests. The joint character of the cult of these three goddesses is attested in letter TCL I 19.[241] The divine triad of Uruk appearing in the texts from the city of Kiš from the end of the Old Babylonian period was transferred there by the inhabitants of Uruk, both priests and worshippers. D. Charpin believes[242] that the priests' migration from Uruk to Kiš took place around the 10th year of Samsu-iluna (1749-1712 BC), because the formula for year 11 contains information about the destruction of the walls of Ur and Uruk.

The possibility of a joint clergy of Inanna/Ištar (designated also as AN-^{d}INANNA) and of Nanāja is further confirmed by a frequent occurrence of personal names incorporating the name of Nanāja (or a patronymic containing the name of the goddess) among the priests of AN-^{d}INANNA (e.g. seal[243] W 16808 e: Ipiq-Eštar, son of Iddin-Nanāja, priest "charmer" of (the goddess) AN-^{d}INANNA; W 16808 a: Sîn-itūram, son of Iddin-Nanāja, priest "charmer" of (the goddess) AN-^{d}INANNA and YBC 4857, 13, where there occurs Iddin-Nanāja s a n g a ^{d}I n a n n a).

---

240 See review of opinions on AN-^{d}INANNA-Unug^{ki} in D. Charpin, *op. cit.*, p. 404 note 1 and p. 412; C. Wilcke, AOAT 247, p. 414-415 and P.-A. Beaulieu, CM 23, p. 109-111 and notes.

The existence of a divinity designated as AN-^{d}INANNA (and not, as some would like, An (and) Inanna) is further attested in a text that records E_2 AN-^{d}INANNA-URUK^{ki} (YOS 13, 435) and in a year formula describing the renovation of E_2 AN-^{d}INANNA LIBIR-RA (W 20038, 18; W 20472, 57; W 20478, 4), as well as by shared temple staff: LU_2.TUG_2 EN AN-^{d}INANNA 'tailor of (the priest of) e n goddess AN-^{d}INANNA' (W 20208 I 20', Irdanene) and IŠIB AN-^{d}INANNA '(priest) charmer of the goddess AN-^{d}INANNA' (W 16808 a, d and others – seals from the times of Rīm-Sîn). The omission of the sign E_2 indicates that a divinity is concerned, and not a name of a sanctuary dedicated to Inanna and An.

241 See Chapter VIII, p. 147.

242 D. Charpin, *op. cit.*, p. 414 and note 4.

243 For seals, see A. Cavigneaux, R. M. Boehmer, AUWE 23, p. 6-10.

From Uruk under the reign of Irdanene (1816-1810 BC) we know of a s a n g a priest of Nanāja who bore the name of Iddin-Nanāja (W 20472, 152).[244] The text (l. 7-10) reports how he paid a fine for tearing down together with others a bronze star from the doors of the temple of Nanāja (1/3 m a - n a *I-din-*^{d}*Na-na-a* s a n g a ^{d}*Na-na-a* (...) m u m u l - z a b a r *ša* ^{giš}i g e_2 - ^{d}*Na-na-a* u_2*-ḫa-am-mi-ṣ*u_2).

Among the texts from Kisurra there is one preserving the following datation:[245] m u g u r_7 A n - n a ^{d}I n a n n a u_3 ^{d}N a - <n a - a> i n i m m u - g i$^{!}$ - n a "Year in which the granary of An, Inanna and Nanāja was checked." It is impossible to assign this date to any of the kings, but the text testifies to the supremacy of the worship of the deities from Uruk at Kisurra.[246] One should presumably also consider in this group a text from Uruk (W 20197, 3),[247] speaking of the offerings made by detachments from Kisurra (l. 10'-11'): [x+]42.1.4.0 š e - g u r / [s a_2] - d u_{11} e r e n_2 K i - s u r - r a^{ki} g i r i_3 DINGIR-*ku-za*. In another part of the same text, the name of Iddin-Nanāja is listed among other names.

In Larsa, in the times of Rīm-Sîn (1822-1763 BC), that is, between this king's 2nd and 39th regnal year, other priests of Nanāja – g u d u_4/*pašīšum* appear as witnesses or participants in rituals.[248] In the second year of the reign of this king there were likely as many as three such priests, while for the 39th year two g u d u_4 priests were attested. In the 2nd regnal year there also occur g a l a - m a h/*kalamaḫum* priests, concurrently with the above mentioned ones.[249]

---

244 Sh. Sanati-Müller, *BaghM* 21 (1990), p. 191, no. 135 7, [Ird 20]; presumably the same person appears in W 20472, 192 (*ibid.*, p. 206, no. 145).

245 B. Kienast, FAOS 2, text 184, where the author writes g u r_7, g u r u_7 in paragraph 17D (Part 1). See C. Wilcke, AOAT 247, p. 415, note 5.

246 On the links between Uruk and Kisurra, see B. Kienast, *op. cit.*, p. 20-21.

247 Sh. Sanati-Müller, *BaghM* 23 (1992), no. 192, p. 157.

248 J. Renger, *ZA* 59 (1969) p. 146-149. See above note 187 on p. 56 on the text UCLMA 9-1845 and also Ch. B. Dyckoff, in: CRRAI 47/1, p. 123-127.

249 J. Renger, *ZA* 59 (1969), p. 196.

A text from Hammurabi's 33rd year (TCL XI 146) evinces yet another s a n g a priest from the temple of Nanāja also in Larsa.

At Ur, in the 28th of the rule of Rīm-Sîn there is proof of the existence of three *pašīšum* priests of Nanāja, who appear as witnesses in various documents.[250] The texts demonstrate that *pašīšum* priests were also active in the 6th year of Abisarē (1905-1895 BC) and the 5th of Nūr-Adad (1865-1850 BC).

In Nippur, a document recording the selling of part the income of a g u d u_4 priest was written up in the 13th year of the rule of Samsu-iluna (1749-1712 BC). The priest was concurrently a brewer of Inanna and Nanāja.[251] Interestingly, the buyer was a woman.

Presumably in the 21st year of Ammīditāna (1683-1647 BC) a document was written up, MLC 1348,[252] confirming the activity of an *ērib-bīti* priest of Nanāja.

No mention of priests of Nanāja fills the gap between the 16th and 11th centuries BC. It does not mean, however, that no priesthood of the goddess actually existed.

The founder of the Second Dynasty of the Sealand that ruled in Babylonia in the late 11th century (1025-1008 BC), one king Simbar-Šipak ordered the building of a throne to Enlil in Nippur. The colophon of this document[253] mentions the descendants (father and son) of Sîn-leqe-unnēnnī, who served as *kalû* priests of Ištar of Uruk and Nanāja, *ērib bīti* priests of Kanisurra and son was also a scribe of the Eanna temple.

A *kudurru* text of the 9th century BC from the reign of Marduk-zākir-šumi (854-819 BC) also attests to the frequent practice of combining offices. The priest mentioned in this document by name was a *kalû* of the temple of Ištar of Uruk, an *ērib-bīti* of Nanāja, *šangû* of Uṣur-amāssa and scribe of the Eanna temple.[254]

---

250 *Ibid.*, p. 157-158.
251 PBS VIII/2 182.
252 J. J. Finkelstein, YOS 13, 174.
253 RIMB 2 B.3.1.1.
254 F. Thureau-Dangin, *RA* XVI (1919) p. 129 col. III, l. 7-12.

From the middle of the 8th century BC comes a *kudurru* document from Borsippa mentioning by name the *ērib-bīti* priest of Nanāja.[255]

The reign of Nabû-apla-iddina (887-855? BC) yielded an enormous list of dispositions regarding offerings made to Ištar of Uruk and Nanāja (W.-B.10).[256] The tablet belonged to the Eanna temple, hence it is to be surmised that the mentioned persons (only the titles of priests and officials with innumerous exceptions were written down) were all involved with the same temple, although there can be no certainty that they actually served as clergy of the cult of Nanāja. The following were listed: *šešgallū*, *ērib-bītāti*, *mašmaššū*, *šatammū* (administrators) and others. We have the oblats of Nanāja in letter YOS 3, 106, l. 37. The formula that appears in text NBC 4913 is "PN_1, son of PN_2, lives on the estates of Nanāja" and at the end (l. 27) the text says: "Total: 26 houses of Nanāja in which the *mār-banî*s live." Maybe certain *mār-banî*s of Uruk worked for Nanāja.[257]

There is no explicit evidence for the presence of separate female personnel in the temples of Nanāja. The woman bearing the title of "beloved l u k u r (priestess) of the journey" of king Būr-Sîn (1895-1874 BC), called ᵈNanāja-ibsa, offered a plaque with votive inscription to the "body" or rather the statue of the goddess.[258] There is nothing to show that she played any kind of role whatsoever in the cult.

Seals are very useful in determining the status of personnel serving Nanāja. Yet the only designation from Old Babylonian times is g e m e₂ ᵈN a - n a - a - (a),[259] which hardly explains what the real status of the slave or servant of the goddess was.

---

[255] VS I 36, 20-24. Three priests of Nanāja are likely concerned.
[256] S. Langdon, OECT I, pl. 20-21.
[257] See CT 23, p. 215 about the possibility of linking certain *mār-banī*s of Uruk to the cult of Nanāja.
[258] RIME 4 1.7.3.
[259] D. Collon, *Catalogue of the Western Asiatic Seals in the British Museum III. Isin-Larsa and Old Babylonian Periods*, London 1986, nos. 545, 572,

A text[260] dated to the 14th year of Nabû-kudurri-uṣur (605-562 BC) mentions Kidin-Marduk referred to as LU_2.UR ^{d}Innin ^{d}XV u ^{d}Na-na-a (rev. 15) "servant of Inanna, Ištar and Nanāja." It is difficult to discern whether this is a designation of a person connected with the cult or a lay person in service at the temple (or temples possibly) of these goddesses.

Text AO 19536[261] from Babylon and dated to the 17th year of Nabû-naʾid (539 BC) constitutes proof that the service of the goddess endured. The document records the following (l. 3-5): ^{fd}*Nanāja-ḫussinni* / $GEME_2$ *ša*$_2$ *kakkabti ritta-šu*$_2$ *šendeti u*$_3$ / *ana* ^{d}*Nanāja šaṭratu* "Nanāja-ḫussinni / – slave girl whose hand is marked with a (tattoo of a) star and / is signed 'for the goddess Nanāja.'" In l. 9-10 this slave girl is called *zakītu ša*$_2$ ^{d}*Nanāja* "oblate[262] of the goddess Nanāja", and in l. 18-19 she herself explains (since the text is the record of a trial in court) that her former owner *ana* ^{d}*Nanāja uzzakkanni* "offered me to Nanāja." An examination of the woman's hand in front of the court revealed another inscription below that saying "for Nanāja", namely "for Ištar of Uruk" (l. 19-26). By sentence of the court the slave girl and her son were included in the group of "basket carriers" from the Eanna temple (l. 39-41: ^{fd}*Nanāja-ḫussinni u* ^{m}*Taddannu* DUMU-*šu*$_2$ / *itti ummanni zābil tupšikku ša*$_2$ E_2.AN.NA / *imnū).*

The name of the slave, as well as the fact that she served two goddesses of Uruk indicates that she must have come from Uruk.

609, 615; M.-L. Vollenweider, *Catalogue raisonnée des sceaux cylindres et intailles*, vol. I, Genève 1967, no. 51; the following designations occur: g e m e$_2$ ^{d}I n a n n a u$_3$ ^{d}N a - n a - a - a – C. Bezold, *Catalogue*... I (1888) 245, no. 217 bis and g e m e$_2$ ^{d}E n - l i l$_2$(?) u$_3$ ^{d}N a - n a - a – L. Speleers, *Catalogue des intailles et empreintes Orientales des Musées Royaux du Cinquantenaire*, Bruxelles 1917, no. 543. One should also mention the seven-day Old Babylonian ritual from Larsa which despite damages obviously confirms the offering of a slave girl to Nanāja (l. 625).

260 See V. Scheil, *RA* XXIV/1 (1927), p. 38-41. The author believes that Kidin-Marduk, here a witness to real-estate sales, was a temple functionary in the service of the goddesses forming the triad from Uruk.

261 D. Arnaud, *RA* LXVII (1973), p. 147-156.

262 The oblate of Nanāja are attested in letter YOS 3, 106, 37.

In the 4th year of Nabû-na'īd (556-539 BC) the office of a *šangû* priest of Nanāja existed (OECT X 110, 11); it lasted through the Persian invasion, being confirmed in a text from the 3rd year of Cambyses II (530-523 BC) (YOS 7, 150, 21 = YBC 3749). The cult of Nanāja and Ištar declined somewhat in view of the presence of the couple, Anu and Antu, who rose to the highest rank in the hierarchy of the Uruk pantheon between the 6th and 5th centuries BC.[263]

Temple personnel of Nanāja in Uruk were known also under the Seleucids.[264] She was then worshipped together with a triad of other goddesses: Ištar, Uṣur-amāssa and Bēlet-ša-Rēš.

The period of about 200 years (from the beginning of the Seleucid era to the beginning of Parthian domination) yielded some 135 transactions concerning prebend sales in two major Uruk temples, Bīt Rēš and Irigal (read also as e š$_3$ - g a l). According to P.-A. Beaulieu,[265] most of the documents list the divinities before whom the duties connected with the office were performed. The number varies of course (from one to fourteen), but there exist two texts that mention all of the gods in the same sequence (OECT IX 61 and BRM 2, 40), which is as follows: Anu, Antu, Enlil, Ea, Sîn, Šamaš, Adad, Marduk, Papsukkal, Ištar, Bēlet-ṣeri, Nanāja, Bēlet-ša-Rēš and Šarraḫītu. The latter goddess appeared in the Ištar circle along with Bēlet-ṣeri not before the 5th century BC. This order demonstrates that Nanāja had lost her standing among the gods, moving down in the hierarchy to a position near the end of the list of worshipped deities at the time. It would signify a regress in the cult of Nanāja in Uruk, which however is not observable with respect to other cities.

The sale of prebends was very common in the Seleucid period,[266] although it is clear from the texts that it had already existed in the

---

263 Favoring this idea is a sudden increase in the number of personal names with the theophoric element Anu compared to the minute number of names incorporating the Ištar element.

264 P.-A. Beaulieu, *ASJ* 14 (1992), p. 55 ff.

265 *Op. cit.*, p. 55-56.

266 See H. Hunger, *BaghM* 5 (1970), p. 193-304; G. J. P. McEwan, FAOS 4, p. 67 ff.; D. B. Weisberg, Bib. Mes. 24, nos. 1, 10, 17, and K. Kessler, AUWE 8, *passim*.

7th[267] and 6th[268] centuries BC. The sale was conducted by *āšipū* – exorcists (e.g. BRM 2 16), as well as persons with the privilege of entering a temple, who sold their *ērib bītūtu* (e.g. BM 93004). Other persons are also evidenced, selling the right to enter the "secret" part[269] and the goldsmith's allowance – *ērib bīt pirištūtu u kutimmūtu* (e.g. Ash. 1923.735). As well as *qerseqqû* priests whose duties are still unclear (e.g. BRM 2 15). Also an *itinnu* – builder (BRM 2 22) voluntarily sold for a year his entire monthly allowance from the temples of Irigal and Rēš and the *akîtu* of Ištar received for performing duties "before Anu, Antu, Nanāja, Ladies of Rēš and all the gods of the temples." The texts bring mentions of cooks – *nuḫatimmū* (e.g. Ash. 1923.738), brewers – *sirāšû* (e.g. BRM 2, 11), oil pressers – *ṣāḫitū* (e.g. VS XV 28), butchers – *ṭābiḫū* (e.g. BRM 2, 40) selling their prebends partly or in whole.

In Neo-Babylonian Uruk we have attested four prebendary offices:[270] *rab-banûtu* (YOS 6, 222), *sarrārūtu* (NBC 5037), several *sirāšûtu* (YOS 6, 241; YOS 17, 126; YOS 17, 360) and *nuḫatimmūtu* (YOS 6, 241; YOS 17, 126; YOS 17, 360).

An analysis of the evidence leads to the conclusion that a priesthood of Nanāja existed since at least the middle of the 21st dynasty BC and endured until practically the end of the Seleucid dynasty in Babylonia. It may also be surmised that Uruk was the cult center, consider-

---

[267] H. Hunger, *BaghM* 5 (1970), nos. 3, 7, 8, 9, 10, 11, 12, 18, 23, 25. See A. C. V. M. Bongenaar, *The Neo-Babylonian Ebabbar Temple at Sippar: Its Administration and its Prosopography*, Leiden 1997, p. 240 note 221: "(...) the days of service for Uṣur-amāssa, Bēlet-Uruk, Bēlet-Rēš and Nanā, (...), are not the days for the service of these goddesses in Eanna at Uruk, but the days of service for the small sanctuaries of these goddesses in Larsa."

[268] H. M. Kümmel, *Familie, Beruf und Amt im spätbabylonischen Uruk. Prosopographische Untersuchungen zu Berufsgruppen des 6. Jahrhunderts v. Chr. in Uruk*, Berlin 1979, p. 119 (text from the 12th year of Nabû-na'īd).

[269] On *bīt pirišti*, see L. T. Doty, in: Studies Hallo, p. 87-89. The text OECT IX 50, which is a sale of prebends, also speaks of a *lubuštu* ceremony for the gods Anu, Enlil, Nanāja and Bēlet-ša-Rēš.

[270] P.-A. Beaulieu, CM 23, p. 214, and references to texts edited by K. Kessler, AUWE 8 (nos 4, 26, 32, 36, 40, 46, 53, 56, 67, 84h, 84z). See also R. da Riva, *AfO* 50 (2003/2004), p. 245-254 (for the 4th year of Nabopolassar).

ing that the biggest number of priests were active there. Other cult centers included Kiš, Kisurra, Larsa and Ur.

It should be assumed that the priesthood of Nanāja was entirely male – š a b r a, g u d u$_4$, s a n g a, g a l a - m a h and *ērib-bīti*. No mention is made of women – priestesses of Nanāja,[271] while the document referring to a woman with a tattoo may simply testify to the presence of temple slaves engaged in inferior services not related to the cult in any way.

II.5 THE IMAGE OF NANĀJA BASED ON RITUALS

Nanāja's name appears also in the rituals. The key texts are the New Year greeting ceremonies, although the goddess is mentioned in other rituals as well. Rituals usually accompanied offerings[272] made in the temples or were part of feasts held for the deities.

According to the Drehem texts, Nanāja takes part in the ritual of *girrānu* (g i - r a - n u m$_2$), at the 6th month in Uruk. The ritual was also common to the goddesses Inanna, Nanāja, Bēlat-suḫnir, Bēlat-tirraban, Anunītum and Ulmašītum. It seems to be a monthly observance.

The only text to be preserved from the Old Babylonian period or to be more precise from the 2nd year of the rule of Rīm-Sîn (1822-1763 BC) is a ritual accompanying seven successive days of feasts held in Larsa, during which offerings were made to different divinities.[273] Nanāja received hers on the nineteenth day of the month (l. 541-626). The ritual devoted to the goddess started in the evening when roasted sheep were laid in offering to her presumably at the moment of her statue being taken ([*i-na*] *e-ri-*[*bi*]*-ša*) into the temple (or temple niche). This was followed by bloody offerings to the

[271] E. C. Kingsbury is of the opinion that the ritual from Larsa speaks of gifts assigned to the priestesses of Nanāja, see a discussion of the ritual on p. 75-76 and note 273.

[272] For example, during the *girrānum* ritual as attested in two texts: PDT 2, 998 [Š 35], AnOr 7, 55 = MVN XVIII 55. Songs to the divinities demonstrate irrefutable links with rituals.

[273] E. C. Kingsbury, *HUCA* 34 (1963), p. 1-34.

king and the temple, among others. In the morning (on the twentieth day of the month, that is) further offerings were made of animals, bread and beer. Following is a list of various offerings to the goddess and rations (mainly food rations) allocated to the cult personnel (singers, male and female sweepers, l u k u r priestesses, hairdressers and doorkeepers). Silver bracelets were given to persons mentioned by name who were, according to E. C. Kingsbury,[274] priestesses of Nanāja, while the male priests (among whom a female miller is recorded!) were assigned mines of wool. During the ceremony of the goddess's "exit" (*i-na ra-bi-ša*) more offerings were made: sheep, oil, butter, also a slave girl and jewelry. In the evening, to close the day (the twentieth of the month) dedicated to the goddess, a feast was held in her name (k a š - d e_2 - a ^{d}N a - n a - a).

The other deities mentioned in this ritual include: Ningunanna, Enki and Asarluḫi, Šamaš, Ištar, Ninegal, Maḫ and Panigingarra, as well as Sîn. The section devoted to Nanāja follows that dedicated to Ištar.

A fragment of a Middle Assyrian New Year ritual celebrated in Aššur mentions Nanāja[275] among the divinities taking part in a procession in honor of Marduk. The name of the goddess appears in the same paragraph as that of Nabû. It has been questioned whether some of the statues of deities (including the statue of Marduk) carried in the procession had not been brought to Aššur only momentarily. Assuming this was the case, one could hardly speak of a cult of Nanāja existing at Aššur in the Middle Assyrian period.

A ritual against misfortunes employing a magic stone is evidenced for the Late Babylonian times.[276] Nanāja appears here next to Ištar (col. I):

13. *šumma amēlu*(NA) *e-nu-ma bir-ṣi i-ta-nam-ma-ru ki-a-am iqabbi*(DU_{11}.GA)
14. *ša*$_2$ ^{d}*En-lil*$_2$ *u* ^{d}*Nin-lil*$_2$ *ana-ku ša*$_2$ ^{d}*Iš-tar u* ^{d}*Na-na-a ana-ku*

---

274 *Ibid.*, p. 24.
275 F. Köcher, *ZA* 50 (1952), p. 196, rev. 19'.
276 W 22669/0, SpTU II 22.

15. *ša* ^{d}*Uraš*(IB) *u* ^{d}*Nin-e*$_2$*-gal ana-ku 3-šu iqabbī-ma iballuṭ*(TIN)

"If a man keeps on seeing light, he should say in consequence:

(Servant?) of the god Enlil and the goddess Ninlil am I, of the goddess Ištar and the goddess Nanāja am I,

of the god Uraš and the goddess Ninegal am I – three times he should say (this) and he will be healthy."

For the Neo-Assyrian period Nanāja is mentioned in a *tākultu* ritual concerning the supplying of offerings to temples and their divine patrons. Text K 252 (III R 66)[277] has come to be called an "address book" as it lists the names of divinities in connection with cities and temples. Nanāja is mentioned repeatedly (col. VIII 32; IX 14; XI 4; XI 26), but only in two cases is the place of her cult mentioned: one is the town of Bīt-Bēlti, the other is the Esagil in Babylon. At the unidentified town of Bīt-Bēlti Nanāja was worshipped alongside gods like (col. VIII 27-35): Bēlet-Agade^{ki}, Dumuzi, Papsukkal, Šita-GAM, Minā^{l}mnū, Biṣilla and Kanisurra. Is then Bīt-Bēlti perhaps a name for Uruk?

The rituals of the Egašankalamma temple,[278] which was reconstructed in honor of Ištar in the reign of Aššur-aḫa-iddina and Aššur-bāni-apli (7th century BC), also mention Nanāja. The text as a whole is not quite understood and the name of the goddess appears in a part that concerns the bringing up of the young Marduk by goddesses which are subsequently turned into dust:

34. [*x x ša*] *uṣṣî*(E$_3$)*-ma ri-gim-ša*$_2$ *ittanaddû*(ŠUB.ŠUB)$^{u}{}_{2}$ ^{d}*Na-na-a*

35. *ki a-na* ^{d}*Bēl šiltaḫa*(GAG.TAG.GA) *parzilli*(AN.BAR) *ta-ḫu-šu*$_2$$^{?}$-[*x x x*]

---

277 R. Frankena, *Takultu*, Leiden 1954, p. 1-22.

278 A. Livingstone, *Mystical and Mythological Explanatory Works of Assyrian and Babylonian Scholars*, Oxford 1986, p. 116 ff. and *idem*, SAA III, no. 38, p. 95-98. The identification of the temple is not certain; it could be the temple of Ištar at Arbela, see A. R. George, *Temples*, no. 351.

"...[who] comes out and shouts all the time (is) the goddess Nanāja,
when she gives (?) the god Bēl an iron arrow."

A short text from the reign of Nabû-kudurri-uṣur (604-562 BC) attests the performing of a ritual, of which we know nothing, in honor of Nanāja of Uruk[279] (l. 4-8): 1/2 GIN$_2$ *a-na par-ṣu* / *a-na ša* ^{d}*Na-na-a* GIŠ / 1/2 GIN$_2$ *a-na* ^{md}*Na-na-a-*[...] / LU$_2$.MUŠEN.DU / *ša*$_2$ *iṣ-ṣur a-na* TIN.TIR.KI GIŠ "1/2 shekels (of silver) for the ceremony / in (honor) of the goddess Nanāja have been brought, / 1/2 shekels for Nanāja-..., / fowler, / for birds to Babylon have been brought."

From the Seleucid period there is text AO 6467[280], which is a list of hymns/lamentations performed by the *kalû* priests in the temple of Anu in Uruk. Notes on which days the texts should be performed and the titles and names of deities to whom particular songs were dedicated leave no doubt as to which pieces were dedicated to Nanāja. On the seventh day of each month the hymn or lamentation a - š e - e r g i$_6$ - t a[281] "Sighs at the Night" was performed for Nanāja (l. 7); its prototype was known already in the Old Babylonian period. The text u r u$_2$ - h u l - a - k e$_4$[282] ("She of the Destroyed City") was devoted to her on the fourteenth day of the month of *araḫšamnu*.

In Seleucid times, the *akītu* feast was celebrated twice at Uruk: at the beginning of the month of *nisannu* and at the beginning of the month of *tašrītu*.[283]

One text (VAT 7849) concerning the feast in the month of *nisannu* (March/April) originates from Uruk. Nanāja plays an active part in this ritual, appearing next to other goddesses designated as

[279] R. H. Sack, *Cuneiform Documents from the Chaldean and Persian Periods*, London 1994, no. 17 (WHM 1571).
[280] F. Thureau-Dangin, *Tablettes d'Uruk*, Paris 1921, no. 48; S. Langdon, *AJSL* 42/2 (1926), p. 120-122.
[281] See p. 132 and note 432.
[282] See p. 131 and note 430.
[283] See TUAT II/2, b) Das Akitu-Fest im Monat Tischrit, p. 223-227.

Mārāt-Uruk and *Mārāt*-Eanna. The instructive character of the text (for it actually lists in sequence all the different activities performed for the statues of the divinities) leads to the conclusion that the statue of Nanāja always stood near the statue of Ištar (directly behind it or abreast of one another).

Nanāja is also mentioned in the second of the two feasts, which was celebrated in the month of *tašrītu* (September/October). The preserved text concerns only the first eleven days of the month of *tašrītu*. Its analysis leaves no doubt that the feast begins with the ritual of marriage (*parṣi ša ḫašādu)* in a chapel[284] called the Eḫilikuga, which was part of the Eḫilianna, temple of Nanāja (AO 6459 l. 4-5). It would thus seem that Nanāja could have been a major figure in the *hieros gamos* ritual, although the text hardly confirms this.

Tablet K 9876[285] is also tied with the *akītu* feast. On the reverse, it bears a number of questions addressed to various deities, including Nabû and Nanāja (l. 24'-27'):

Rev. 24'. [^{d}A]G KI.MIN *am-me-ni ina* BAR.SIP.KI *la aš$_2$-ba-ta-ma*

25'. [*ina*] E$_2$.ZI.DA *la na-di-i ku-su-ka*

26'. ⸢^{d}⸣*Na-bi-ia-nu-u$_2$-a la iq-bu-nik-ka*

27'. ^{d}*Na-na-a* ^{d}*Su-ti-ti la il$^{!}$-su-ka-a-ma*

"Nabû ditto. Why don't you reside in Borsippa?

---

284 *Ibid.*, note 4, where the author surmises that Ehilikuga defined as *e$_2$-nir* was presumably a bedroom. He translates the name as "House of sacred abundance", and Ehilianna as „House of the abundance of the heavens." M. E. Cohen does not have these doubts, providing in his study on *The Cultic Calendars of the Ancient Near East*, Bethesda 1993, the following translation (p. 431): "On the first day of the month Tašrītu (...). The marriage rites in the Eḫilikuga-chapel, the bedchamber of the Eḫilianna, the tempel of Nanâ, are performed".

285 W. G. Lambert adds to this K 19534; see B. Pongratz-Leisten, BaghForsch 16, p. 229-231. The only analysis of tablet K 9876 that the author cites is H. Zimmern, BSGW 58, p. 136-143, while there is also the study by P. Jensen, KB 6/2, Berlin 1915 (Amsterdam 1970), p. 32-37.

Why in (the temple of) the Ezida your throne has not been set up?

Why don't they call you our small Nabû?

Nanāja! (The goddess) Sutīti (why) don't they call you?"

Another ritual known from Uruk is the "Feast of Ištar" (AO 7439 + AO 8648 + AO 8649),[286] which was celebrated presumably on the 8th and 9th day of the *akītu* feast of Anu (obv.) and included a procession of Ištar to the temple called *bīt akīti* (rev.).[287]

Nanāja appears in this text a number of times together with Anu, Ištar and the goddess Bēlti-ša-Rēš ("Lady of (the temple of) Rēš"), known from the sources from Uruk. Offerings were made to these divinities during the ritual (l. 20'-21', 24'), a special throne to Anu and Nanāja was erected and seats were taken in their temples (rev. 29': ^{giš}*kussû ša* ^{d}*Anu ša ni-me-du u* ^{d}*Na-na-a irrubū*^{pl}*-ma ina bīt pa-pa-ḫa-šu*$_2$*-nu uššab*^{ab}). Golden vessels were filled with incense before the goddesses Nanāja and Bēlti-ša-Rēš (rev. 35').

Tablet VAT 14524[288] is a list of cult ceremonies connected with the Eanna temple in Uruk. Perhaps, considering that the surviving lines describe the feasts taking place over ten months, it was meant as a detailed catalogue of feasts held throughout the year. Nanāja participates in the ceremonies of the month of *Du'uzu/Tam(m)uz* with three other goddesses: Uṣur-amāssa, Aškajītum/Urkajītu and Bēlet-ša-Uruk. On the first day the throne of the goddess Aškajītum was carried to the *bīt ḫilṣi* and a procession around the Eanna was prepared. During this procession, an offering of a sheep was made in each of the eight temple gates. Actors (*kurgarrû*) were dressed in caps or masks (*rēs-su irakkas*), and regular offerings were made.

---

[286] S. Lackenbacher, *RA* LXXI (1977), p. 45 ff.

[287] See W. G. Lambert, *RA* XCI (1997), p. 58 (K 10282, l. 11) and p. 67-68 (81-2-4, 309, l. 3) – fragments of tablets concerning the procession to the *bīt akīti*.

[288] LKU 51, p. 17-21, pl. XVII-XVIII; P.-A. Beaulieu, CM 23, Appendix 2, p. 373-377.

There follows an unclear fragment (l. 20'): [xxx] *ina* UGU $BARA_2$-*An-zu-u*$_2$ *a-na* ^{d}*Na-na-a i-maḫ-ḫa-aṣ-m*[*a* ...].[289] The goddess (l. 22'-23') moved to the "house of the oracle" and then she climbed to the top of the ziggurat in the Eanna called E_2.GI_6.PAR_3.IMIN.BI in order to take her place there on the left hand side of the goddess Bēlet-ša-Uruk: [^{d}]*Na-na-a i-teb-bi-ma a-na* E_2 *te-rit ir-ru-ub-ma il-lak-ku* [...] / E_2.GI_6.PAR_3.IMIN.BI *i-lam-ma-am-ma a-na šumēli* (MIN.EŠ) *ša* ^{d}GAŠAN-*ša*$_2$-UNUG.KI *uš-*[*ša-ab li-li-si*]. Then the first procession took place and after a meal at noon and another one in the evening the second procession around the Eanna was performed. The *lilissu* drum played an important role.

For the Seleucid period there is a text that tells of the sacred marriage ritual of Nanāja and Nabû. The ceremony was assigned to the month of *ajjaru* and lasted for several days; perhaps the procession of the statues of the deities from Borsippa first to Babylon and then to Uruk and even Nippur was connected with it.[290]

A small tablet counting only 10 lines, BM 34030,[291] presumably refers to an unknown ritual. It is composed of two parts: the words of a priest addressed to five divinities (persuading them to take part in a procession) and explanations of divine names through the names of divinities identified with them (first comes the name of the "newer" god followed by that of the "older" one). Undoubtedly, the text reflects the outcome of the process of religious syncretism, a process that was widespread in the Ancient Near Eastern religion in the first millennium BC.

---

289 A. Falkenstein's translation (LKU) is as follows: "Er (= *kurgarû*) erschlägt ^{d}Nannâ den ^{d}Zû, [...];" P.-A. Beaulieu (CM 23) translated: "...on the Dais of Anzû for Nanaya he strikes/kills (?) and ..."
290 So M. E. Cohen, *The Cultic Calendars of the Ancient Near East*, Bethesda 1993, p. 311, although other scholars do not share his opinion. See below, notes 411 and 412 on p. 124, where this ceremony has been discussed in more detail in chapter V devoted to love lyrics.
291 W. G. Lambert, *AoF* 24/1 (1997), p. 158-162. Lambert considers this to be a school tablet, perhaps not used at all in the cult.

The following is a translation of the entire text (after W.G. Lambert):

Obv. 1. [Process, Bēl, Enlil of] heavens and netherworld,
[...] king of the great gods,

2. [Process, Zarpānītum], Bēlet-ilī, the beautiful, the bride, queen of Esagil, queen of Nippur,

3. Process, Tašmētum, Gula, mistress of Isin, counsellor of the great gods,

4. Process, Nanāya, Ishtar, mistress of the lands, mistress of Uruk, mistress of Ezida,

5. Process, Nabû, Anum, king of the pure heavens, foremost of the great gods.

Rev. 1. Bēl is present like Enlil.

2. Zarpānītum is present like Bēlet-ilī.

3. Tašmētum is present like Gula.

4. Nanāya is present like Ishtar.

5. Nabû is present like Anum.

From Hellenistic-period Uruk comes a ritual (CT 49, 150), during which 30 *sibtu* breads each were offered to the goddesses Antu, Ištar and Nanāja (l. 30).

Another ceremony known from this period was the dressing of statues, including that of Nanāja (Ash. 1923.739, 7).

In this context, one should be reminded of the words of E. Matsushima, who studied the *lubuštu* ceremony in reference to the statues of divinities:[292] "The clothing and fashioning of divine statues, as well as the feeding of them, was a very important aspect of religious life in the cities of Ancient Mesopotamia. It was essentially a part of the 'official cult.'"

---

[292] E. Matsushima, "Divine Statues in Ancient Mesopotamia: their Fashioning and Clothing and their Interaction with the Society", in: *eadem* (ed.), *Official Cult and Popular Religion in the Ancient Near East*, Heidelberg 1993, p. 217.

The rituals listed here evince the official cult of Nanāja. Whether there also existed a private cult of the goddess with separate rituals to be performed by individuals cannot be more than surmised (AUCT 3, 508 could be proof of a female ritual). The Old Babylonian ritual from Larsa, describing the feast of Nanāja on the 19th and 20th day of the month is further proof for the worship of Nanāja in this city. The number of rituals attesting the participation of Nanāja's statue grows dramatically in the Seleucid period; they were all localized at Uruk. In this aspect, too, Nanāja is connected with Ištar, a fact best demonstrated by the *akītu* rituals. The text BM 34030 is naturally the principal source documenting the link between Nanāja and Ištar. The sacred marriage rites reflect an important aspect of Nanāja, which was providing for the prosperity of the entire district or land.

II.6 PERSONAL NAMES WITH THE NAME OF NANĀJA

Next to temples and offerings performed there, personal names containing the appellation of a god or goddess are direct evidence for the existence of the cult of a given deity. It is assumed that the frequency with which the name of a divinity appears in the names of people testifies to the deity's popularity and is indirect proof of the number of his worshippers.

Personal names constructed with the element of the name of a god or goddess contain a determinative preceding the deity's appellation. I have decided to omit these in this section. In cases where a female name is concerned, this has been noted, for male names are undoubtedly in an overwhelming majority.

In presenting the number of personal names with an element of the name of Nanāja I have drawn heavily on data collected by F. Pomponio[293] in his monograph of the god Nabû who was Nanāja's con-

293 F. Pomponio, *Nabû. Il culto e la figura di un dio del Pantheon babilonese ed assiro*, Roma 1978. See tables with the names of deities occurring in the personal names of particular periods: Old Babylonian (p. 35), Neo-Assyrian (p. 89), Neo-Babylonian and Persian (p. 110). The author cau-

sort. In spite of the thirty years that have followed the publication of Pomponio's study and the publication of new texts, the quantitative relations of personal names with the Nanāja element and with that of Inanna/Ištar have not undergone any substantial change.

Old Babylonian period	Nanāja	Inanna/Ištar
Sippar (47 texts)[294]	1	3
Sippar (119 texts)	0	9
Sippar (32 texts)	0	3
Sippar (71 texts)	0	3
Tell ed-Dēr (191 texts)[295]	1	20
Tell ed-Dēr (30 texts)	0	3
Lagaba (120 texts	0	15
Kiš (77 texts)	0	1
Kiš (23 texts)	0	1
Dilbat (57 texts)[296]	1	7
Northern Babylonia (Dilbat, Sippar, Kiš: 538 texts)[297]	10	29

tioned with regard to the approximate nature of the statistics that he had presented (p. 34: "Va precisato che questa indagine statistica vuole avere un fine puramente orientativo, senza pretese di completezza o di assoluta precisione.") The designation of a city is followed in parentheses by the number of texts considered, references to which are given in the notes. I have refrained from copying this system in its entirety, preferring to give references to studies of groups of texts only if names with the Nanāja element are present in them.

[294] T. Friedrich, BA 5/4, p. 413-529. Index of names p. 478-483. Tests dated from the reign of Hammurabi to Ammī-ṣaduqa.

[295] TIM 7, 1-26, 28, 32-37, 43, 51, 54-201. Index of names: D. O. Edzard, *Altbabylonische Rechts- und Wirtschaftsurkunden aus Tell ed-Dēr im Iraq Museum*, Baghdad – Wiesbaden 1971, p. 219-234. Texts dated to the rule of Sumu-abum, Sumu-la-El and Sabium.

[296] I. E. Gautier, *Archives d'une famille de Dilbat au temps de la première dynastie de Babylone*, Mémoires publiés par les membres de l'Institut Français d'Archéologie Orientale du Caire 26, Le Caire 1908. Index of names p. 105-114.

Nippur (68 texts)	0	11
Nippur (160 texts)	0	19
Nippur (257 texts)	0	26
Nippur (56 texts)	0	3
Adab (57 texts)	0	3
Larsa (68 texts)[298]	3	10
Larsa (176 texts)[299]	6	9
Larsa (152 texts)[300]	1	7
Ur (883 texts)[301]	10	44
Iščali	0	13

In the Old Babylonian period personal names with the Nanāja element are seldom encountered. Assuming that the presence of a theophoric element in the names of individuals is a reflection of a given deity's popularity, it should be said that Nanāja was hardly a popular goddess. Inanna/Ištar enjoyed much greater popularity. In turn, Tašmētum is evidenced in this period only twice.

The rareness of Nanāja's name occurring in personal names, when compared to the alacrity with which Isin-Larsa and Old Babylonian rulers constructed chapels and temples to the goddess, is highly surprising. Could it perhaps reflect the stage at which the inception of the cult occurred with Nanāja gradually entering the Sumero-Akkadian pantheon?

Presented below are merely examples of personal names from the Isin-Larsa and Old Babylonian periods, complete with translation of the meaning of particular names.

---

297 J. J. Finkelstein, YOS 13 (Index of names p. 45-78). Texts dated to the last four kings of the Old Babylonian dynasty.
298 TLB 1, 1-68 (Index of names: W. F. Leemans, SLB 1/2, p. 98-103). Texts dated to the rule of Warad-Sîn and Rīm-Sîn.
299 D. E. Faust, YOS 8 (Index of names p. 29-34). Texts dated to the times of Rīm-Sîn.
300 H. F. Lutz, YOS 2 (Index of names p. 29-34). Texts dated to the times of the First Babylonian Dynasty.
301 H. H. Figulla, W. J. Martin, UET V (Index of names p. 27-66). Texts dated to the times of Isin-Larsa and the First Babylonian Dynasty.

A tablet from Uruk (W 20472, 75),[302] dated to the reign of Anam (1821-1817 BC), mentions an i š i b priest named Iddin-Nanāja ("Nanāja gave") and a s u k k a l official of the same name.

Under Irdanene (1816-1810 BC), a s a n g a priest of Nanāja from the same city bore the name of Iddin-Nanāja (W 20472, 125).[303] Also recorded is a slave who was a son of Šu-Nanāja "The one (who belongs to) Nanāja" – W 20472, 16 and W 20472, 76[304] and another slave of the name Inu-Nanāja "The Eye (?) of Nanāja" – W 20472, 202.[305] Another name to occur was Warad-Nanāja "Slave of Nanāja" – W 20472, 92.[306]

An undated text from Uruk (W 20472, 187)[307] gives the name Nanāja-AG$_2$[ ].

Personal names could also take on a form that was identical with the goddess's appellation (YOS 14, 59, 3 Na-na-a-a.)[308] The name Qiš-Nanāja is evidenced from Kiš (written as Qi$_2$-iš-Na-na-a/ia "Gift of Nanāja.") In Larsa there is Šu-Nanāja and at Tell ed-Dēr we have the female name Nanāja-ulamaši ("Nanāja releases (?) for her.")

The reign of Rīm-Sîn in Larsa (1822-1763 BC) witnesses a substantial increase in the number of names with the Nanāja element. Evidenced are new male names like Nanāja-ummī "Nanāja (is) my mother", Nanāja-lamassī "Nanāja (is) my protection", Ipqu-Nanāja "The friendly embrace of Nanāja", Nanāja-bēltī "Nanāja (is) my mistress", Puṭur-Nanāja "Release, Nanāja!" and female names: Nanāja-gamilat "Nanāja is the one who protects", Nanāja-imgur "Nanāja has granted (me)." In the reign of Samsu-iluna the female names of Nanāja-ša-

---

302 Sh. Sanati-Müller, *BaghM* 21 (1990), p. 209, no. 148; tablet W 20472, 66 (*eadem*, *BaghM* 20, 1989, no. 71, p. 290) mentions one Iddin-Nanāja as a witness.

303 *eadem*, *BaghM* 21 (1990), p. 191, no. 135, see also p. 28.

304 *eadem*, *BaghM* 19 (1988), p. 513, no. 30 (W 20472, 16) and *eadem*, *BaghM* 21 (1990), p. 186, no. 131 (W 20472, 76).

305 *eadem*, *BaghM* 19 (1988), p. 538, no. 43, seal b.

306 *eadem*, *BaghM* 21 (1990), p. 180, no. 126, l. 10: ni$_3$-ba Ir$_3$-^{d}*Na-na-a* GAR$_3$?.

307 *eadem*, *BaghM* 22 (1991), p. 328, no. 162, col. II' 5'.

308 See seal UE X, 213 where the name of the engraver is Na-na-a.

takālim "Nanāja of trust" and Nanāja-ēkalli "Nanāja (of) the palace"[309] are evinced in Larsa. Originating also from Larsa is the male name Nanāja-kuzub-mātim "Nanāja (is) the potency/abundance of the land" which illustrates Nanāja's aspect as a goddess-mistress who contributes to the development of the land.

The document AO 5421,[310] which comes from Babylon, from the Old Babylonian period (year "q" of the reign of Abī-ešuḫ), records the court proceedings in the case of a woman named Nanāja-šamḫat "Nanāja is the most beautiful,"[311] a daughter of Ša-Nanāja "The one who (belongs) to Nanāja." The witness was presumably one Ibni-Nanāja "Nanāja created."

Old Babylonian texts collected in YOS 13 present 11 names with the Nanāja element. The most popular name of the period is Nanāja-ibni (and the variant Nanāja-ibnī-šu) and Nanāja-ēriš "Nanāja entreated." Other names include: Ēribam-Nanāja/Nanāja-ēribam "Nanāja ascends there" and Etelpī-Nanāja "Grow along with (the child), Nanāja!" Also appearing are the names of Nanāja-ummī (both male and female) and the male name Nanāja-ilu(DINGIR)[312] "Nanāja is (my) deity." Other types are Gimil-Nanāja "Protect, goddess Nanāja!" and Idin-Nanāja "Give, goddess Nanāja!"

Old Babylonian texts and seals provide very interesting material[313], namely, the i š i b/*išippu* priests of the deity AN-^{d}INANNA (that is, Ištar of Uruk or Anum and Ištar) bear personal names with the theophoric element of ^{d}Nanāja:[314]

---

309 PTS 2187, see in: B. Lafont, *RA* LXXXVI/2 (1992), p. 104.

310 C. Wilcke, AOAT 247, p. 413-429.

311 See *šamāḫu* CAD Š/1 288b 2. "to flourish, to attain extraordinary beauty or stature"; stat. G *šamkat/šamḫat*. See also *šamḫatu* CAD Š/1 311b ("a prostitute, a woman connected with the temple"), there also the personal name Ša-am-ḫa-tum.

312 J. J. Finkelstein, YOS 13, 198, l. 1 and 9. In the index of names J. J. Finkelstein lists ^{d}Na-na-a-ilu, but this could also be read as Nanāja-iltu.

313 My observations concern primarily the documents studied by J. J. Finkelstein, in: YOS 13.

314 See above II.4, p. 67-68.

YOS 13, 44 (Abī-ešuḫ?)	*Nanāja-ibni* i š i b AN-[d]INANNA;
YOS 13, 262 (Samsu-ditāna 2)	*Nanāja-ēriš* i š i b AN-[d]INANNA;
YOS 13, 297 (Samsu-ditāna 5)	*Nanāja-ēriš* i š i b AN-[d]INANNA *mār Uruk*[ki]*-libluṭ warad*(IR$_3$) *Ammī-ṣaduqa* (see RIME 4 3.10.2014);
YOS 13, 435 (Samsu-ditāna 13)	*Nanāja-ēriš* i š i b AN-[d]INANNA.

A seal from Uruk (UVB IX 16) is evidence for the existence of one *Sîn-itūram mār Iddin-Nanāja* i š i b AN-[d]INANNA.

R. Pientka[315] is his work about the late Old Babylonian time gathered all the names with the element Nanāja from this period. They total 64 in number and the table I cite here (from p. 187) presents their distribution (see the next page).

According to Pientka, 67% of the names cames from Dilbat and Kiš, confirming a continued worship by émigrés from Uruk around the 10th year of Samsu-iluna's rule.

Among the personal names evinced in the texts from Nuzi, Nanāja occurs three times: Iddin-Nanāja "Nanāja gave", Nanāja-ummī "Nanāja (is) my mother" and the name of a woman Nanāja.

No personal names with the Nanāja element have been recorded for the Kassite period, presumably because of the gap in the Uruk sources. The sole exception is a *kudurru* document of the 12th century BC mentioning a royal daughter of the name of Ḫannubat-Nanāja. Names with the Ištar element are present:[316]

Nippur (A. T. Clay, CPN)	39
Dūr-Kurigalzu (44 texts; *Iraq* 11 (1949), p. 131-149 and *Sumer* 9 (1953), p. 21-34)	1

Few names continued to be constructed with the Nanāja element in the Neo-Assyrian period. According to Pomponio, the numbers are as follows (as before, the last column gives the number of personal names with the Ištar element in the same center):

---

315 R. Pientka, *Die spätaltbabylonische Zeit. Abiešuh bis Samsuditana. Jahresdaten, Quellen, Geschichte*, Marburg 1998.
316 F. Pomponio, *op. cit.*, p. 54.

Town	Abī-ešuḫ	Ammī-ditāna	Ammī-ṣaduqa	Samsu-ditāna	No date	Total
Dilbat	–	1	10	1	1	13
Kiš	1	3	11	13	1	29
Dilbat/Kiš	–	–	1	–	–	1
Babylon	3	3	1	1	–	8
Sippar	–	6	2	–	1	9
Others	–	–	1	1	2	4
Total	**4**	**13**	**26**	**16**	**5**	**64**

Kalaḫ (353 texts of the 8th century BC)	0	22
Kalaḫ (89 texts of the 7th century BC)[317]	2	27
Balawat (29 texts from the time of Sîn-aḫḫē-erība Aššur-aḫa-iddina)	0	3
Niniveh (678 texts from the reign of Sargon until the end of the Assyrian empire)[318]	5	58
Aššur (172 texts of the 7th century BC)[319]	1	39
Northwest Assyria (33 texts of the 7th century BC)	0	4

The name Nanāja-karābī "Nanāja my prayer (has answered)"– W 22657 comes from the reign of Sīn-šar-iškun (630-612 BC). The most popular names are Amēl-Nanāja "Servant of Nanāja" and Gimil-Nanāja "The grace of Nanāja."

The number of personal names with the Nanāja element increased rapidly in the Neo-Babylonian and Persian periods. Names with the Inanna/Ištar element continued to appear in approximately the same quantity (again given in the last column):

Babylonia (460 texts from the times of Nabuchodonozor II)[320]	2	1
Babylonia (102 texts from the times of Awēl-Marduk Neriglissar and Labaši-Marduk)[321]	1	0
Babylonia (1134 texts from the times of Nabonid)[322]	1	2

[317] J. Kohler, A. Ungnad, *Assyrische Rechtsurkunden*, Leipzig 1913, 44-45; B. Parker, *Iraq* 16 (1952), p. 29-58 (64 texts); B. Parker, *Iraq* 19 (1957), p. 125-138 (23 texts).
[318] J. Kohler, A. Ungnad, *op. cit.*, texts beside nos. 44-45, 76, 166, 170, 174, 553.
[319] CT 33, nos. 15A, 16A, 16B, 17A, 17B, 18A, 18B, 19A, 19B; KAJ 189 and 208, as well as 160 texts from the Museum in Berlin.
[320] J. N. Strassmaier, BT 5 and 6A (Index of names p. 19-38).
[321] B. T. A. Evetts, BT 6B (Index of names p. 6-20).
[322] J. N. Strassmaier, BT 1-4 (Index of names p. 40-68).

Babylonia (825 texts from the times of Cyrus and Cambyses)[323]	1	1
Sippar (247 texts from the Neo-Babylonian dynasty and the first three Persian kings)[324]	2	4
Nippur (74 texts from the Nabopolassar-Cambyses period)[325]	2	1
Nippur (109 texts from the reign of Artaxerxes I: 464-424 BC)[326]	6	0
Nippur (360 texts from the reign of Darius II: 424-404 BC)[327]	6	1
Uruk (163 texts from the Nabuchodonozor – Cambyses period)[328]	4	17
Uruk (177 texts from the Nabonid – Cambyses period)[329]	17	36
Uruk (56 texts from the Seleucid period)[330]	9	12
Ur (84 texts from the Merodach-baladan II – Cambyses period)[331]	2	2
Ur (75 texts from the Darius I – Seleucid period)[332]	5	4

323 J. N. Strassmaier, BT 7 (Index of names p. 15-26) and BT 8-9 (Index of names p. 16-28).
324 CT 22, 1-247.
325 A. T. Clay, BE VIII/1, nos. 10, 12-13, 15, 17-23, 25-29, 31, 33, 36-37, 39-42, 45-46, 48-63, 65-68, 69-78, 80-92, 94-99 (Index of names p. 39-69).
326 H. V. Hilprecht, A. T. Clay, BE IX (Index of names p. 47-74).
327 A. T. Clay, BE X (Index of names p. 37-67) and A. T. Clay, PBS II/1 (Index of names p. 9-41).
328 H. Freydank, *Spätbabylonische Wirtschaftstexte aus Uruk*, Deutsche Akademie der Wissenschaften zu Berlin, Institut für Orientforschung 71, I-II, Berlin 1971 (Index of names I, p. 134-145).
329 C. E. Keiser, BIN 1 (Index of names p. 11-22).
330 A. T. Clay, BRM 2 (Index of names p. 41-78).
331 UET IV nos 6-7, 9, 13-16, 23-24, 27, 32-33, 36, 51, 56, 61-63, 68-84, 86-90, 112-114, 117-121, 126-127, 130, 139, 146-148, 154-156, 158-161, 163-164, 171-172, 176-177, 182-188, 190-192, 195-199, 201-203, 207.

In his study devoted to the prosopography of professional groups in sixth-century BC Uruk, H. M. Kümmel[333] listed 16 different names with the Nanāja element. Some of these were known from earlier times: Amēl-Nanāja "Nanāja's man", Arad-Nanāja "Servant of Nanāja" and Gimil-Nanāja "The grace of Nanāja." New ones include the very telling names of Nanāja-naṣir-aḫī-rabî "Nanāja guards my elder brother", Nanāja-aḫa-iddin "Nanāja gave (me) a brother" and Nanāja-aḫa-uṣur "Nanāja, guard (my) brother!" The following names should be presumably considered as abbreviated forms: Nanāja-iddin "Nanāja gave", Nanāja-ibni "Nanāja created", Nanāja-ēriš "Nanāja planted" and even Nanāja-uṣalli/a "I pray/I prayed (to) Nanāja." The names: Ina-ṣilli-Nanāja "Under Nanāja's protection (I remain)", lit. "In the shade of Nanāja" and an abbreviation of the previous one – Ṣilli-Nanāja, and also Nanāja-šuma-uṣur "Nanāja, protect my name!" all refer to the aspect of motherly care. Personal names like Nanāja-šamšīja "Nanāja (is) my sun" and Ša-Nanāja-tašmet "The one whom Nanāja answers" appeared. From the same period come the names:[334] Itti-Nanāja-īnī-ja "With Nanāja my eyes" and the female names Ina-Nanāja-ultarraḫ "Thanks to Nanāja I can glorify", Itti-Nanāja-gūzu "Security with Nanāja", Ina-qāt-Nanāja-šakin[335] "Rests in Nanāja's hand", Li'utu-Nanāja "Able (for) Nanāja" and Nanāja-bēl-bīti "Nanāja (is) the Lord of the house." Also attested is a male name composed of merely the two divine names: Nanāja-Nabû.[336]

New texts from the Chaldean and Persian periods published in 1994[337] have not enriched the set of known names: Amēl-Nanāja,

332 UET IV nos 1-5, 10-12, 17-20, 25-26, 28-30, 34-35, 37-50, 52-55, 57-60, 64-67, 85, 91-97, 99-101, 111, 115-116, 124, 128, 136, 145, 193-194, 205.

333 H. M. Kümmel, *Familie, Beruf und Amt im spätbabylonischen Uruk. Prosopographische Untersuchungen zu Berufsgruppen des 6. Jahrhunderts v. Chr. in Uruk*, Abhandlungen der Deutschen Orient-Gesellschaft 20, Berlin 1979.

334 A. Tremayne, YOS 7, see list of names.

335 R. P. Dougherty, YOS 6, see list of names.

336 H. F. Lutz, UCP IX/2, 2, 2.

337 R. H. Sack, *Cuneiform Documents from the Chaldean and Persian Periods*, London 1994; index of names p. 62-86.

Arad-Nanāja, Gimil-Nanāja, Nanāja-aḫa-iddina, Nanāja-ēriš, Nanāja-ibni, Nanāja-iddina, Nanāja-naṣir, Nanāja-uṣalli keep on being repeated. A new name is Nanāja-šarra-uṣur "Nanāja, protect the king!" Attested in the same period are Nanāja-ilu'a "Nanāja (is) my god" (the form Nanāja-ilu should be treated as an abbreviation) and Nanāja-kiširat "Nanāja endows with success."

The following names occur as names of slave girls:[338] Nanāja-ana-bītīšu "Nanāja (let her enter) his family", Nanāja-bēla-uṣur "Nanāja, protect the master!", Nanāja-ittī-ja "Nanāja (is) with me" and Ana-muḫḫi-Nanāja-taklak "I trust in Nanāja." The female name Ša-Nanāja-nīnni "We (are) assigned to Nanāja" is also attested.

A variety of female names with the element of the goddess's name comes from the 3rd century BC:[339] Erēštum-Nanāja "Desiring the goddess Nanāja", Nidinti-Nanāja "Present of Nanāja", Nuptum-Nanāja "Present of Nanāja", Ṭābat-Nanāja "Good (is) Nanāja."

Among the Hittite personal names[340] the name of Nanāja can also be found, as well as other forms composed with the Nana-element (Nananta, Nananza, Nanapi, Nanatalli, Nanaziti next to Nani, Na(n)nija, Nanijanza). The form Pīḫananājaš is also known (KBo 12.53 + obv. 14', 15').

Cappadocian texts also provide personal names that could be linked to the goddess (notation: Na-na, Na-na-a, Na-na-a-a, Na-ni-a, Na-na-nim).

The element *-naja* is frequent among Hurrite names known from Nuzi; it is characteristic of female names (a shorter form is *-na*). The names originating from there,[341] such as Ḫanannija and Nanija, should be linked with the goddess Nanni known from Mari rather than with Nanāja.

Personal names connected with Nanāja are also attested in the Aramaic texts, e.g. the abbreviated name nn'.[342]

---

338 K. Tallqvist, *Neubabylonische Namenbuch*, Helsingfors 1905, p. 266 ff.

339 D. B. Weisberg, Bib. Mes. 24, see index of names.

340 E. Laroche, *Les Noms des Hittites*, Paris 1966, no. 855 ff.

341 See M. P. Maidman, SCCNH 6, p. 369; NPN, p. 236-237 and AAN I, p. 97.

342 E. Lipiński, *Studies in Aramaic Inscriptions and Onomastics*, Leuven 1975, p. 86. The author remains doubtful about whether it has a connection

A review of personal names composed with the use of the Nanāja element clearly demonstrates that no theophoric name linked to this goddess is attested for the Ur III period despite the confirmed existence of her cult in this period. Hence, her popularity does not begin until the Old Babylonian period. It occurs seldom, while the extensive number of mentions in building inscriptions and in other royal sources leads one to think that there was a substantial difference between official and private worship. Also in Neo-Assyrian times few names refer to this goddess. The number grows rapidly in Neo-Babylonian and Persian times, outdistancing even in some centers the names with the Ištar element. It is found most frequently in texts from Uruk which once again would confirm the theory about this city being the major center of Nanāja's cult.

with Nanāja, considering it rather as a Neo-Hittite or Eastern Luwian name (he compares it with words from the Luwian hieroglyphic language, Greek and Indo-European tongues). He emphasizes that elements like *-nana*, *-nani*, *nan-* appear in Hurrian names.

CHAPTER III

THE IMAGE OF NANĀJA BASED ON MAGIC AND DIVINATION TEXTS

Nanāja's domain also incorporated the sphere of magic and divination. Her name was evoked in a variety of spells: purifying (*Šurpu*), magic (*Maqlû*) and "releasing" (*Namburbû*), female love spells (discussed in the chapter devoted to love lyrics) and male potency spells; medical texts are also close to these. Nanāja appears twice in omens and in mono- or bilingual oath formulas.

III.1 THE ROLE PLAYED BY NANĀJA IN MAGIC SPELLS

Šurpu

In the collection of Sumerian and Akkadian purifying spells *Šurpu*,[343] Nanāja's name occurs once, on tablet II. The last part on this tablet mentions different divinities who are supposed to cleanse a person of unconscious sin (the text was also known in Late Babylonian Uruk – W 22743/2,[344] IV 18-19):

155. ^{d}*Nabû u* ^{d}*Na-na-a lip-ṭu-ru ina* E$_2$.ZI.DA

156. ^{d}*Taš-me-tum lip-ṭur kal-la-tum rabītum*^{tum}

"Nabû and Nanāja, may release in Ezida,

Tašmētum, may release, the great daughter-in-law."

Nanāja is paired here with her spouse Nabû; both are connected with the Ezida temple.[345] Ištar of Uruk and the goddesses connected with her (or aspects of Ištar) are evoked starting with line 168.

Nanāja's name, as I have already noted above, occurs only once, while the names of other deities are repeated several times.

343 E. Reiner, *Šurpu*, Graz 1958.

344 E. von Weiher, SpTU II, no. 13.

345 The Neo-Babylonian colophon reads as follows (D. C. Snell, *RA* LXXXVIII (1994), p. 59 ff.): *ana* E$_2$.ZI.DA *bīt* ^{d}*Nabû u* ^{d}*Nanāja bīt bēli u bēlti* "For the Ezida, temple of the god Nabû and the goddess Nanāja, house of the Lord and Lady" (l. 17), demonstrating that at this time Nanāja had her own chapel in the Ezida, which was a sanctuary of Nabû (presumably at Kalḫu).

On tablet III, which is a list of different oaths and spells, Nabû is paired not with Nanāja, but with the goddess Tašmētum (l. 158), designated before as "great daughter-in-law" (*kallatum*). Tablet IV, addressed to Marduk as the greatest force capable of releasing from all kinds of sin, also evokes other divinities. In a supporting role (third in sequence) there is Ištar, mentioned together with the goddesses Bau and Anunītu (l. 62). As the Mistress of all lands, Ištar is also asked to intervene on behalf of the sinner (l. 106). Tablets V-VI, which refer to, among others, a ritual burning of various objects that are symbolic of the sins of the sufferer, mention Ištar aiding the goddess of weaving Uttu in manufacturing thread (l. 144-147). Tablet VIII, which also mentions deities releasing from misfortune, again mentions Tašmētum coupled with Nabû.

The situation in which Nabû is mentioned in this particular category of spells once in a pair with Nanāja and at other times coupled with Tašmētum is likely a reflection of where the text was composed. E. Matsushima has demonstrated beyond all doubt that Nanāja appears with Nabû in texts referring to the sacred marriage rites from the territory of Babylonia, while in the Assyrian texts her place next to Nabû is taken by Tašmētum. The goddess appears in tandem with Nabû already in a list of gods from the Old Babylonian period (TCL XV, pl. 25 and following, l. 110-111). The text, which presents deities who had undergone syncretism, gives Tašmētum as the "former" Gula, goddess of healing. Thus, it may be assumed that the *Šurpu* collection, which was written down somewhere in Assyria, but had been composed (possibly as a prototype) in Babylonia, reflects the chaos of mutually clashing traditions.

Maqlû

In the *Maqlû*[346] series of purifying spells, Nanāja is evoked on tablet V, among the names of other divinities:

59. *i-na* qi_2*-bit* ^{d}*Ištar* ^{d}*Dumu-zi* ^{d}*Na-na-a be-let ra-a-mi*

60. u_3 ^{d}*Ka-ni-sur-ra be-let* ^{f}*kaššapāti*^{pl} EN_2

[346] G. Meier, *Die Assyrische Beschwörungssamlung* Maqlû, *AfO* 2, Berlin 1937.

"At the command of Ištar, the god Dumuzi, the goddess Nanāja, Mistress of love,

and the goddess Kanisurra, Lady of Magic. Spell."

In the quoted fragment of the text, Ištar appears together with her beloved Dumuzi. The author attached Nanāja to this pair, designating her as the "Mistress of Love", as well as Nanāja's daughter, the "Lady of Magic", Kanisurra. The epithet *bēlet ru'āmi* refers to Nanāja's role as guardian of lovers and the betrothed of kings.

The author of the text (tablet IX, l. 42) states: *ši-na mārāti*^{pl} ^{d}*Anim ša*$_2$ *šamê*^{e} "Two (are) the daughters of the god of the heavens, Anu."[347] Nanāja was, like Ištar, entitled probably to this epithet.

Namburbû

The *Namburbû* rituals, created in order to remove a person from a variety of evils and to aid him or her, evoke the name of Nanāja only once. It is a spell intended to ensure profit from selling beer,[348] which is connected with this ritual. The taverner or his wife should kneel on the roof and remaining in this position they should call to Ištar, Nanāja and Gazbaba for aid (l. 10). Further on in the text, Ištar alone, referred to by a plenty of epithets, is called upon for aid. Perhaps this is tantamount to calling upon also Nanāja and her daughter Gazbaba.

Potency spells

Sexual potency spells, i n i m . i n i m . m a š a$_3$. z i. g a/*nīš libbi*, aided the proper treatment of patients by priests-exorcists. They were recited most often by those instituting a cure. The texts come from different centers, but Nanāja is mentioned solely in tablets from Sultantepe and Aššur, in both cases from the first millennium BC.

In the collection prepared by R. D. Biggs,[349] Nanāja occurs a total of six times,[350] usually in combination with other goddesses: Ištar,

347 See B. R. Foster, *Before the Muses*, Bethesda 1993, p. 853.
348 E. Ebeling, *RA* XLIX/4 (1955), p. 178 ff., no. 26 (KAR III, no. 144).
349 R. D. Biggs, TCS II.
350 *Op. cit.* no. 3, l. 24; no. 5, l. 13; no. 10, l. 36; no. 12, l. 22; no. 25, l. 12, 16.

Gazbaba, Kanisurra and Išḫara. Text no. 12 gives the titles of Ištar and Nanāja, which are helpful in separating the different competences of the goddesses (l. 22): *ina qibīt* ^{d}*Ištar bēlet ru'āme* ^{d}*Nanāja bēlet* h i . l i "According to the command of Ištar, goddess of feminine charms (and) Nanāja, goddess of sexual attractiveness."[351] In text no. 25 we read (l. 11-13): *ša* ^{d}*Ištar ana* ^{d}*Dumuzi ēpuš*[352] / *ša* ^{d}*Nanāja ana ḫa'īriša ēpuš* / *ša* ^{d}*Išḫara ana lamanīša ēpuš* "What Ištar did for Dumuzi, / what Nanāja did for her lover, / what Išḫara did for her husband (let me do for my lover!)"[353]

The epithet *bēlet kuzbi* used in text no. 12 (in contrast to *bēlet ru'āmi*) seems to reflect a characteristic trait of Nanāja, who ruled over female appeal, as well as the other senses.[354] This title can be viewed as derivative of "Mistress of love" and reflecting Nanāja's "specialization" in physical love. The second of the texts seems to confirm this as the woman is shown asking for herself a fluency in the art of love equal to the goddesses.

The last of the texts, an Akkadian magic-medical text, was found at Hattuša.[355] Nanāja appears only in a fragment (l. 15'-23'), which is a spell inserted between medical prescriptions. It is the only case of Nanāja appearing without the dingir determinative. The same concerns the goddess-demon Kilili (l. 20') which is her counterpart.

Here is the appropriate fragment:[356]

15' ⸢TU$_6$⸣ E$_2$.NU.RU *ag-ra-aḫ-ki Na-na-a*

---

[351] Cf. h i. l i/*kuzbu* above: note 176 on p. 54 (n i n h i - l i (- a) š u - d u$_7$), p. 56 (n i n h i - l i š e - e r - k a - a n - d i), p. 57 (e$_2$ - h i - l i - a n - n a), p. 87 (the name *Nanāja-kuzub-mātim*), p. 107 (h i - l i z i d - d a u l - š c$_3$ p a d$_3$ - d a h i n h i - l i - a t u m$_2$ - m a), p. 116-117 and note 394; R. D. Biggs, TCS II, p. 31 note 22.

[352] The notation DU$_3$-*uš*, which justifies the reading *ēpuš*, *īpuš*, *lūpuš* and *līpuš* (R. D. Biggs, *op. cit.*, p. 44 note 10).

[353] Cf. translation by B. R. Foster, *Before the Muses*, Bethesda 1993, p. 885.

[354] Some scholars have translated this epithet as "Mistress of sensuality."

[355] KBo 36.27; the transliteration and translation D. Schwemer, *ZA* 94/1 (2004), p. 59-79.

[356] Transliteration and translation after D. Schwemer, *op. cit.*, p. 62-64.

16’ *ag-ra-aḫ-ki Na-na-a ⸢ki⸣-ma im-me-ri*
17’ *a-la-⸢la⸣-ma ⸢ki⸣-ma a-ri-ti ta-nu-qa-tum*[!?] (⸢*am*⸣[?]) - *ma*
18’ ⸢IM⸣-KUM PA-⸢KI⸣-*ti-a* BI[!?]-*ta-a-*⸢*ki*⸣
19’ IM-KUM PA-⸢KI⸣-*ti-a ma-ia-a-al-ki*
20’ *a-ra-am* ⸢*Ki-li-li*⸣ *a-na-ak Ki-li-li*
21’ UŠ te UŠ ⸢te da⸣.ga.an.ni
22’ da.zi.da.an.ni
23’ ga$_2$.an.ga da.⸢ga⸣.an.ni ⸢mah⸣.ha
15’ “Bechwörungsformel. Hiermit begatte ich dich, Nanaja,
16’ hiermit begatte ich dich, Nanaja! Wie bei einem Widder
17’ is der Freudenschrei, wie bei einer Schwangen *das Gebrüll.*
18’ .....
19’.... dein Bett!
20’ Ich liebe (*dich,*) Kilili, ich beschlafe (*dich,*) Kilili!
21’-23’ ... Abrakadabra ...”

Medical spells

Nanāja’s role in female illness was well known in Assyria of the first millennium BC. Medical texts from the times of Aššur-aḫa-iddina and Aššur-bani-apli,[357] which open with the phrase: “Samaš, great lord, whom I ask, answer me with a real ‘yes’”, mention *qāti* (*qātē*[pl]) [d]*Nanāja ša Uruk*[358] “the hand (hands) of the goddess Nanāja of Uruk”, which was placed on the sick person.

Also the commentary of a text dealing with illness caused by the spirits of the dead (SpTU I 49 – W 22307/17) mention the name of the goddess (l. 10).

Nanāja stands next to Ištar in a spell against the female demon of illness, Lamaštu. The sense of the quoted words is not clear, howev-

357 Cf. J. A. Knudtzon, *Assyrische Gebete an den Sonnengott für Staat und Königlisches Haus aus der Zeit Asarhaddons und Asurbanipals*, I and II, Leipzig 1893.
358 J. A. Knudtzon, *op. cit.*, nos. 102 and 103; I. Starr (ed.), SAA IV, nos 191-194.

er[359] (l. 49-50): ^{d}*Ištar pī kalbīki ṣabtī* / ^{d}*Nanāja ṣubbitī pī mūrānīki* "Ištar! Catch your dog by the muzzle! / Nanāja! Catch your puppy by the muzzle!"

The goddess appears also in the company of other divinities (Šamaš, Sîn, Bēl and Nergal) in an Aramaic spell from Nippur,[360] originating from the 5th or 6th century AD. The magical objective of the text was to tame an evil spirit and by the same protect the woman from losing her reproductive capabilities. The gods listed here are supposed to imbue the future mother with strength. What is surprising is that, to judge by the forms of the verbs, the masculine was used for Nanāja. This is presumably due to the fact that all the other divinities here listed are male and that in this late period the goddess's true identity had been lost. The divinities evoked here came from a bygone time even though the belief in their instrumental power was still well engrained.

The medical texts discussed above reveal Nanāja as having the power to make sick or protect (in the case of the last text) the ability to have offspring. In this Nanāja is like Ištar, the guardian of mothers.

III.2 THE OMENS OF NANĀJA

Nanāja is seldom mentioned in predictions. Texts with her name are restricted to Old Babylonian and Kassite times.

The Akkadian oracle text from Uruk (W 19900, 1),[361] discovered in the palace of Sîn-kāšid (c. 1865/60-1833 BC), contains merely a mention of the goddess Nanāja (l. 6): *iš-tu* u_4*-um* ^{d}*Na-na-a i-ru-ba-kum* "Since the day (that) Nanāja visited you." The main characters in the prediction were *rē'û kīnu* "the rightful shepherd" and the goddess Ištar.

---

359 Cf. D. W. Myhrman, *ZA* 16 (1902), p. 176-177 and D. R. West, AOAT 233, p. 255.

360 J. Montgomery, *Aramaic Incantation Texts from Nippur*, Philadelphia 1913, no. 36.

361 UVB XVIII, pl. 28c, p. 61-62; ANET Suppl., p. 604; J. G. Westenholz, AS 27, p. 305-324.

The period of the Kassite dynasty is represented by text YBC 4363,[362] which is a report on oracles read from the viscera of lambs. The offering was made to two goddesses: Nanāja (obv. 1) and Ištar (rev. 1), probably with the purpose of double-checking the oracle.

Text YBC 4634[363] in five columns is a systematically described prediction divined from a liver. The name of Nanāja appears in very similar stanzas:

> ᵈ*Na-na-a se*$_2$*-[ek]-re-tam i-na si*$_2$*-ik-ri-im [u*$_2$*-ši-ṣi]-a[m]* (II 53),
>
> ᵈ*Na-na-a se*$_2$*-ek-re-tam na-ra-am-ti šar-ri-im / i-na si*$_2$*-ik-ri-im u*$_2$*-ši-ṣi* (IV 49-50).

The term *sekretu*[364] and derivative form *sikru*[365] pose a problem. Nanāja's role is reduced to releasing a woman called *sekretu* (designated as "beloved of the king") from a place known as the *sikru*. Does it mean that prayers addressed to the guardian of the betrothed (Nanāja, that is) were capable of raising the status of the praying woman? Was the exit of the "favorite (?)" from the *sikru* "seclusion (?), harem (?)" tantamount to her assuming the title of royal wife?

This text reveals Nanāja as the guardian of the royal concubines. Let it be recalled that in a votive inscription of the 19th century BC a l u k u r priestess of Būr-Sîn, ruler of Isin, called Nanāja her mistress. In the intention of the lives of the king and her own, she of-

---

[362] YBT X 2. Cf. also A. Goetze, *JCS* 11 (1957), p. 103-104 and J. Nougayrol, *RA* XLIV (1950), p. 8.

[363] YBT X 46. Cf. J. Nougayrol, *RA* XLIV (1950), p. 22.

[364] AHw 1036a: 'Abgesperrte' (eine Frauenklasse); CAD S 215a, 1. ("a woman of high rank, possibly cloistered"), 2. ("a woman of the palace household, court lady"), cf. 1b). Cf. p. 58 (text of Aššur-aḫa-iddina, who calls the goddess *sekrat na'itti*).

[365] AHw 1043a is consistent in giving "*Absperrung*", cf. 1. CAD S 259b in 2. "seclusion, cloistering", and the translation is as follows: "Nanâ will remove the concubine, the king's favorite, from the enclosure." Translation, s.v. *narāmtu* (CAD N 342a), is somewhat different: "Nanâ will let the palace woman, the favorite of the king, leave the harem." Another translation, s.v. *aṣû* (CAD A 373a, 6. *šūṣû* m) 2', runs as follows: "love (lit. Nanâ) will drive out the lady of the harem, the favorite of the king, from the harem." Cf. also W. von Soden, *ZA* 49 (1949), p. 162.

fered the goddess a plaque of agate. Perhaps these two texts should be viewed as evidence for a special worship of Nanāja as guardian of the royal concubines.

III.3 NANĀJA IN OATH FORMULAS

A collection of oath formulas prepared by E. Ebeling[366] offers evidence for the fact that Nanāja was evoked among other divinities in order to emphasize the importance of an oath. She appears in a Sumero-Akkadian model (VAT 13662+13883, col. II 28-34):

zi ^{d}Na-na-a	: *niš* ^{d}*Na-na-a*
nir-gal$_2$ E$_2$-an-na	: *e-tel-lit* E$_2$-an-na
E$_2$-zi-da ti-la	: *a-ši*$^{!}$*-bat* E$_2$-zi-da
nitalam(SAL.UŠ.DAM) ^{d}PA	: *ḫi-rat* ^{d}*Nabû*
dumu-nita E$_2$-sag-ila-ke$_4$	: *a-pil* E$_2$-sag-ila
ur$_4$ gašam	: *ḫa-mi-mat ni-me-qi*$_2$
abzu-ke$_2$$^{?}$-e-ne$^{!}$ he$_2$-pad$_3$	: *ap-si-i*

"(An oath) on the life of (the goddess) Nanāja,
princess of (the temple of) the Eanna,
resident of (the temple of) the Ezida,
spouse of (the god) Nabû,
firstborn of (the temple of) the Esagila,
collecting the wisdom of
apsû (you should take this oath!)."

The goddess Tašmētum appears immediately before the lines in which Nanāja is mentioned (col. II 20-27). Yet the author did not designate her as the spouse of Nabû.

Another text is the bilingual tablet K 3179+, on which Nanāja is referred to as the daughter of Ištar (col. III 13-14):

zi ^{d}Na-na-a [DUMU.M]I$_2$.SAG$^{!}$ ^{d}Innin[-na-ke$_2$ he$_2$]

[366] E. Ebeling, "Sammlungen von Beschwörungsformeln", *ArOr* XXI (1953), p. 357 ff.

niš ^{d}Na-na-a mar-ti reš$^{!}$-ti$^{!}$-ti ša$_2$ [^{d}*Ištar lu-u$_2$*]

"(The oath) on the life of (the goddess) Nanāja, firstborn daughter of Ištar, you should [take]."

J. J. Finkelstein published a text (YOS 13, 192) that bears witness to the birth of a girl. The mother was a slave girl belonging to an *ugbabtum* priestess of the god Zababa. The text runs as follows (l. 11-13): *a-ma-at* / ^{d}*Na-na-a pi$_2$-ḫa-as-sa* / *i-ip-pa-a*[*l*] "(the mother) before / the goddess Nanāja will be for her (= the priestess's) duties / responsible."[367] The name of Nanāja was used here as a form of confirmation of one's word, like an oath formula. The text further contains information that the birth had taken place in a new house on Nanāja's street (l. 6: *ina* E$_2$.GIBIL *ša* SILA ^{d}*Nanāja*).

Magic and divination sources provide a homogeneous picture of Nanāja, the goddess of love. It is best highlighted by the *Maqlû* spells which are straight-forward in using this title to designate Nanāja. For the same reason she is listed among the other divinities in potency spells. They evince her power in the sphere of the senses and carnal pleasures. The term h i . l i,[368] frequently used in reference to Nanāja, can be understood after all as sexual desire as much as charm, appeal, attractiveness. Nanāja was simultaneously treated as a cause for female illness and repelling the Lamaštu demon that endangered the fetus and small children.

The second of the Kassite fortune-telling texts, while not entirely clear, leads one to surmise that Nanāja was the target of prayers by women living in the harems. Thus, she may be taken to be the guardian of mistresses, a fact which is made especially well evident by the love spells from Isin and the love dialogue from Sippar to be discussed in chapter V.

---

367 Cf. J. J. Finkelstein, YOS 13, p. 15: "The responsibility of Amat-Bau to the goddess Nana would consist of aiding her mistress to carry out the latter's function as an ugbabtu, by washing her feet, carrying her chair to the goddess's temple, or providing other services in support of her mistress's cultic role."

368 See RlA IX, p. 378 s.v. Nin-hilisu (^{d}Nin-hi-li-su$_3$) "Anmutige Herrin", and S. N. Kramer, in: Fs Mikasa, p. 207, l. 153.

CHAPTER IV
HYMNS AND PRAYERS TO THE GODDESS NANĀJA

It should be emphasized that the compositions presented here are a reflection of the official cult of Nanāja. The oldest known hymn[369] to the goddess, written in Sumerian, dates to the reign of Išbi-Erra (2017-1985 BC), ruler of Isin.

According to the legend, it is a t i g i composition, meaning it was performed to the beating of a drum. It combines an extolling of the goddess with a plea to her to bless the king. It is the sole known t i g i composition dedicated to Nanāja.

Nanāja does not come through clearly in this piece. Her great dependence on Inanna is emphasized: "created for the Goddess" (i n - n i n - r a t u m_2 - m a, l. 2), "by the Hierodula to be mistress of all lands chosen appropriately" (n u - u_8 - g i g - g e n i n k u r - k u r - r a z i - d e_3 - e š - š e_3 p a_3 - d a, l. 3), "properly educated by the holy Inanna" (k u g ^{d}I n a n n a - k e_4 z i - d e_3 - e š u m u n_2 a k, l. 7), "counselled by the holy Inanna" (u m u š k u g ^{d}I n a n n a - k e_4 a k, l. 10), "verily chosen with you(?), Nanāja of the land, by Hierodula – your beloved!" (š a - m u - d a - p a d_3 ^{d}N a - n a - a k a l a m - m a n u - u_8 - g i g - g e k i a $\hat{g}_2$ - z u, l. 26), "the glorious divine powers (m e) have been generously given to you by Hierodula" (m e - g i r i_{17} - z a l š u d a ĝ a l n u - u_8 - g i g - e m a - r a - a n - š u m_2, l. 30), and finally "the Goddess verily caused the growth of your sacred powers (m e) for you" (I n n i n m e k u g - z u KA$^{?}$ š a - r a - m u_2 - m u_2, l. 39).

The role of An, the chief god in the Sumerian pantheon, was emphasized next to Inanna's great influence (l. 18-19):

> A n - e i g i s a g_9 k a l a m - m a l u g a l - k u r - k u r - r a [...]
> ^{d}N a - n a - a k a l a m E_2 - a n - [n a ...] h i - l i [...]
> "By An, the benevolent eye of the homeland, the king of all lands,

369 YBC 9859, W. W. Hallo, *BiOr* 23, 5/6 (1966), p. 239-247; see also G. Zólyomi, *N.A.B.U.* 2003/4, no. 91 (Ni 4058); ETCSL 2.5.1.3 (Išbi-Erra C), P. Lapinkivi, SAAS XV, p. 50, no. 34.

Nanāja, the land of (the temple of) the Eanna ... charm / beauty..."

Below we read the telling words (l. 33-34):

^{d}N a - n a - a i n i m d u g_4 [A n - n a - t a n i n] k u r - k u r - r a z a - e - m e - e n

e $š_3$ - e K u l - a b a_4 I N š a - m u - n a - a b - b e_2

"Nanāja! You are the lady of all lands based on the words uttered by An,

In the temple, in Kullaba ... indeed he declared it to her."

Nanāja's link with the two deities mentioned here is further emphasized by the epithets referring to the Eanna temple in Uruk, where both An and Inanna were worshipped: "Nanāja – the ornament of the Eanna" (^{d}N a - n a - a m e - t e E_2 - a n - k a, l. 2), "elevated head / pride of the Eanna" (s a ĝ i l_2 E_2 - a n - k a, l. 16) and by the designation "you teach science in the land of the Eanna" (k a l a m E_2 - a n - k a i g i - ĝ a l_2 š u m_2 - m u b a - e - z u, l. 4), "the deity who occupies the high throne of the land of Uruk" (d i n g i r d u r_2 m a h k i - U n u g^{ki} - g a t i l_3 - l a, l. 11).

The remaining attributes of Nanāja concentrate around her astral nature: "emerging like the daylight" (ud - g i n_7 d a l l a e_3, l. 1), "woman – star of the heavens (or: star of An), whom you verily are" (m u n u s m u l - a n / A n h e_2 - m e - a, l. 8).

Nanāja's connection with the powers is underlined, the "great" powers"[370] (n i n m e - n u n - n a, l. 1) and the divine ones, which Inanna endowed her with (l. 30) and which Inanna also intervened to magnify (l. 39).

Nanāja bears the title of "great judge" (^{d}N a - n a - a d i - k u d g a l, l. 11), emphasized still further by other stanzas: "righteous woman, who is the favorable verdict[371] of the land, who knows all

370 See the study by W. W. Hallo, who translates "Lady of the 'princely' attributes..."

371 ETCSL: "worthy source of inspiration."

its laws; / Nanāja, who knows justice for cities and numerous people" (m u n u s z i d e š - b a r d u g_3 k a l a m - m a - k a m d i - d i - b i g a l - z u / ^{d}N a - n a - a s i s a_2 i r i u $\hat{g}_3$ l u - a i g i - $\hat{g}$ a l_2, l. 13-14). The phrase: "created in the place of living beings" (š a g_4 k i z i - š a g_4 - $\hat{g}$ a l_2 t u m_2 - m a) was repeated twice (l. 29 and 31). Two further definitions: "eternally in appropriate beauty chosen" (h i - l i z i d - d a u l - š e_3 p a d_3 - d a, l. 1) and "Lady in beauty created"[372] (n i n h i - l i - a t u m_2 - m a, l. 15), albeit in somewhat modified form, kept on being used to describe Nanāja even in Neo-Assyrian times.

Other epithets are common enough not to constitute a distinguishing feature of the goddess (e.g. "wise", "good as An", "righteous woman", "lofty woman", "great Lady" or "Lady of all the lands"), perhaps with the exception of the fairly unclear designation "woman with a pure / holy head" (m u n u s s a $\hat{g}$ - m a $\check{s}_3$, l. 6).

The above hymn does not contain any clearly formulated plea for a blessing for the reigning Išbi-Erra, merely words addressed to the king: "Išbi-Erra, may you always be eulogized by her" (l. 27) and the statement addressed to Nanāja: "verily you opened the favorable eye of life on (his) bed"[373] (l. 40).

In conclusion, I would cite J. G. Westenholz who wrote the reputed article "Nanaya: Lady of Mystery":[374] "This hymn expresses explicitly some of the ideas that underlay the relationship of the Ur III kings and Nanaya. The relationship seems to have been an erotic one, perhaps related to some type of 'sacred marriage' ritual, and it was a necessary aspect of true kingship (...)."

---

372 ETCSL: "lady fitted for beauty."

373 In the personal letter to the author, W. W. Hallo referred to suggestions concerning the royal bed put forward by D. R. Frayne in: *The Historical Correlations of the Sumerian Royal Hymns*, Yale Diss. (1981): "He suggested a possible correlation between our hymn with its concluding reference to a bedstead (of Nanaia at Uruk?) and the construction of a bed for Inanna (in Isin?) in Ishbi-Irra's date formula B."

374 J. G. Westenholz, CM 7, p. 68-69.

In honor of the reigning king of Uruk Anam (1821-1817 BC), a hymn[375] was composed in Sumerian. In it Nanāja was called a m a n i ĝ$_2$ - n a m - m a "mother of everything" (l. 17) and n i n e m e d a - a ^{d}N a - n a - a b a d$_3$ g a l b a - g u b - b u? "Lady of nurses,[376] the goddess Nanāja, like a 'great wall' standing" (l. 36). It is she, as we read in the piece, who assigned the king z i n u m u n h i - l i that is, "life, seed (offspring) and abundance (of riches)" (l. 37). The name of Nanāja occurs in connection with the renovation of the Emeurur temple by the king and the reinstating of the repaired statues of the divinities in the Eanna and Emeurur sanctuaries (l. 29: [e$_2$] - a n - n a e$_2$ - m e - u r$_4$ - u r$_4$ a l a n - g i$_{16}$ s u g$_2$ - g a).

The next of the hymns to Nanāja[377] is already written in Akkadian and contains a clearly formulated plea for a blessing for Samsu-iluna, then ruler of Babylonia (1749-1712 BC).

Through its style, structure (14 stanzas) and topic, the composition reveals similarities with the hymn to Ištar from the reign of Ammī-ditāna, hence it may be seen as a model of sorts. The name of Nanāja occurs four times (obv. l. 2, 8, rev. l. 14, 21).

The epithets that Ištar is known under were also used to designate Nanāja, who was her ward, if the above discussed hymn from the times of Išbi-Erra is taken into consideration.

In this composition special emphasis was placed on the astral nature of the goddess. She is compared to the sun of her worshippers (*il-ta-am ša-ma-aš ni-ši-i-ša*, l. 1) and the moon with its afterglow, throwing a shadow, meaning that it protects (*ša-tu ki-ma ar-ḫi-im a-na-ṭa-li-im / i-gi-zu ṣi-il-la-ša ša-ru-ri za-a'-nu*, l. 3-4). The ex-

---

375 (W 20477), A. Falkenstein, *BaghM* 2 (1963), p. 80-82 and ETCSL 2.7.1.1 (Anam A).

376 Cf. another translation by A. Falkenstein, *op. cit.*, p. 82: "die Herrin, die Amme, Nanâ, die wie eine 'grosse Mauer' dasteht..." The construction n i n e m e d a - a seems to consist of a noun with another noun in the genetive.

377 VAT 5798, VS X 1913, no. 215; edit. cf. W. von Soden, *ZA* 44 (1938), p. 32-35; SAHG, p. 237-239; M.-J. Seux, *Hymnes et prières aux dieux de Babylonie et d'Assyrie*, Paris 1976, p. 42-45; TUAT II/5, p. 724-726; B. R. Foster, *Before the Muses*, Bethesda 1993, p. 69-71; P. Lapinkivi, SAAS XV, p. 55.

pression in l. 12 is presumably a direct reference to the planet Venus:[378] "her way (through the heavens will remain) forever a good sign" (*al-ka-as-sa*$_3$ *ad-da-ar da-mi-iq-tum it-tu-um*).

Nanāja owes a great deal to her father Anu, the god of the heavens. Anu elevated her among the goddesses (l. 17-18), filled her heart with benevolence (l. 15), decorated with a necklace (l. 16) and allotted her joy, pleasure and abundance (l. 20). He also addressed her with the command of happiness: *be-le-e-ti ša da-ad-mi ab-ra-ti-ši-in / pa-al-sa*$_3$*-a-ši*$^!$*-im ki* ^{d}*Šamaš ni-šu nu-ri-iš-ki* ("You will rule the seats and their populace, the people shall look upon your light as (if it were the light of) Šamaš!" l. 23-24).[379]

The character traits attributed to Nanāja in this hymn are typically feminine: "She overflows with fertility, light, sweetness and charm; she is endowed with joy, laughter and loveliness" (*uḫ-ta-an-na-mu e-lu-uš-ša / na-na-bu ma-aš-ra-ḫu du-šu-pu ku-uz*$_2$*-bu / ḫu-di ṣi-ḫa-tum u*$_3$ *ru-a-mi tu-uš-ta-az-na-an*, l. 5-7), and still more, "(her) clothing is joyful play" (lit. "she is clothed in play") (*lu-ub-bu-ša-at šu-a-ra-am*, l. 13).

She also has more universal characteristics: "Stepping at her side are truth, listening, dignity and a pleasant appearance" (*it-ta-al-la-ku i-du-uš-ša ki-na-tum / te-eš-mu-um ba-aš-tu-um si-im-tu-um / ma-lu-u*$_2$ *ša šu-ul-mi u*$_3$ *ba-la-ṭim*, l. 9-11), she is "proud and honored among the goddesses" (l. 19). Other epithets that appear include such as "capable", and a title taken over from Ištar, the meaning of which is still unclear tytuł – *telītu* ("good?"/ "tender"?).

Nanāja also bore the title of goddess of victory – "fierce Irnina"(^{d}*Ir-ni-na ga-aṣ-ṣa-tum*, l. 26), which is slightly at odds with the image of an alluring and sweet goddess. She is also described as: "the

---

378 Cf. B. Landsberger, *WO* III (1964), p. 73, note 97a, who believes that this sentence concerns Ištar.

379 For the new reading of l. 21-22, see N. Wasserman, *N.A.B.U.* 1992/3, no. 80: "Laughingly he (Anu) said to her a word of happiness, making her heart radiant."

most valiant among the Igigi, you are superior to them (lit. you are the tallest among them); your name is held high among them" (^{d}*Ir-ni-na ga-aṣ-ṣa-tum ga-še-er-ti I-gi-gi / e-li*$^{!}$*-šu-un a-še-ra-su*$_2$$^{!}$*-un*$^{!}$ / *qe*$_2$*-er-bu-uš-šu-uš*$^{!}$ *šu-qu-ru šu-mu-u*$_2$*-ki*,[380] l. 26-28).

On the reverse of the tablet there is a plea addressed directly to the goddess, asking her first to shine and make happy her heart (l. 1), so she would enjoy (respect) in the chapels (l. 2); she would be presented with cypress wood (l. 3), and also would come and cause the fields to be fertile and abundant (l. 4).

The last six stanzas concern the relation between Nanāja and Samsu-iluna, that is, the god-king relation. The ruler who is called her favorite, a king chosen by the goddess and striving for her pleasure (rev. 5-6), is also the one whom the goddess gave a name to[381] (rev. 18-20). He is obliged to make offerings to her (rev. 6). On her side the goddess ensures him years of justice and stability, a fortified throne and health (rev. 10-11), apart from the scepter of life (rev. 9) and income from the lands and mountains (rev. 7). Nor was the doubling of royal wealth forgotten (rev. 22) and ensuring the king a long life (rev. 21). Nanāja is also supposed to dedicate the sun as light to her beloved Samsu-iluna (rev. 23-24). In this composition, the goddess is revealed beyond doubt as guardian of the king and through the king of the entire land that he rules. The last lines are very expressive in this respect (rev. 25-27):

> *qi*$_2$*-bi-tu-uš-ša mi-i*[*g-ru-u*]*š e-te-el*
>
> [*e*]*l ur*$_2$*-ša-ni š*[*a-qi*$_2$] *i-n*[*a*] *ki-ib-ra-tim*
>
> [...]*-i-ma* [*l*]*i-ri-iš na-bi-i-*[*ša*]
>
> "By her command her favorite is ruler,
>
> Higher than any hero in the world he is elevated above the warriors in the lands.
>
> ... Let him rejoice, whom she has named."

---

[380] Cf. M.-J. Seux, *RA* LXIII (1969), p. 95, no. 5 who reads *e-mu-*<*qu*$_2$>*-u*$_2$*-ki*.

[381] The instrumental power of a word said by a divinity existing in Sumerian-Akkadian religion should be emphasized.

From the Old Babylonian period comes a short fragment of an Akkadian hymn,[382] in which the name of Nanāja appears three times (l. 3, 9, 11). The text is exceptionally difficult. Line 4 begins with the word *kuzbu* "fullness, abundance; potency; allure" (sum. h i. l i), l. 5 may be read as *mārti Ani*[*m*], l. 8 as *šarum waštum* "destructive wind", and in l. 10 we read *gišperru* "trap."

A gap of a thousand years follows with the next preserved hymn to Nanāja dating from the 8th century BC. This composition is an example of syncretism, that is, the combining of divinities with similar characteristics.

Written in Sumerian and Akkadian, this hymn[383] to Nanāja is known from eight fragmentary copies coming from Assyria as well as Babylonia. The preserved colophon of text C (LKA 37) from Aššur gives a *limmu* name that dates the copy to the second half of the 8th century BC. This is one of the few Akkadian texts in which the goddess appears under a number of different names, in connection with different cities and temples. This kind of text is more broadly represented in Sumerian literature. It should be underscored that the hymn is hardly a typical bilingual text[384] – the introductory line of each stanza is written in Sumerian, the rest of the text and the refrain in Akkadian. Horizontal lines separate the particular stanzas one from the other in virtually all of the copies. Each gives a city, temple or chapel, the name of the goddess which Nanāja has appropriated for herself, her title – epithet and the name of the spouse. The repeated refrain (*iqabbūni*) *anākuma* ^{d}*Nanāja* can be translated as follows: "(they call me) / by this name /, and (still) I am Nanāja."

The goddess thus bears eighteen different names that permit the various attributed aspects of her nature to be described. As Damkianna and Irnina she is the Lady of the Heavens and Earth, as Gula,

---

[382] UET VI/2, 404, pl. CCXCI.

[383] E. Reiner, *JNES* 33/2 (1974), p. 221-236.

[384] According to generally accepted criteria, a typical bilingual text has identical versions of the text in two languages found on the same object.

Ninkarrak, Ungal-Nibru, Nisaba and Bau, she is a great doctor, guardian and goddess of vegetation. Her identification with the goddesses whose names are Išḫara, Ṣarpanītu, Anunītum, Mammītu, Šerua, and ultimately also Ištar makes her the great Mother, Queen of the Underworld and warrior goddess. She also bears the names of the goddesses Manzat of Elamite origin and Šimalija of Kassite provenance.

The titles used to define her in this composition also speak of her position: *bēlet dadmē* "Lady of all the inhabited places", *lē'āt Igigi* "strong Igigi", *nāṣirat kullat nišē* "defender of all people", *aḫāt Šamaš māšītu* "twin sister of Šamaš", *bēlet Eanna* "Lady of (the temple of) the Eanna", *bānīt ilī u šarrī* "creator of the gods and kings", *mubbibat ḫiṭāti* "exonerating of sin" and *šākinat nūri* "bringing light."

The cities and temples mentioned here were the cult centers of different divinities, the spouses of the goddesses identified with Nanāja. These gods include: Ea, Enzag and Meskilak, Zababa, Marduk, Nabû, Adad, Ištarān, Haja, Meslamtaea, Nergal and Aššur. Starting with stanza II the following cities are cited: Ur, Eridu and Kullaba, Dilmun, Isin, Nippur, Hursagkalama, Kuara, Babylon, Borsippa, Sippar, Agade, Karkar, Dēr, Diniktu, Kuta, Me-Turna, Uruk, Šubria?, Aššur and Raqanan.

Stanza I,[385] which is slightly different from the others, makes use of the attributes and titles of Ištar to present Nanāja:

1. "My Lady, Sîn, Inanna, born of ..., similarly (?)/ I am the same (?).
2. Wise daughter of Sîn, beloved sister of Samaš, I am powerful in Borsippa,
3. I am a hierodule in Uruk, I have heavy breasts in Daduni,
4. I have a beard in Babylon, still I am Nanāja."

The second stanza also presents Nanāja personified as Ištar. The next 24 stanzas are preserved more or less fragmentarily. The se-

385 E. Reiner, *op. cit.*, p. 233.

quence of identification with various goddesses imposes a certain hierarchy of similarities, hence the closeness between Inanna/Ištar and Nanāja is once again confirmed.[386]

The ritual discussed earlier (on p. 81-82), which uses the phrase *ašbat* ^{d}*Nanāja kīma* ^{d}*Ištar* ("Nanāja is present like/as/instead of Ištar") seems to originate from exactly the same period, although obviously there is hardly any way to date the process of syncretism.

The group of Neo-Assyrian texts is formed of three hymns. The first, from the 8th century BC, was composed by an anonymous author and addressed to Nanāja; it contains a plea for Šarru-kīn II (721-705 BC). The composition (K 3600+DT 76)[387] underscores particularly the elements of power – an accent heretofore unknown and related to the military prowess of Assyrian kings. The goddess's divine insignia include a naked sword (*namṣāru petû*, l. 2') and sharp axe (*qulmû zaqtu*, l. 3'). Combat is her element (*ašaritti ilāni ša mēlulša qablum*, l. 5'), she has a heart that knows no mercy toward warriors (*libbi lā gāmelu muqtabli*, col. II 7'). On both sides she arranges the battle lines (*imna u šumēla suddur tamḫaru*, l. 4') and elevates the warrior role (*mudammeqat paraṣ qarrādi*, col. II 6'). These epithets no doubt bring to mind the Assyrian Ištar.

Her interest in song and music has also been emphasized distinctly (l. 7'-11'): "Skilled singers kneel before her, / those (playing) the lyre, the small harp and the clappers, / (playing) the flute, oboe and long pipes; / actors (*kurgarrû*) with the aid of a spindle, switches of a whip / (and incense made of) 'sweet' cane soothe her heart."[388] The gracious Lady, spouse of Mu'ati, robed in shining

---

386 After E. Reiner also P. Lapinkivi (SAAS XV, p. 233 ff.) repeats that the term *qadištu* used here (associated maybe with Lilitu) referring to the demonic nature of Nanāja. Personally, I doubt this!
387 K. D. Macmillan, BA 5/5, p. 626-629; J. A. Craig, ABRT I, p. 54-55; H. Winckler, *Sammlung von Keilschrifttexten* II, Leipzig 1894, p. 2-3; edit. K. D. Macmillan, BA 5/5, p. 564-567; M.-J. Seux, *Hymnes et prières aux dieux de Babylonie et d'Assyrie*, Paris 1976, p. 107-109; A. Livingstone, SAA III, p. 13-16, no. 4; B. R. Foster, *Before the Muses*, Bethesda 1993, p. 709-710.
388 Cf. the newest translation of the fragment (l. 2'-11') B. Groneberg, in: MARI 8 (1997), p. 292.

glimmer is still beautiful, splendid and powerful, a goddess to whom prayers should be addressed incessantly. Gods like Enlil and Tutu (Marduk) listen to her and she is revered even by the Lady of the gods. Her power over locusts is surprising, but nor the respect she enjoys from the guardian deities *šēdu* and *lamassu*.

The damages of column III and the opening lines of column IV deprive us of a considerable part of the text, hindering a full understanding. Lines 5-7 col. IV concern the relation between Nanāja and Marduk, who is called here a "medical expert", deprived of his power without her cooperation. The very expressive words *ēla šâša mannu mīna ippuš* "Without her, who can do anything?" (l. 9) predestinate Nanāja to a position equivalent to Ištar and even the Mother Goddess.[389] In the following lines (10-16), the author of the hymn encourages listeners to worship Nanāja:

"Go and hasten to learn of her glory!
In the future, every month, worship the gracious,
(the one) who can make a poor (man) rich (and a man) in rags affluent.
Listen regions of the fame of queen Nanāja!
Praise the beautiful one, make her the great thundering (one)!
Exalt the splendid one, hail the mighty one,
Address your prayers to her and do not cease to entreat her!"

Following these multiplied imperatives one reads the next line with some surprise (l. 17): "Calm down, daughter of Sîn, take up in your abode!" The line is an introduction to entreaties for a blessing for the reigning king, a worshipper of Nanāja (l. 18-19). All the entreaties are composed as imperative statements; therefore, the goddess ought to ensure the ruler a long life (l. 20), an enduring throne and heirs (l. 21) and (sic!) choice horses in the royal team (l. 22), as well as avert all sickness and disabilities from the king (l. 23).

[389] In Anam's hymn the term is "Mother of everything" (a m a n i ĝ$_2$ - n a m - m a).

The process of syncretism with Inanna made Nanāja a daughter of Sîn. At the same time, as the spouse of Nabû-Mu'ati, she rose in the hierarchy to become the daughter-in-law of Marduk (lit. daughter-in-law of the Esagila temple).

The hymn of Aššur-bāni-apli (668-627 BC) to Nanāja (K 226)[390] uses the title "Lady of the Great Gods" in reference to the goddess. The lines 13-14: "In your holy city which .../ she accepted his prayers..." presumably also refer to her.

Nanāja is one of the goddesses evoked by the king (l. 3 and 11) next to divinities like Aššur, Nabû, Sîn, Urkittu and Ninlil. Damages to the text, however, hinder a full understanding.

The last of the royal hymns to the goddess (K 9480),[391] also from Niniveh, has survived in fragmentary form, missing the name of the ruler. Nanāja is designated as *mārtu rēštītu* (l. 1) – "firstborn daughter", *binti* ^{d}*Sîn* (l. 3) – "daughter of Sîn", *qarittu narāmti ilāni aḫḫēša* (l. 2) – "gallant beloved of the gods, her brothers", *talīmat* ^{d}*Šamaš* (l. 3) – "favorite sister of Šamaš." She also bears the epithet *ilat tanādāti* (l. 2) – "goddess of glory." Her cheeks are ruddy – *zīmē ruššūti* (l. 2), and she possesses the ornaments of joy – *ša ulṣa zā'nat* (l. 2).

To a ruler who remains nameless the goddess allocates prosperity and causes him to take pride in his offspring.

In a damaged fragment we read of the seat of the goddess Irnina, a resident of Niniveh, and of the god Mu'ati, whose name is written without a determinative.

Hymns to cities are well known ever since Sumerian times. In a composition to the town of Arbela (K 173/4b),[392] which was created around the 7th century BC, Nanāja appears next to Ištar, Irnina and

390 J. A. Craig, ABRT I, pl. 9-10; edit. F. Martin, TRAB, p. 42-44; A. Livingstone, SAA III, p. 16-17 no. 5.
391 K. D. Macmillan, BA 5/5, p. 664-665; edit. *ibid.*, p. 601-602.
392 LKA 32; edit. E. Ebeling, *JkF* II/3 (1953), p. 274-282; A. Livingstone, SAA III, p. 20-22, no. 8; TUAT II/5, p. 768-770.

Ištartu. She is called the daughter of Sîn, and Arbela, a city of music and joy, is assigned to her (l. 22 ff.).

Nanāja is mentioned in only one prayer (Rm. 97),[393] recited during a ritual performed when the house of a god was being constructed or reconstructed.

The prayer, which is a Sumerian-Akkadian bilingual text surviving in fragmentary form, most likely concerns the Eanna temple in Uruk, because its lord is Anu and its lady Nanāja. In the line written down in Sumerian there is the goddess N i n - z i l_2 - z i l_2, in the Akkadian version – Nanāja. She is designated with the titles *bēltum ša kullat parṣī šuklulat* – "Lady who imparts the final shape on all rites" and *ša kīma ušumgallu ajjābi*... "(the one) who like the great dragon (goggles) at the enemy..." Here is the fragment of interest to the discussion:

12. n i n - z u n i n m e - š a r_2 - r a š u - d u_7 ^{d}N i n - z i l_2 - z i l_2
13. ^{lu_2}u š u m g a l (GAL.BUR_2) - g i n_7 ^{lu_2}e r i m_2 (NE.RU) - m a i g i a n - d a - a b - s u h - x
14. *be-let-ka be-el-tum ša₂ kul-lat par-ṣi šuk-lu-lat* ^{d}*Na*-[*na-a*]
15. *ša₂ ki-ma u₂-šum-gal-lu a-a-bi* [...]

Textual analysis reveals the scribe's fluency in translation. The Sumerian n i n m e - š a r_2 - r a š u - d u_7 corresponds to the Akkadian phrase *bēltum ša₂ kullat parṣī šuklulat.* Line 13 corresponds to line 15 which does not have a verbal form: "(the one) who like a great dragon goggles at the enemy", resulting in associations with the cobra which hypnotizes its enemies.

Summing up the hymns dedicated to Nanāja, one should foremost emphasize the links with Inanna, An and Uruk, her original seat, all of which are very evident from the Sumerian composition of the turn of the third millennium BC. Compared to a star the goddess is empowered with the divine m e, although indeed only thanks to Inanna. The term h i - l i appearing in the hymn and translated as

---

393 S. Langdon, OECT VI 27.

"beauty, allure" can take one more erotic accents and mean "sensuallity, sex appeal", and even "sexual lust."[394]

An Akkadian piece of the 18th century BC also compares Nanāja to an astral divinity, the sun and the moon. As a woman, the goddess is endowed with sweetness, charm and allure, she shines and is joyful. As the king's guardian, she gives him independently health and graces him with prosperous rule.

The thousand-year-long gap in the literary sources (strictly speaking: the absence of hymns and prayers to Nanāja) does not permit a precise tracing of the modified scope of her powers over time. A Sumerian-Akkadian hymn of the first millennium BC, an example of syncretic thinking, demonstrates Nanāja to possess a variety of different aspects of other goddesses, thus considerably, even if perhaps largely fictionally increasing her domain. In Aššur-bāni-apli's hymn she was called Lady of the Great Gods.

The oldest of the Neo-Assyrian texts emphasizes the warrior-like aspect of the goddess and her ties to music and song. For the first time in compositions of this genre does the goddess appear with the designation "daughter of Sîn." She continues to be represented as a beautiful and alluring woman and a potent goddess.

---

394 The name of the ship of Ištar contained on the boat list is ^{giš}m a$_2$ h i - l i - a n - n a (Hh IV, l. 329), and may be rendered as "Ship of heavenly charm." Interestingly, Dumuzi's boat used to deliver supplies during the feast of drinking malt in the Lagaš region in the Ur III period is called m a$_2$ n i n - h i - l i - s u$_3$ ^{d}D u m u - z i "The boat (called) 'Lady sprinkled with charm' of the god Dumuzi" (AO 4209, 2; cf. R. Kutscher, *ASJ* 5 (1983), p. 60-61). Nanāja's boat (more properly, the boat of Ištar and Nanāja) occurs in a text YOS 3, 86, but it is clear that the bark of An was used already in the times of the III Dynasty of Ur to transport offerings also for Inanna and Nanāja. Thus we remain still in the sphere of An-Inanna-Dumuzi-Nanāja.

CHAPTER V

LOVE LYRICS CONNECTED WITH THE GODDESS NANĀJA

The Akkadian love dialogue (YBC 4643)[395] between a priestess and Rīm-Sîn of Larsa (1822-1763 BC) is the oldest lyric text to mention the goddess Nanāja. It was likely composed on the occasion of the cultic liaison of the pair during the New Year Festival celebrated in spring; therefore, it must have accompanied the sacred marriage rites. The priestess presumably played the role of Nanāja whose name is mentioned but once, in l. 27: *ša-li šar-ra-tum* d*Na-na-a* "Oh, Queen Nanāja, ask!" Another possible translation is "Oh, queen, ask Nanāja!", which would then constitute a form of calling the goddess who was a guardian of the lovers. Incorporated in the dialogue are comments by a chorus that had probably stood outside the bedchamber of the couple lying in bed.

This piece refers to Sumerian love lyrics connected with the sacred marriage rites in which the king took it upon himself to represent the goddess's lover.

The next text (VAT 17347)[396] is also a dialogue concerning marriage rites. In this case the main characters are Nanāja and a god called Mu'ati, later identified with Nabû. The tablet is damaged to the extent that the sequence of obverse and reverse cannot be established. Apart from the above two characters there is also a narrator. Expressions of an erotic nature are interrupted with a plea addressed to the goddess requesting a blessing for Abi-ešuh (1711-1684 BC), ruler of Babylonia (l. 14). According to the text, she looks upon her capital with good eyes (rev.? l. 3), and also protects the health of the

---

395 YBT XI, no. 24; edit. *ibid.*, p. 28 and 66; cf. also TUAT II/5, p. 747-750 and B. R. Foster, *Before the Muses*, Bethesda 1993, p. 98-99, P. Lapinkivi, SAAS XV, p. 54-55.

396 W. G. Lambert, *MIO* XII/2 (1966), pl. following p. 48; edit. *ibid.*, p. 41-56; TUAT II/5, p. 741-743; B. R. Foster, *Before the Muses*, Bethesda 1993, p. 96-97. See also G. Leick, *Sex and Eroticism in Mesopotamian Literature*, London – New York 1994, p. 183-185; P. Lapinkivi, SAAS XV, p. 1 (the author calls Nanāja as a hypostase of Inanna/Ištar) and p. 55-56.

king (rev.? l. 5-6). A statue, presumably to be offered to the god Mu'ati[397] is also mentioned there (l. 11-13).

According to P. Lapinkivi,[398] the Mu'ati is probably the king himself, playing his role of Dumuzi and Nanāja the role of Inanna/Ištar.

Contrary to the above two texts, a dialogue between lovers discovered at Sippar (Si 57)[399] treats on real people. It has become known to scholars under the title "The Faithful Lover" (Der "Treue Liebhaber"). Nanāja is shown here as the guardian of disillusioned lovers. The piece basically boils down to a young girl persuading her lover to bestow his affection again on her. She evokes Nanāja's help in this task – in l. 24 we read that she keeps on praying to Nanāja to be granted the affections of her beloved. The lover in turn calls upon Nanāja and king Hammurabi to witness his words. The appearance of the name of the ruler dates the text potentially to the 18th century BC, while according to B. Groneberg it is in the Late Old-Babylonian language.

From the Old Babylonian period there is a collection of eleven love spells found at Isin (IB 1554).[400] In view of their substantive similarity to lyrics, I have included them in this chapter.

These spells are generally referred to as i n i m . i n i m . m a k i . a g₂ . g a₂ . k a m "love spells." Nanāja is evoked, although sporadically. She is seen as personifying sexual desire (wild lust)[401] – *uzzum ša* ᵈ*Nanāja*, which is "to leap" on the person saying the spell

[397] Cf. G. Leick, *op. cit.*, p. 185, where the author suggests that the text was composed specially for the occasion of dedicating a statue.
[398] P. Lapinkivi, SAAS XV, p. 55.
[399] W. von Soden, *ZA* 49 (1950), p. 168-169; edit. *ibid.*, p. 151-194; M. Held, *JCS* 15 (1961), p. 1-26; M. Held, *JCS* 16 (1962), p. 37-39; TUAT II/5, p. 743-747; B. R. Foster, *Before the Muses*, Bethesda 1993, p. 92-95; M. Stolarczyk, *Przegląd Orientalistyczny* 1986/1-2, p. 69-73, B. Groneberg, in: CRRAI 47, p. 165-183; P. Lapinkivi, SAAS XV, p. 57-58.
[400] C. Wilcke, *ZA* 75/2 (1985), p. 188-209.
[401] Cf. the meaning of *uzzum* in the translations by C. Wilcke, *op. cit.*, p. 203 and 205 ("Wildheit") and B. R. Foster, *Before the Muses*, Berthesda 1993, p. 144 ("arousal"). Cf. also R. M. Whiting, *ZA* 75/2 (1985), p. 187 and J. Assante, in: CRRAI 47/1, p. 47 with note 86.

or else leave this person.[402] It should be noted that love spells were mostly used by women.

A. W. Sjöberg published among others a b a l - b a l - e song for Inanna, duplicates of which (or similar fragments) bear the subscript b a l - b a l - e ᵈN a - n a - a - k a m "this is the (song) b a l b a - l e of the goddess Nanāja."[403] The text ROM 721 is the most extensive of these hymns and quite well preserved with the above mentioned gloss. In l. 1-2 we read: A n - n a t u m_2 - m a x[. . . . . .] / x AN x x n a m - n i n - e d i [b? - b a - a m_3], which can be understood as follows: "Worthy of the god An, . . [. . . . . .] / . . . . . unsurp[assed] in her femininity." A few lines later (l. 13-14) it is: [t u m_2 - m a] - d a n i n - m u t u m_2 - m a - d a / [k a - p a] - p a h - a - t a t u m_2 - m a - d a "Being [brought out], my lady, being brought out, / being brought out of [the entrance of] the [ce]lla."[404]

The goddess is referred to here as the very essence of femininity (l. 16-20):

[š u - z u m u n u s] - a m_3 g i r i_3 - z u m u n u s - a m_3
[i n i m] l u_2 - d a b a l - e - z u m u n u s - a m_3
[i g] i l u_2 - d a b a r - r e - z u m u n u s - a m_3
[z a] - e - d a LUM - d a g u b - b u - n a m š a_3 - s u_3 i_3 - s [a]$_6$
[GAM] - x - d a i b_2 - i b_2 i_3 - s a_6 - s a_6

"[Your hand] is [womanly], your foot is womanly,
When you converse with a man it is womanly,
When you [lo]ok at a man it is womanly,
...(your) remote heart is gracious,
[Bow]ing [down], (your) hips are pleasing."

---

[402] Cf. B. R. Foster, *op. cit.*, p. 144 note 1 and p. 123.

[403] A. W. Sjöberg, *JCS* 29/1 (1977), p. 16-27, P. Lapinkivi, SAAS XV, p. 45-46.

[404] Cf. B. Alster, in: Studies Hallo, p. 15-27, especially the author's note that the hymn contains no obvious reference to the temple or ritual (p. 15). It should be kept in mind that there exist offerings made „to gain entry", cf. p. 36 (AnOr 7 56) and above, note 111.

The reverse of this tablet contains an invitation from the goddess to have sex,[405] cleverly concealed, as is the rule in love lyrics, under agricultural terms (rev. 21-25):

> [i$_7$] n a - a n - b a - a l - l e i$_7$ - z [u h e$_2$ - m e - e n]
> [a - š a$_3$] n a - a n - u r$_x$ - r u a - š a$_3$ - z u h e$_2$ - m e - e [n]
> [m u - u]n - g a r$_3$ k i - d u r u$_5$ n a - a n - k i n - k i n - e
> [z e$_2$ - b]a - k a l - l a - m u k i - d u r u$_5$ - z u h e$_2$ - a m$_3$
> [x (x)] - e a b - s i n$_2$ - z u h e$_2$ - a m$_3$
> "Do not dig a [canal], [let me be yo]ur canal!
> Do not plough [a field], let me be your field!
> [Far]mer, do not search for a wet place,
> My precious [swe]et, let me! Be your wet place!
> [. . . . .] . . let me! be your furrow!"

The song terminates with a call to the beloved sister (meaning lover) to come (rev. 30: DU n i n$_9$ - k i - a g$_2$ - m u) and granting permission to kiss (l. 31: ^{d}N a - n a - a n e g e$_4$ - s u - u b).

The text CBS 8530 is very close to the text discussed above. Initially, the song consisted of 26 or 27 lines, followed by a signature (even though according to the caption this is a b a l b a l e song of Inanna, the goddess mentioned in the text is Nanāja). The legible lines (obv. I 10-23, obv. II 10-14) help to find the repeated fragments (CBS 8540 obv. I 11-14 = ROM 721 obv. 11-14; 17-20 = 15-18 etc.)[406]

---

[405] According to B. Alster, in: Studies Hallo, p. 15, 4 texts published by A. W. Sjöberg unambiguously present the words said by the man to a prostitute and her response.

[406] Cf. translation of CBS 8530, obv. I 13-18 by B. Alster, in: Studies Hallo, p. 19-20 (also note 42):

13. D U - m a - d a n i n$_9$ - m u DU - m a - d a
"Come with me, my sister, come with me",
14. k a p a - p a h - a - t a DU - m a - d a
"Come with me from the entrance of the cella",
15. i n i m l u$_2$ - d a b a l - a - z u m u n u s - a m$_3$
"When you talk to a man, what a woman (lit. it is a women)!"
16. i g i l u$_2$ - r a b a r - r e - z u m u n u s - a m$_3$
"When you look at a man, what a woman!"

The last[407] of the b a l b a l e texts, CBS 13915, is a small fragment. According to A. W. Sjöberg,[408] the text mentions Nanāja (^{d}N a - n a - a, obv. 6'), who is referred to as "my beloved sister" (rev. 2').

The catalogue of titles of songs (VAT 10101),[409] composed around the 12th century BC in Aššur, constitutes proof for the existence of a number of unknown pieces. Of the close to 400 titles of songs and hymns only about 275 have been preserved and of these a fifth is made up of Sumerian texts, while the rest are in Akkadian.

The first part of this text covers 93 titles of Akkadian songs (*zamāru*), divided into three sections entitled one by one: "Oh, young man loving me" (*māruma rā'imni*), "Lovers" (*murtāmi*) and "My shepherd, my shepherd" (*re'î re'î*). Each of the sections is further subdivided into groups of 5 or 6 titles. J. A. Black believes that these songs can be defined as "ballads."[410] The following were addressed to Nanāja: *Nanāja at*(?)*tīma šulma ana šarri kī tašimî* "Oh, Nanāja, how do you dedicate the king's prosperity?" (col. II 23-24), *tuktennî šarratu Nanāja* "You are honored, oh, Queen Nanāja!" (col. II 25), *Nanāja libbaša hadâ ublamma* "The heart of Nanāja brought joy" (col. II 44) and *rešī Nanāja ina kirê* E_2 . b a b b a r *ša tarammî*

17. z a g e_2 - g a r_8 - d a g u b - b u š a_3 - [s u_3] - z u i_3 - s a_6
"When you lean the side against the wall, your nakedness is sweet."
18. GAM - e - d e_3 i b_2 - i b_2 i_3 - s a_6 - s a_6
"When (you) bow down, the hips are sweet."

See also B. Alster, *ZA* 82 (1992), p. 186-201.

407 I omit text SRT 9 1-21, published with the previous ones and referred to in the caption as a b a l b a l e of Inanna but failing to mention Nanāja and a fragmentarily preserved text UM 29-16-560, where a goddess not identified by name is referred to as n i n_9 - k i - a g_2 - m u "my beloved sister" – on the grounds of the next text (CBS 13915) this designation could be construed as referring to Nanāja.

408 A. W. Sjöberg, *JCS* 29/1 (1977), p. 17. On p. 23: "Because of the fragmentary condition of the text no translation is offered here."

409 KAR 158: edit. E. Ebeling, Berliner Beiträge zur Keilschriftforschung 1/ III, Berlin 1923, p. 1-32; A. Falkenstein, *ZA* 15 (1949), p. 91 ff.; M. Held, *JCS* 15 (1961), p. 10-26; J. A. Black, *JAOS* 103/1 (1983), p. 25 ff.

410 Cf. J. A. Black, *op. cit.*, p. 29.

"Rejoice, oh, Nanāja, in the gardens of the Ebabbar, which you love" ("rev. II" l. 38).

The Seleucid ritual calendar from Babylon describes the sacred marriage rites between Nanāja and Nabû (VAT 662).[411] They took place in the second month of the year, *ajjaru*, when oxen were harnesses and work began in the fields. The rites started on the second day of the month. We do not have any description of the preparations for the ceremony nor an image of the goddess during the act. Her future spouse, robed in "superior power", shining like the moon, moved from the Ezida (most likely in Borsippa) to the Euršaba,[412] temple of Nanāja, where he became *ana maḫar* ᵈ*Bēlti* – before the Lady, that is, Nanāja. There, *ina majjāltum mūši ṭābi ittanalū šitta ṭābta* "in the bed of sweet nights they lie in sweet sleep night after night" until the sixth day, when Nabû goes into the garden alone. On the next day he directed his steps to the Emeurur inside the Eanna sanctuary; he went into the garden and received the symbols of superior power. Not until the seventeenth day did the goddess get up from the bed and go into the mountain garden.

The texts collected here as love lyrics substantiate Nanāja's title of the "goddess of love." The category includes just as well texts concerning sacred marriage rites (confirming the enduring performance of the ritual for over 1500 years) and texts speaking of the carnal pleasures. It seems that this aspect of physical love, best documented in the b a l b a l e songs and the love spells, is of particular importance for the personality of Nanāja.

---

[411] G. Reisner, SBH VIII, p. 145-146; cf. E. Matsushima, *ASJ* 9 (1987), p. 158-161; M. E. Cohen, *The Cultic Calendars of the Ancient Near East*, Bethesda 1993, p. 311; E. Unger, *Babylon*, Berlin 1970, p. 264 ff., no. 13; T. Jacobsen, *Unity and Diversity*, Baltimore 1975, p. 74-76.

[412] There existed two temples of Nanāja both bearing the same name, one in Borsippa and the other in Babylon; cf. A. R. George, *The Temples*, nos. 1195 and 1196. On the subject of where the ritual took place, cf. also E. Matsushima, *Orient* XXX-XXXI (1995), p. 177 and above p. 81.

The love dialogue of the 19th century BC between the king and Nanāja, as well as the sacred marriage ceremonies between Nanāja and Mu'ati (in the Old Babylonian period) or between Nanāja and Nabû (Seleucid period) are connected with the ritual that was intended as a means of ensuring the fertility of the fields and the constancy of the ruling dynasty. Thus, the sexual act is tantamount to future prosperity and its participants personify the two joining elements of manhood and womanhood. In the Sumerian period the male role was played by the king and the female one most frequently by a priestess of Inanna.[413] Starting already in the 18th century BC, it became accepted to have the lovers personified by statues of the gods, including the goddess Nanāja. Thus, her role was that of a lover.

Love spells demonstrate that Nanāja ruled the sphere of sexual desire and was capable of depriving as well as endowing with desire. The rejected lover from the Sippar dialogue refers to this aspect of the goddess in an attempt to retrieve her lover's affections. The b a l b a l e songs reveal that charm and sexual lust are characteristics of the goddess herself, with which she deigns to endow human beings.

413 See P. Lapinkivi, SAAS XV, p. 69 f., 81 ff.

CHAPTER VI
NANĀJA IN TEXTS OF LAMENTS

In compositions from four categories of the Sumerian genre of cultic lyrics written in e m e - s a l (b a l a g, e r$_2$ - š e m$_3$ - m a, š u - i l$_2$ - l a and e r$_2$ - š a$_3$ - h u n - g a$_2$), Nanāja appears sporadically at best. All the categories were present already in the Old Babylonian period, although they are best known from the Neo-Assyrian and Late Babylonian times.

The b a l a g lamentations, performed by the g a l a/*kalû* priests to the music of harps, served like the other categories to pacify the god's anger. While none of these lamentations is addressed directly to Nanāja, twelve texts actually mention her name.

The first of these, u r u$_2$ a - š e - e r - r a[414] "City in Sighing", attested from the Old Babylonian period, but in a number of copies from the first millennium BC and existing also as an independent e r š e m m a song, says (l. b+67 - b+71):[415]

[e$_2$ - g i$_4$ - a] - e$_2$ - s a g - i l$_2$ - l a gu$_3$
[d u m u - s a g - ^{d}]U r a š - a gu$_3$
[d u m u - s a g - e$_2$] - i - b i$_2$ - ^{d}A - n u - u m gu$_3$
[g a š a n - g u$_3$ - t e š$_2$ - a] - s i$_3$ - g a - k e$_4$ gu$_3$
[^{d}N a] - n a - a gu$_3$

"The [daughter-in-law] of the Esagil cried out in it.
[The foremost child of] Uraš cried out in it.
[The foremost child] of the Eibianum cried out in it.
Gašangutešasiga cried out in it.
Nanāja cried out in it."

The title "daughter-in-law of (the temple of) the Esagil" *kallat Esagil* determines the degree of kinship between Nanāja and Marduk as the Lord of the Esagil temple, the next two lines link her to the god Uraš: "firstborn daughter of the god Uraš" (or Ninurta, iden-

414 M. E. Cohen, *CLAM*, p. 65 ff.

415 The transliteration and translation of all the b a l a g lamentations are given after M. E. Cohen, *CLAM*. Cf. his commentary to the above lines, *ibid.*, p. 72.

tified with Nabû, the spouse of Nanāja) and "firstborn daughter of (the temple of) the Eibianum" – temple of Uraš at Dilbat. The last title-epithet, Gašangutešasiga, usually refers to the goddess Tašmētum, for it means "Lady of listening", rendering the meaning of her name in Akkadian.

The next text is u$_4$-dam ki am$_3$-us$_2$[416] "It Touches the Earth Like a Storm", in the Old Babylonian version of which we read (l. f+240 - f+242):

ama mu-gi$_{17}$-ib gašan-e$_2$-tur$_3$-kalam-ma
kur-gul-gul gašan-e$_2$-an-na-ra
egi$_2$-zi-da gašan-mu ^{d}Na-na-a
^{d}Gašan-gu$_3$-ni-sur-ra

"The mother, the hierodule, the lady of the Eturkalama,
The devastatrix of the land, the lady of the Eanna,
the faithful princess, my lady Nanāja,
Gašangunisurra."

The fragment refers to Inanna, the mother, ravaging the land, represented also as a "righteous princess." The name of Nanāja is therefore equivalent to that of Inanna.

M. E. Cohen adds to the above lamentations a fragment[417] from sources N, O and P, in which the name of Nanāja occurs (l. 138-141):

[e$_2$-gi$_4$-a dumu-sag-^{d}Uraš-a]
[dumu-e$_2$-a dumu-sag-e$_2$-i-bi$_2$-^{d}A-nu-um]
egi$_2$-zi-da g[ašan-gu$_3$]-teš$_2$-a-s[i$_3$-ga-ke$_4$]
egi$_2$-gu-la gašan-mu ^{d}Na-na-a

"Daughter-in-law, first born of Uraš,
child of the house, first child of the Eibianum,
faithful princess, Gašangutešasiga,[418]
great princess, my lady Nanāja."

[416] M. E. Cohen, *ibid.*, p. 120 ff. In the translation on p. 142 there appears in l. f+243 the goddess Lillaenna, missing from the transliteration on p. 135.
[417] M. E. Cohen, *ibid.*, p. 146 ff.
[418] In the translation on p. 149, M. E. Cohen writes in l. 140: "Ninguteshasiga."

Nanāja's name does not seem to be used here merely as a synonym for Inanna. A new epithet is the not very telling designation – "child of the house/temple."

The next lamentation, which is entitled "The Bull in His Fold"[419] a m - e a m a š - a - n a, mentions Nanāja's name a number of times (l. 60; a+105 - a+106; b+158'; b+153 - b+155), but without giving any new epithets.

"The Honored One Who Wanders About" e - l u m d i - d a - r a,[420] a lamentation from the first millennium BC provides us with the following fragment (l. b+73 - b+79):

e g i_2 - r e e g i_2 - r e g u_3 a m_3 - m e u r u_2 i n - g a - a m_3 - m e u_3 - l i - l i

ru-ba-tu$_4$ MIN *ši-si-it* URU *i-šas-si ina lal-la-ra-a-ti*

a g a š a n - m u n u - n u z - š a_6 - g a u_3-

e_2 - g i_4 - a - e_2 - s a g - i l_2 - l a u_3-

d u m u - s a g - ^{d}U r a š - a u_3-

d u m u - s a g - e_2 - i - b i_2 - ^{d}A - n u - u m u_3-

g a š a n - g u_3 - t e $š_2$ - a - s i_3 - k e - a - k e_4 u_3-

g a š a n - m u ^{d}N a - n a - a u_3-

"Princess! Princess! Is the cry which the city utters. Alas!

Oh, my lady, the beautiful woman! Alas!

Daughter-in-law of the Esagil! Alas!

Firstborn of Uraš! Alas!

Firstborn of the Eibianum! Alas!

Gašangutešasiga! Alas!

My Lady, Nanāja! Alas!"

In subsequent texts: e - l u m g u_4 - s u n_2[421] "Honored One, Wild Ox", a - a b - b a h u - l u h - h a[422] "The Raging Sea" and u n k i n -

---

[419] *Op. cit.*, p. 152 ff.

[420] *Op. cit.*, p. 175 ff.

[421] *Op. cit.*, p. 272 ff. Lines 38-39 and 88-89 of the version from the first millennium BC refer to Nanāja.

[422] *Ibid.*, p. 374 ff. Lines c+156 - c+157 of the recension of the first millennium BC refer to Nanāja.

ta eš-bar til-la[423] "He Who Makes Decisions in the Council" there are no new designations.

A version of a lamentation ^{d}Utu-gin$_7$ e$_3$-ta[424] "Come Out Like The Sun!", which is not a standard one, originating from the first millennium BC, appears to be entirely devoted to Nanāja,[425] although the lack of a subscript precludes a reliable determination. The goddess is represented here as weeping, banished[426] from her temple and her city of Nippur. She is mentioned in combination with a variety of temples: she is Lady of the Ekur, princess of the Kiur, mother of the Esagil, firstborn of the Eibianum, banished from the Enamtila, the Ebabbar, the Ezida, the Emahtila and the Edaranna. Also Sippar, Tintir and Borsippa have banished her. She is known by her name and beside that as Gašan-bara$_2$-ge-si$_3$ "Lady who fill the temple (with wealth)", ^{d}Pa$_4$-nun-an-ki "First princess of the heavens and earth" and Gašan-gu$_3$-teš$_2$-a-si$_3$-ga "Lady of listening."

A very fragmentary text of a lamentation to Inanna from the Old Babylonian period ab$_2$-gin$_7$ gu$_3$-de$_2$-de$_2$,[427] "Lowing like a cow", provides new designations of Nanāja (l. 7):

> [^{d}Na-na-a] du-mu-ša$_6$-e$_2$-e-ke$_4$
>
> "[Nanāja], the beautiful child of the house."

It should be noted that the preceding lines (2-6) constitute a series of epithets and names uttered by Inanna:

> mu-gig-an-na ga-ša-an-an-na-men$_3$
>
> kur-gul-gul ga-ša-an-e$_2$-an-na-men$_3$

---

[423] *Ibid.*, p. 479 ff. Three reconstructed lines after l. f+207 refer to Nanāja. The fact that as many as three lines are devoted to Nanāja should be underscored; other divinities merited no more than one line as a rule in this composition.

[424] *Ibid.*, p. 519 ff.

[425] See l. a+9 - a+13 on p. 520.

[426] Compare the texts of Aššur-bāni-apli telling of the statue of Nanāja which he had brought back after 1635 (or 1535) years from Elam. It seems more likely, however, that the lamentation referred to the carrying off of the statue of Nanāja by the Elamites in the 12th century BC.

[427] M. E. Cohen, *CLAM*, p. 533 ff.

a [n a l - d] u b_2 - b a g a - š a - a n - g i_6 - p a r_3 - r a - m e n_3
[^{d}L i l_2 - l a_2] - e n - n a g a - š a - a n - t u r_3 - a m a š - a - m e n_3
[a m a - e_2 - a ^{d}]D a - d a n u - n u z - š a_6 - g a
"I, the celestial hierodule, Inanna,
I, the destroyer of the land, the lady of Eanna,
I, who causes the heavens to tremble, the lady of the g i p a r,
I, the Lillaenna, the lady of the cattle pen and sheepfold,
I, the mother of the house, Dada, the beautiful lady."

It may be assumed that the construction of this text followed a well known model of suggesting the main character through successive versions of designations and epithets. The name of Nanāja appearing at the end of the series would suggest who the main character of the composition was. Yet the designations mentioned here point rather to Inanna.

The next text mentioning Nanāja is known from many copies (Old Babylonian and from the first millennium BC). It is a lamentation addressed to Inanna, u r u_2 a m_3 - i - r a - b i[428] "That City Which Has Been Pillaged!" The version of the 1st millennium BC brings the following designations (l. 110): [^{d}N a - n a - a d u m u - s] a g - e_2 - a [(x)] "Nanāja – firstborn of the temple", while the fragment consisting of negated questions asked by Inanna of herself (starting from l. c+329) contains a line (c+338) concerning Nanāja: g a š a n - m u ^{d}N a - n a - a m e - e n u - [m e n_3]: *be-el-tu₂* *^{d}Na-na-[a]* *ul* MIN "I am not the lady Nanāja?"[429]

Inanna's lamentation u r u_2 - h u l - a - k e_4[430] "She of the Destroyed City" (known from Old Babylonian and first millennium texts), mentions Nanāja's name among the other names and epithets used to refer to Inanna. According to the discussed text AO 6467 this

[428] M. E. Cohen, *op. cit.*, p. 536 ff.
[429] M. E. Cohen, *op. cit.*, p. 574; cf. also K. Volk, FAOS 18, p. 135 and 148 (tablet 20, l. 11, sources B and C) and SpTU II, no. 27 (W 22760/0).
[430] M. E. Cohen, *op. cit.*, p. 650 ff. Line 7 of the recension of the first millennium BC refers to Nanāja.

song was performed in honor of Nanāja on the fourteenth day of the eight month.

The text SLTNi 71, which Cohen links with the lamentation e d e n - n a u_2 - s a g - g a_2 - k e_4[431] "In the Steppe in the Early Grass", also puts down a link between Nanāja and Inanna.

The last of the lamentations – a - š e - e r g i_6 - t a[432] "Sighs at the Night", was known already in Old Babylonian times. Nanāja occurs in the many texts from the first millennium BC (l. b+138, b+193). According to the list of songs AO 6467, it was performed on the seventh day of each month. J. A. Black, who studied this text, wrote:[433] "Sometimes the names of other goddesses are used as if they were no more then synonyms for Inanna." Having collected the epithets of Inanna used in this text, he defined Nanāja as belonging to Inanna's entourage.[434]

An analysis of the b a l a g lamentations, known from the beginning of the second millennium BC albeit attested more frequently in the first millennium BC, provides distinct proof of the ties between Inanna and Nanāja, who is indubitably a secondary deity, a shadow of the prototype. The name of the goddess occurs in twelve[435] lamentations directed to other divinities.

"The wailing of the š e m drum" or otherwise the song e r_2 - š e m_3 - m a, composed also in the eme-sal dialect and also performed by

---

431 *Ibid.*, p. 668 ff.; SLTNi 71 on p. 690-691.

432 *Ibid.*, p. 704 ff. and J. A. Black, *ASJ* 7 (1985), p. 11-87; Lines 230 and 285 concern Nanāja.

433 J. A. Black, *op. cit.*, p. 17.

434 *Ibid.*, p. 51.

435 M. E. Cohen on p. 611 (lamentation i m - m a - a l g u_3 - d e_2 - d e_2) gives for l. a+107: a m a - m u ^{d}N a - a n - n a - k e_4 u_4, while in the translation on p. 627 there is: "my mother, Nanâ, cries out all day long." The list of names of divinities lists ^{d}Na-an-na separately from ^{d}Na-na-a. According to the list of texts (p. 604), this line is contained in only two of the sources (J = SBH 66 and K = SBH 82). I have found it only in the text SBH 66, rev. 40, where the name of the goddess was written as NA.AN.NA, without the determinative, hence a simple scribal error is possible. Thus, the number of b a l a g texts with the name of Nanāja may actually be thirteen.

the g a l a/*kalû* priests in the first millennium BC, were surely connected very closely with the b a l a g lamentations.[436]

It is noteworthy that none of the known e r š e m m a texts was ever dedicated to Nanāja, although they were sung before the statue of this goddess.[437]

The e r š e m m a for Inanna[438] known from an Old Babylonian copy, gives in l. 8: ^{d}N a - n a - a d u m u - š a g_5 - e_2 - e - m e n_3, which designation M. E. Cohen believes to be a variant of the epithet d u m u - s a g - e_2 - a.[439]

Among the e r š e m m a known from Old Babylonian and first-millennium BC copies, only two record the name of Nanāja. The first composition is addressed to Inanna;[440] it says (l. 39): e g i_2 g a š a n - m u ^{d}N a - n a - a š a_3 - z u "Princess, my lady, Nanāja, (let him calm) your heart!" The receiver of this beseeching is likely Inanna, so the name of Nanāja is a synonym here.

In the second composition directed to Marduk[441] we read (l. 29): e g i_2 - g u - l a g a š a n - z u ^{d}N a - n a - a a - r a - [z u] "(Let) the highest princess, your lady, Nanāja, (utter) a prayer to you!"

In e r š e m m a compositions known from the first millenium BC Nanāja's name is found four times. In three of these (e r š e m m a

---

436 M. E. Cohen, *Sumerian Hymnology: the Eršemma*, Cincinnati 1981, p. 25-26: "As is known from colophons, catalogues, ritual texts and ritual calendars, by the First Millennium B.C.E. many eršemmas were recited by the gala-priests in conjunction with the balag-lamentations and in fact were considered to be the concluding portion of the total balag-composition." On p. 41 we read: "In the First Millennium B.C.E., the ritual use of the eršemma is better documented. Eršemma were preserved as appendages to balag-lamentations or on tablets consisting of several eršemmas." Cf. also p. 42-47.

437 The Neo-Babylonian text MLC 382 rev. (without the song preserved) attests ITI-*us-su* UD.3.KAM *x x x x ti ina* E_2 *pa-pa-ha ana* IGI ^{d}*Na-na-a iz-za-mu-ur*.

438 M. E. Cohen, *ibid.*, eršemma 32, p. 66.

439 *ibid.*, p. 158. Cf. Old Babylonian lamentation a b_2 - g i n_7 g u_3 - d e_2 - d e_2, l. 7: ^{d}N a - n a - a d u m u - š a_6 - e_2 - e - k e_4 "Nanāja, the beautiful child of the house."

440 M. E. Cohen, *op. cit.*, eršemma 34.2, p. 131.

441 *Ibid.*, eršemma 13, p. 136.

for Ninurta,[442] for Enlil[443] and for Inanna[444]) there is talk of soothing the heart of Nanāja who is called "my lady" (š a_3 g a š a n - m u ^{d}N a - n a - a). The fourth e r š e m m a song,[445] composed together with a b a l a g song a b z u p e - e l - l a_2 - a m_3 "The Defiled a b z u", runs as follows (rev. 13-15):

[e_2 - g i]$_4$ - a d u m u - s a g ^{d}U r a š - a: *kal-lat mārtu*^{tu_4} *rēštītu*^{tu_4} *ša*$_2$ ^{d}*Nin*[*urta*]

[g a š a n - z] i - d a G a š a n - g u_3 - t e $š_2$ - a - s i_3 - g a - k e_4: *ru-bat rēštītu*^{tu_4} ^{d}*Taš-me-tum x*

[g a š a n - g] u - l a g a š a n - m u ^{d}N a - n a - a: *ru-bat ra-bi-tu*$_4$ *be-el-tu*$_2$ ^{d}*x*

"The daughter-in-law, firstborn of the god Uraš (Akkad. Ninurta),

Righteous lady, the goddess Gašangutešasiga (Akkad. Firstborn princess, the goddess Tašmētum...),

Great lady, my lady, Nanāja (Akkad. Great princess, lady, the goddess...).

The e r š e m m a songs use the name of Nanāja as a synonim for Inanna. In the last mentioned piece Nanāja was also made the equivalent of Tašmētum, who was also a spouse of Nabû.

The š u - i l_2 - l a constitute the third category of cultic songs. Their designation indicates that their performing was accompanied by the priests raising their hands. The oldest song of this category mentioning Nanāja comes from Nimrud and is dated to the reign of king Sîn-šar-iškun (630-612 BC). This is a composition directed to Marduk and performed during the New Year Festival in Babylon. The text[446] runs as follows (l. 23-24):

---

442 *Ibid.*, eršemma 45, p. 143.
443 *Ibid.*, eršemma 53, p. 145.
444 *Ibid.*, eršemma 59, p. 147.
445 G. Reisner, SBH 35 (VA.Th. 418+424+Fragment). Cf. M. E. Cohen, *CLAM*, p. 47, who writes the following of source F (SBH 35) of the b a l a g song: "The reverse contains the closing heart pacification unit of the *eršemma* with the part of the section which preceded it in the *eršemma*."
446 J. S. Cooper, *Iraq* 32 (1970), p. 60.

[n i n - z i - d a ^{d}]G a š a n - g u$_3$ - t e š$_2$ - a - s i$_3$ - g a - k e$_4$ n a - n a h u n - g a$_2$ h u - [m u - r a - a b - b e$_2$]

[*ru-ba-tum kit-tu*]*m* ^{d}*Taš-me-tum ma-ti nu-uḫ l*[*iq-bi-ka*]

[n i n - g u - l] a g a š a n - m u ^{d}N a - n a - a m e - n a

[*r*]*u-ba-tum ra-bi-tum be-el-tum* ^{d}MIN

"Let the righteous lady (Akkad. princess), Gašangutešasiga (Akkad. Tašmētum) tell you 'How long? Calm yourself!'

Let the great lady (Akkad. princess), my lady (Akkad. lady) Nanāja tell you 'How long? Calm yourself!'"

Again we have standing together the names of the two spouses[447] of Nabû: Tašmētum and Nanāja. The fact indicates clearly that despite the prevalent tendency toward combining goddesses of similar function, these two continued to be distinguished. A *kudurru* document, which will be discussed in the next chapter, confirms the presence of this triad already in the 12th century BC. The cult of Tašmētum, however, did not last as long as the cult of Nanāja.

The second of the š u - i l$_2$ - l a texts also originates from Nimrud; it was recorded solely in Akkadian. The tablet IM 67630,[448] containing seven prayers to different goddesses along with the rituals, was according to the colophon a collection of [?ŠU.IL$_2$].LA$_2$$^{?}$ x x x IŠ$_8$.TAR.MEŠ *ra-ba-te u ṣi-ra-te* "(prayers) š u - i l$_2$ - l a (for) the great and august goddesses." This big two-column tablet thus contains two prayers addressed to the goddess Nisaba, one to Ištar, three to Tašmētum and one to Nanāja. According to a gloss, the set was directed to the goddess Išḫara, "the queen of the lands."

Nanāja has had numerous epithets bestowed upon her here: *šarrat kibrāti* "queen of the world", *ilat bēlēti* "goddess of the la-

447 About the syncretism between Nanāja and Tašmētum, see P.-A. Beaulieu, CM 23, p. 186 and notes 48-49.

448 D. J. Wiseman, J. A. Black, *Literary Texts from the Temple of Nabû*, London 1996, no. 168, Appendix 2. Col. IV 31-52 concern Nanāja; the next line is a gloss, after which there comes the ritual and another gloss (l. 54-57).

dies",[449] *rubat* ^{d}*Igigi* "princess of the Igigi", as well as *šaruḫti ilāni* "pride of the gods" and *kanūt ajjaki* "the dignity of the temple." She naturally remains *narāmti bēli* "the beloved of the lord" (that is, of her spouse Nabû), on whose behalf she is to plead (l. 49) and *bēltī* (GAŠAN.MU). The damaged middle part of the tablet hinders the understanding of the exact relation between Nabû and Nanāja. The last three lines of this prayer contain the words of the supplicant:

50. *al-si-ki bēltī* (GAŠAN.MU) *ši-me-e su-pe-ia*

51. *us-ḫi lum-na ša*$_2$ *zu-um-ri-ia*

52. *gi-im-li-ni-ma da*$_3$*-li*$_2$*-[li*$_2$*-ki] lud-lul*

"I called you, my Lady, answer my pleas!

Remove the misfortunes from my body

So I can pay homage to you!"

The letter[450] written by a priest-exorcist to Aššur-aḫa-iddina (ca. 671 BC) describes the preparations made before an upcoming lunar eclipse. The author mentions a prayer of "raised hands" to Nanāja (beside others addressed to other divinities) performed on the sixteenth and seventeenth day of the month of *kanūnu* (the tenth month).

In the š u - i l$_2$ - l a songs Nanāja was recognized as one of the "great and august goddesses" next to the other goddesses: Nisaba (also a daughter of An, considered to be the spouse of Nabû as she was the goddess of scribal knowledge), Ištar, Tašmētum and Išḫara (goddess of love identified with Ištar).

The recitation of prayers to pacify the hearts of divinities – e r$_2$ - š a$_3$ - h u n - g a, was another duty of the g a l a/*kalû* priests. In the

---

449 In col. IV 32 there is the notation x k i? t u$_2$ ^{d}A - n i m u ^{d}D a - g a n : *ru-bat* ^{d}*I*$_2$*-gi*$_3$*-gi*$_3$. I should think the best way to fill the gap is to give the kinship, but I know of no other text in which the goddess would have any ties with the god Dagan.

450 ABL 23 = LAS 185 = SAA X 240.

collection studied by S. Maul,[451] the goddess Nanāja can be found eight times, but none of the texts was actually composed especially for her. Nanāja mediates in pacifying gods like Enlil,[452] Enki/Ea,[453] Iškur/Adad,[454] Marduk[455] and Inanna/Ištar.[456] She is designated most often as e g i$_2$ - g u - l a / *ru-ba-tum ra-bi-tum* "great princess" or e g i$_2$ - z i - d a "righteous princess" and g a š a n - m u[457] "my lady." Equally often the goddess to appear in the next line is G a š a n - g u t e š a s i g a - Tašmētum.

The Neo-Babylonian text pleading for the soothing of Nabû's heart, published in 1991 (83-1-18, 1871),[458] somewhat damaged, mentions Nanāja as the only goddess whose help is requested:

9' [e$_2$ - g i$_4$ - a E$_2$ - s] a g - i l$_2$ - l a d u m u - s a g ^{d}U r a š - a i m i n a - r a$_2$ i m i n n a - a m$_2$ - (t a g - g a - m u d u$_8$ - a - a b)

10' [e g i$_2$ E$_2$ - z i - d a] g a š a n - m u ^{d}N a - n a - a i m i n a - r a$_2$ i m i n n a - a m$_2$ - (t a g - g a - m u d u$_8$ - a - a b)
[*bēltu*(*m*) ^{d}]*Na-na-a rubāt*(EGI) *E$_2$-zi-da*

11' [n a - a m$_2$ - t a] g - g a - m u d u$_8$ - a - a b š e - e r - d a - m u b u r$_2$ - r a - a b
[*arnī/annī pu*]-*ṭur še-er-ti pu-šur*

12' [n a - a m$_2$ - t a g - g a g u -l a (?) u d - t u r - r] a - n i - t a i m i n a - r a$_2$ i m i n n a - a m$_2$ - (t a g - g a - m u d u$_8$ - a - a b)
[*ištu ūm ṣ*]*e-eḫ*[!]*-ri*[!]*-ia se-bet a-di se-bet*

451 S. M. Maul, *'Herzberuhigungsklagen'. Die sumerisch-akkadischen Eršaḫunga-Gebete*, Wiesbaden 1988.
452 *Op. cit.*, Ešh n3, rev. l. 11'-12'.
453 *Op. cit.*, Ešh n12, rev. l. 3'.
454 *Op. cit.*, Ešh n19c, l. 1'-2'
455 *Op. cit.*, G. Reisner, SBH 30, l. 22-23 and Ešh n26, rev. l. 5'.
456 *Op. cit.*, Ešh n70a, l. 14' and Ešh n73, rev. l. 20.
457 In the commentary on p. 96 S. Maul writes: "Nanâ wird in der sumerischen Zeile stats als gašan-mu ("Madonna") bezeichnet..."
458 S. Maul, *RA* LXXXV (1991), p. 67-70.

Rev.

1 [n a - a m_2 - t a g - g] a - m u d u_8 - a - a b
k a - t a r - z u g a - a n - s i - i l

2 [š a_3 - z u] [š a_3⌉ - a m a - t u - u d - d a - g i n_7
k i - b a d e_3 - e n - g i_4 - g i_4

3 [a m a - t u - u d] - ⌊d a a - a - t u - u d - d a - g i n_7
k i - b a d e_3 - e n - g i_4 - g i_4

[ ]
k i - b i - š e_3 h a - m a g i_4 - g i_4

9' "[The daughter-in-law of (the temple of) the Es]agil, the first-born child of the god Uraš, (he is) seven times seven, (my) sin remove!

10' Princess of (the temple of) the Ezida, (Sum.: my) Lady Nanāja, (he is) seven times seven, (my) si(n remove!)

11' My [si]n remove, my guilt abolish!

12' [Sin (Akkad. perhaps: my sin) is? great (?)], from [the day], when I (Sum.: he) was small, he is seven times seven, (my) s(in) remove!)"

Rev.

1 "My [si]n remove, (then) I will praise you!

2 [Your heart] like the heart of my own mother, to its place let it return!

3 Like (my) own mother], (my) own father, let it return to its place!

[ ] , let it for me to its place return!"

The text of a prayer addressed to Inanna/Ištar (Ešh n70a) clearly indicates that the name of Nanāja is treated as an epithet or designation of equivalent stature as others found in the composition: e g i_2 g a š a n - E_2 - a n - n a, e g i_2 g a š a n - k i - U n u g[ki], e g i_2 g a š a n - k i - Z a b a l a m[ki], e g i_2 g a š a n - h u r - s a g - k a l a m - m a, e g i_2 g a š a n - E_2 - t u r_3 - k a l a m - m a or e g i_2 g a š a n - T i n - t i r[ki].

This demonstrates that the early identification of Nanāja with Inanna/Ištar had not prevented worshippers from distinguishing the two goddesses in compositions of another type. Let it be recalled that the genre of cult songs in the eme-sal dialect became established already in the Old Babylonian period when the prototypes were created. The Sumerian language in these compositions of the first millennium BC falls under the influence of the interlinear Akkadian version and is fossilized, even though still lexically rich. The analysis of the epithets in particular bears out this opinion.

The figure of Nanāja in poetic texts written down in the e m e - s a l dialect is manifested solely in the epithets and designations assigned to her. She is attributed to a variety of cities and temples, but the most frequently repeated phrase is "firstborn of the god Uraš." As said already above, Uraš is identified with Ninurta and with Nabû. He was the son of the god Anu or a synonym for him, as well as the father of the goddess Tašmētum (counterpartner of the goddess Nanāja). Tašmētum appears in these compositions under a different name, that of G a š a n - g u t e š a s i g a "Lady of listening." Her epithet is "Righteous lady", while Nanāja bears the title of "Great Lady."

To judge by the cult poetry texts presented above, Nanāja appears in this genre seldom and merely as a synonym for the goddess Inanna/Ištar. Contrary to compositions belonging to other genres, however, her ties with the god Uraš, a local deity of the city of Dilbat, are strongly emphasized.

The epithets used for Nanāja in these compositions are, as noted, repeated and bring little information on her status; indeed the reader is given the impression that she is a deity of secondary importance despite the fact that in the "raised hands" composition from Nimrud she was included in the set of "great and august goddesses." In the same text she appears with the epithets of the goddess Ištar, while in a Neo-Babylonian request for the pacification of Nabû's heart, she is called upon because of their marital relationship. The supplicant appeals to Nanāja's parental feelings.

CHAPTER VII
THE GODDESS NANĀJA IN *KUDURRU* DOCUMENTS

Inscriptions on *kudurru* incorporating the name of Nanāja start appearing in the second half of the second millennium BC. These steles were acts documenting land grants, usually confirming the owner's right to a given territory, an exemption from fees or additional privileges resulting from ownership. The steles could also be offered or presented to the gods, as revealed by the first and last of the documents discussed here. These inscriptions were duplicates of tablets sealed by the witnesses.

The oldest *kudurru* inscription[459] evoking Nanāja is a land grant to the princess Hannubat-Nanāja made by her father, ruler of Babylonia, a Kassite of the name Melišipak (1188-1174 BC). The goddess guarantees the grant; she was also represented (beside the king and his daughter) on a relief carving accompanying the inscription.[460] Differently from other *kudurru* reliefs, this one illustrates the actual act of land bestowal, which is described in the text as follows (col. II 9-15): *ṭuppa zakut alāni*^{pl} *iknukma / iddinši / u mala iddinuši / in* ^{aban}*narî išṭurma / in maḫar* ^{d}*Nanāja / ...* ^{d}*Nanāja / an dār ušziz* "The tablet (instituting) the exemption of the cities he (Melišipak) sealed and / gave to her (Hannubat-Nanāja), / and everything that he had given her, / he recorded on the boundary stone and / before the goddess Nanāja / ... to the goddess Nanāja / he laid down forever."

The relief on the *kudurru* stele is a traditional scene of presentation (the best known example of which is the relief carving on the basalt obelisk with Hammurabi's codex). King Melišipak is shown leading his daughter by the hand towards the goddess. Nanāja sits on a throne which is in the form of a temple standing on a podium with lion's paws. Her robes are frilled and on her head there is a cylindrical crown of feathers. Seen above the goddess are the emblems

459 V. Scheil, MDP X, p. 87-94, pl. 11-13.
460 U. Seidl, *Die babylonischen Kudurru-Reliefs*, Freiburg 1989, pl. 11a and 11b (damaged copy), and also V. Scheil, MDP X, pl. 13.

of three celestial deities: the solar disc of Šamaš, the crescent of Sîn and the star of Ištar.

It should be noted that col. VIII,[461] which is written in reverse direction, tells of offering the stele to Ištar, Lady of the Lands.

The next document is a *kudurru* IM 67953[462] from the reign of Marduk-apla-iddina (1173-1161 BC). It testifies to the existence in this period of the divine triad of Nabû and his two spouses: Nanāja and Tašmētum. It should be emphasized that this divine triangle was considered as natural to judge by the texts and there does not seem to be any tendency to confuse the two goddesses; quite the opposite is true – the two goddesses are clearly distinguished. In inscriptions not concerned with the *hieros gamos* rites, their names occur side by side without specific reference to their relation with the god Nabû.

These three deities appear together in a curse formula (col. III 22-27): ^{d}*Nabû* ^{d}*Nanāja / u* ^{d}*Tašmētum / bēlē*^{pl} *šipti u purussê / ana lemutti lisḫuruš / ana la ṭabti*^{ti} *lište'uš* "Nabû, Nanāja / and Tašmētum / – rulers of spells and settlements of disputes, / let them look for it in anger / (and) for punishment (lit. for misfortune) (let them) find it."

The triad appears next to other deities, called upon to annihilate anyone potentially wishing to destroy the document. These other divinities are: Anu, Enlil, Ea and Ninmaḫ – the great gods (*ilāni rabûti*), Sîn, Samaš, Adad and Marduk – the revered gods (*ilāni ṣirūti*), Uraš, Ninekalli, Nusku, Sadarnunna, Šuqamuna and Šimalija – the shining gods (*ilāni rašbūtum*) and Gula – Great Lady (*bēltum rabîtum*).

The reign of Marduk-apla-iddina has also yielded another *kudurru* document[463] confirming a land grant by the dead king Melišipak, to part of which a neighbor of the rightful owner laid claim. The fragment of interest to the study at hand is the curse formula listing a substantial number of different divinities (col. V 12 – col. VI 9).

[461] V. Scheil, MDP X, p. 93.
[462] S. Page, *Sumer* 23 (1967), p. 45-67.
[463] V. Scheil, MDP VI, p. 31-39.

Nabû appears in one line with the goddess Tašmētum, while Nanāja is listed together with Ištar a few lines lower down. In this case, therefore, the triad was not called upon and instead the closeness between Nanāja and Ištar was emphasized.

Being the goddess of Namar, Nanāja appears next to Adad and Nergal on the *kudurru* of Nabû-kudurri-uṣur I (1124-1103 BC):[464] ^{d}ISKUR ^{d}U.GAR *u* ^{d}N a - n a - a DINGIR.MEŠ *ša*$_2$ KUR *Na-mar*. According to RGTC 5, p. 202, the land of Namar lay on the Dijala River, in the Hamrin depression.

Nanāja is mentioned a few more times in curse formulas[465] occurring on *kudurru* documents. She is called *bēlet Uruk*^{ki} *u Eanna* – "Lady of the city of Uruk and of (the temple of) the Eanna."

The next donation act (AO 6684)[466] comes from the reign of Marduk-zakir-šumi (854-819 BC). The document was drawn up in Babylon in the second regnal year of this king, but was discovered at Uruk. The endowed is one Ibni-Ištar, who performs a variety of duties in the Eanna temple in Uruk: he is a *kalû* priest of Ištar, *ērib-bīti* of Nanāja, *šangû* of the goddess Uṣur-amāssa and scribe of the Eanna temple (col. III 7-12).

Ibni-Ištar received land estates, eight houses and a slave with family. Apart from this he was endowed with the right to part of the income from the temple of Nanāja and the bread and beer offerings brought for this goddess (l. 19-20).

In the termination of the document containing the curse formula targeted at anyone daring to challenge the genuineness of the document, Nanāja is mentioned along with Nabû (col. IV 2-5): ^{d}*Nabû u* ^{d}*Nanāja / ilāni ṣirūti / išissu lissuḫū / u zēršu lilqutū* "Nabû and Nanāja, / august divinities, / 'his roots' let them pull out / and his offspring (lit. seed) let them destroy." The other deities evoked in the curse formula include: Anu, Enlil, Ea and Bēlet-ilāni – the great

464 Cf. L. W. King, BBSt, no. VI col. II 48 (no. 90858).
465 D. Arnaud, *RA* LXVI (1972), p. 172 ff.
466 F. Thureau-Dangin, *RA* XVI (1919), p. 117-141.

gods, Marduk and his spouse Ṣarpanītum, Sîn, Šamaš and Ištar, referred to as rulers of the heavens and earth, Ninurta, Zababa and Nergal, and again at the end Nabû and Marduk.

The next *kudurru* to attest the name of the goddess is a document from Borsippa (VA 3031),[467] dated to the eight regnal year of Nabû-šuma-iškun (760-748 BC). It is an unique example of a donation act in which the gods, Nanāja and Mār-bīti, are the donators. Together they endow one Nabû-mutakkil, son of Aššur, who is introduced into the temple service.

Nanāja and Mār-bīti are both described in column I (l. 1-21), but Nanāja's description is much more substantial (l. 1-16): *ᵈNanāja bēlti ṣirti / šurbūti ilīᵐᵉ qaritti / ilat ilāti šaqut bēlētiᵐᵉ / šemâti supê / maḫirat unninnu ḫirat ᵈNabû / talīmmat ᵈŠamši narāmti ᵈMarduk / bukurti ᵈAnu rēštiti / ša qibītsu magrat / ša ina puḫur ilīᵐᵉ rabûti / la iššannanu bēlūtsu / mālikat ᵈIgigi mušaddiḫat ḫarranu / ša ina Esaggil ekal šamê u erṣēti / šitluṭat bēlussu / ša ṣīt pîšu la uttakkaru / la ininnu qibītsu / ša kima abi rēmēnî nasḫuršu ṭâbu* "The goddess Nanāja, honored lady, / the greatest (among) the gods, gallant, / goddess of goddesses, the greatest among rulers, / (the one who) answers prayers (and) / accepts pleas, spouse of Nabû, / favorite sister of Šamaš, beloved of Marduk, / firstborn daughter of Anu, / whose orders are fulfilled, / (the one) who has in the assembly of the great gods / power is unmatched, / counselor of the Igigi deities, taking the (procession) way, / (the one) who is in the Esagil, temple of heavens and earth / power is predominates, / whose command cannot be changes / (nor) order abrogated, / (the one) who like the merciful father turns (to the supplicant) with benevolence." Together with the gallant and powerful Mār-bīti who steps before her, "(they) with the shining countenances" – as is written in the text – "looked upon Nabû-mutakkil, son of Aššur / with joy and / on that day to the temple of the god Nabû / in Borsippa they brought him inside" (col. I 21-col. II 4). The endowed received the gifts appropriate for

[467] VAS I 36.

an *ērib-bīti* priest and a document sealed by the gods confirming the donation. Should anyone in the future desire to change this binding state of affairs, both the divinities, Nanāja and Mār-bīti, are to judge him (lit. they are to be "masters of his sentence").

The document also informs that the seals on the tablet presented the "signatures" of all the *ērib-bīti* priests and the *kiništu* college of priests of the Ezida temple. A total of 18 names was mentioned, of which 10 were priests of Nabû, one was a *šangû* priest of the god Adad, three were priests of Nanāja, one a priest of Mār-bīti, one a priest of the goddess Sutītu and a chief of cooks and a chief of brewers. Also present was the scribe of the Ezida temple who was also a *šangû* priest of Sutītu and a *kalû* priest of Nabû.

Nanāja is mentioned yet twice more in this document. When future rulers are evoked, each one of them *ana amat* ^{d}*Nanāja u* ^{d}*Mār-bīti / liplaḫ likkudma atriš / liqissu* "on the command of Nanāja and the god Mār-bīti / let him remain in fear and trembling; additional / offerings let him make to them" (col. IV 17-19). Anyone daring to destroy this stele could expect to be punished by having his line annihilated by the gods who *ina muḫḫi narî annî / šuršudu nanzazu* "on that stele / appear (lit. 'have a well grounded position.')"

The presented *kudurru* documents in which Nanāja is mentioned among the divinities, most often connect the name of the goddess with the curse formula directed against anyone destroying this proof. Two texts are an exception to the rule. The first is an act of endowment from Melišipak to his daughter Hannubat-Nanāja, drawn up in the 12th century BC. In it the goddess guarantees the genuineness of the act and is further represented in the relief scene. In the other text, which was composed about 500 years later, Nanāja and Mār-bīti together endow a person entering the service of the god Nabû. The description of the goddess cited above reflects her very high position in the divine hierarchy of Borsippa at the time.

CHAPTER VIII
THE IMAGE OF NANĀJA BASED ON LETTERS

Letters, those documents of everyday life, are next to offerings, temple buildings and personal names the best proof for the existence of the cult of a given deity or deities. To my knowledge, there are just four such documents mentioning Nanāja from the Old Babylonian period.

The first is text AO 4620,[468] where in l. 4-6 we read: AN-^{d}INANNA u_3 ^{d}*Na-na-a* / *aš-šum-ia da-ri-iš* u_4*-mi-im* / *li-ba-al-li-ṭu*$_2$*-ka* "An-Inanna and Nanāja, / for my sake, eternal / let they make your life!" The author of the letter goes on to list the offerings intended (l. 10-12) *a-na* AN-^{d}INANNA / ^{d}*Na-na-a* u_3 ^{d}*Ka-ni-sur-ra* / *be-le-ti-ia* "for An-Inanna, / Nanāja and Kanisurra, / my ladies." At the close of the letter the sender asks for a prayer in his behalf to An-Inanna and Nanāja, his mistresses (l. 21-23): *ma-ḫa-ar* AN-^{d}INA[NNA] / u_3 ^{d}*Na-na-a be-l*[*e*]*-* / *ti-ia ku-ur-ba-am*. We have thus returned to the issue of a joint cult of the deity AN-^{d}INANNA (believed to be Ištar of Uruk by D. Charpin) and Nanāja.[469]

Another letter from the Old Babylonian period is AbB 12, 178 (BM 29649). It is addressed to a woman, to judge by the pronoun used with the form of the noun and verb (l. 3-4): ^{d}*Ištar* u_3 ^{d}*Na-na-a be-le-tu-ki* / *li-ba-al-li-ṭu*$_3$*-ki* "The goddesses Ištar and Nanāja – your (fem.) mistresses, / may they keep you (fem.) in good health." The content of the letter is not clear, but Nanāja appears at Ištar's side as a guardian divinity.

An undated fragment of a letter AbB 10, 95 speaks of the temple e_2 ^{d}*Na-na-a*, while a damaged text published by S. Greengus, *Old Babylonian Tablets* no. 234 gives ^{d}Na-na-a-a (l. 4).

No more texts are recorded until a thousand years later.

In his study *Royal Correspondence of the Assyrian Empire*, Ann Arbor 1936, L. Waterman included 37 letters in which Nanāja's

---

468 TCL I 19, pl. XIV; for the transliteration and translation, cf. D. Charpin, *Le clergé d'Ur au siècle d'Hammurabi*, Genève 1986, p. 411-412. Cf. another translation, C. Wilcke, AOAT 247, p. 415; cf. also CAD M 330a *s.v. maṣḫatu*.

469 Cf. p. 67-68 and note 240.

name is attested.[470] Most of these are addressed to Aššur-bāni-apli (probably 26 texts); Aššur-aḫa-iddina was the addressee of 3 or 4 texts; the remaining letters were addressed to different people. The name of the goddess, next to that of Ištar (most often: ^{d}*Ištar Uruk*^{ki} u_3 ^{d}*Na-na-a*, but also: ^{d}*Bēlet-ša-Uruk*^{ki} *u* ^{d}*Na-na-a*; ^{d}*Ištar Ninua*^{ki} [*u* ^{d}*Na-na-a*]; ^{d}*Šarrat-ša-Uruk*^{ki} *u* ^{d}*Na-na-a*; ^{d}*Ištar u* ^{d}*Na-na-a*), appears in the greetings formula for the king. Noteworthy is the superior number of letters addressed to Aššur-bāni-apli from Uruk. They treat on city affairs (e.g. 753) and neighboring Elam (e.g. 269-272), and they inform of events taking place in the Uruk region (e.g. 754).

In turn, Aššur-bāni-apli's letter (518) is sent to one Kudurru and the residents of Uruk, and it concerns the feast in the month of *simānu* (3rd calendar month); it mentions three goddesses of Uruk: Nanāja, Uṣur-amāssa and Arkajītu. To judge by the letter content, lamentations were performed then "because of the gods' anger" (l. 9: *ultu ilāni*^{meš} *iznū*), it was necessary to offer libations and dress the mentioned goddesses in special robes.

Letter 1105 is highly interesting as it documents a treaty between the king and the sender or senders (the destroyed beginning must have contained information about the sender).[471] Among the deities called upon to affirm what the sender writes there is Aššur, Marduk, Nabû, Šamaš, Sîn, Ea, Adad, and a few female divinities including Nanāja. Each divinity is assigned an epithet. Nanāja is called (rev. l. 22) "Mistress of mercy/pity" *bēlet rēmi*, which may also be translated as "Mistress of the (maternal) womb."[472] Ištar on the other hand

---

[470] Nos 23, 54, 119, 120, 219, 266, 267, 268, 269, 270, 272, 274, 277, 278, 324, 426, 469, 476, 518, 751, 752, 753, 754, 815, 859, 866, 880, 964, 1007, 1062, 1105, 1124, 1135, 1200, 1202, 1385, 1387. The goddess Tašmētum is attested in 30 documents; 6 documents mention Nanāja and Tašmētum together (nos 23, 54, 119, 120, 426, 1385). See also L. Waterman, *op. cit.*, part IV, p. 211 (YOS 3, 7 = NBU 1, 7).

[471] The authors of SAA II have entitled the text *Assurbanipal's Treaty with Babylonian Allies* (no. 9).

[472] Cf. *rēmu* I, AHw 970a 1b) "Mutterleib; Erbarmen, Mitleid." S. Parpola, K. Watanabe, SAA II, p. 68 gives an interesting transliteration and translation of rev. 22-23: ^{d}*Na-na-a be-lit re-e-mu u* [*x x x*] / IDIM *u* NUN *tu-šam-ri-iṣ-an-na-ši* "May Nanāja, mistress of love and [peace, ...] make us an abomination to (both) nobleman and prince [...]."

has her warrior-like aspect emphasized (rev. l. 24) – "residing in the city of Arbela, goddess of battles" (*ašibat Arba-ilu*[ki] *ilat tāḫāzāti*).

Letter 866, also addressed to Aššur-bāni-apli, speaks of an official named Arad-[d]Nanāja.

Four other letters sent to Aššur-bāni-apli (119, 120, 426, 1385) should also be discussed here. The first two are documents of an official, perhaps a builder or a person supervising building works; they concern work carried out on the Esagila temple in Babylon and the cedars allocated for the rebuilding of a temple in the town of Karkemiš. In the other two documents Nanāja is listed in the greetings formula for the king (119, l. 5-8; 120, l. 5-9): [d]*Marduk* [d]*Ṣar-pa-ni-tum* [d]*Nabû* [d]*Taš-me-tum* [d]*Na-na-a* u_3 *ilāni*[meš] *am-mar ina* E_2*-sag-ila kam-mu-su-ni umē*[meš] *ša*$_2$ *šarri be-li*$_2$*-ia*$_2$ *lu-ur-ri-ku* "Marduk, Ṣarpānītum, Nabû, Tašmētum, Nanāja and the gods, so many as in the Esagila reside, days of the king, my Lord, let them extend these."

The next two letters were written by Šamaš-šum-ukīn (668-648 BC), who also listed Nanāja together with Bēl, Bēlit, Nabû and Tašmētum in the greetings formula.

As I said above, the number of letters to Aššur-aḫa-iddina mentioning Nanāja is not substantial. One of the king's officials, Mār-Ištar,[473] reported in his letter to the king on the progress made in repair work on the statues of Nanāja, Uṣur-amāssa, Arkajītu and Anunītum of Uruk. In l. 12 and l. 13 we read the following: [*ša*$_2$*-kut-tu*$_2$ *ša* [d]*N*]*a-na-a* / *ma-aṭ-ṭi-ia-at* ... "[Decorating (the statue of) the goddess N]anāja / is not yet finished, ...", and in l. 24-26: *ki-ma dul-lu ša* [d]*U-ṣur-a-mat-sa* u_3 *ša bīt*(E_2) / [d]*Mu-um-mu nig-da-mar bīt*(E_2) *is-si-li-im* / *ḫa-ra-ma-ma ša*$_2$*-kut-tu*$_2$ *ša* [d]*Na-na-a ne*$_2$*-e-pa-aš*$_2$ "When the work on (the statue of) the goddess Uṣur-amāssa and on the temple / of the god Mummu will be finished, (and when) the temple is finished, / then the ornaments of (the statue of) the goddess Nanāja we finished." These words cannot have concerned the

473 ABL 476 = LAS 277 = SAA X 349. The sender's name is missing, but S. Parpola believes it could not have been anybody else but Mār-Ištar (LAS, part II, 1983, p. 265).

statue of Nanāja that Aššur-bāni-apli, son of Aššur-aḫa-iddina, brought back from Elam; hence, it must have been another statue of the goddess that was being repaired and renovated.[474]

In letter 1202 = SAA X 353, addressed to the king, the same official, Mār-Ištar, writes of some hearsay information that the bull offered to Nanāja had been missing the right kidney (rev. l. 1-3 *ištu lib*$_3$*-bi alpu rēštu* LU.LU *ša*$_2$ *ka-ri-bi* / *ša*$_2$ *pa-an* ^{d}*Na-na-a e-piš-u-ni a-si-me ma-a* / *kalītu imnī-šu la-aš-šu*).

The letter of a priest-exorcist[475] to Aššur-aḫa-iddina, already mentioned above, concerned a š u - i l$_2$ - l a prayer to Nanāja (and other divinities, including Tašmētum) performed on the 16th and 17th day of the month of *kanūnu* as part of the preparations for a lunar eclipse (rev. l. 2-8).

In two letters (219 and 324) Nanāja follows after the name of Nabû. The deities were mentioned in order to inform the addressee that everyday the sender of the letter prays to this particular pair of deities on their behalf.

In six texts Nanāja takes her place next to Tašmētum. The official writing to the daughter of Sîn-aḫe-erība (705-681 BC), includes in the greetings formula also Bēl, Ṣarpānītum, Nabû, Nanāja and Tašmētum. He writes that he prays daily to these gods for the good life of the king and his daughter.

From the 6th year of Nabû-na'īd's reign (556-539 BC) there are two letters (YOS 6, 71 and 72) concerning the *kusītu* robes of Nanāja.[476] It is easy to identify the goddesses named ^{d}GAŠAN-*ša*-UNUG.KI *u* ^{d}*Na-na-a* (l. 21) as Ištar-of-Uruk and Nanāja, but the goddess ^{d}*Na-na-a ša E*$_2$*-zi-da* from l. 20 could be an appellation of,

---

474 See F. M. Fales, J. N. Postgate, SAA VII 60: List of Temple Treasures Sent to Elam (K 8247 + K 13182), l. 1: "[These are] the objects [of the god]s of Akkad, [which we]nt [to] Elam." In col. II, the making of new rings of gold for Nanāja is mentioned.

475 ABL 23 = LAS 185 = SAA X 240.

476 E. Matsushima, in: H.I.H. Prince Takahito Mikasa (ed.), *Cult and Ritual in the Ancient Near East*, Wiesbaden 1992, p. 12-14 and *eadem*, *Orient* XXX-XXXI (1995), p. 173 ff.

according to E. Matsushima,[477] both Nanāja from the Ezida temple in Borsippa and Nanāja from the Ezida temple existing in Uruk or its vicinity. The analysis of another text (SBH VIII) led the author to suggest that a temple of the name Ezida dedicated to the worship of Nabû and his spouse Nanāja was actually situated in Uruk, in the Eanna sanctuary.[478]

One Nabû-šuma-iškun in a letter from Borsippa[479] relates the journey by boat of statues of the goddesses Nanāja and Ištar of Uruk (who is designated with the name Bēlet-ša-Uruk). These statues, which were returning from Babylon to Uruk, remained under the care of the college of priests from the Esagil temple (l. 8-13: *kinal-tum / ša* E_2.SAG.ILA / *i-na lib₃-bi it-ti* ᵈ*Na-na-a* / *u₃* ᵈ*Bēlet-ša-*Uruk^{ki} / *a-na* Uruk^{ki}).

Letters of the 7th-6th centuries BC confirm the existence of the cult of Nanāja. It should be noted, however, that the goddess is mentioned more frequently in letters addressed to Aššur-bāni-apli,[480] most probably originating from Uruk or Babylon. Listing Nanāja in the greetings formula for the addressee may indicate, although it is hardly ultimate proof, that the person to whom the letter was sent was a worshipper of the goddess. Šamaš-šum-ukīn is known to have

477 *Ibid.*, p. 175.

478 *Ibid.*, p. 177. The distinguishing of the goddess Nanāja from the Euršaba/Eḫuršaba temple is obvious in the text BM 41239 (A. R. George, BTT, tab. 45) l. 1-4: "The deities, who [go] with Bēl to Kiš: / IGI.HUR.RI, Daughters of (the temple of) the Ezida, [...], / Anunnaki, the goddesses Ištarātu, Sîn, Nin[gal, Nanāja (?)] from E_2.UR_5.$ŠA_3$.BA, / Uṣur-amāssa, Ka[nisurra], Ninurta, Mār-bīti, Ištar-bīti." Line 3 in the transliteration: ^{d}9 ^{d}$MUŠ_3$.MEŠ ^{d}30 ^{d}NIN.[GAL ^{d}X] *ša₂* E_2.UR_5.$ŠA_3$.BA. A text from the 8th regnal year of Darius also records distinctly (BE VIII/1, 108, l. 9): *ina* ^{iti}*šabāti*(ZIZ_2) *ina Bābili*(TIN.TIR)^{ki} *pa-ni* ᵈ*Na-na-a* E_2.UR_5.ŠA.BA ...

479 A. T. Clay, YOS 3, 86. On the possible dating of the text, see above, p. 47 and note 159.

480 Of the documents mentioning Tašmētum twelfe are likely to refer to Aššur-aḫa-iddina. The goddess occurs in the greetings formula next to Nabû, but the letters also concern a statue of the goddess, rituals (including *hieros gamos*), offerings and processions dedicated to the goddess.

been an Assyrian who ruled Babylonia from the city of Babylon. The continued existence of the cult of Nanāja in the Babylonian Esagila temple demanded from the king that in a letter to his brother he list Nanāja, who was after all also connected with Nabû, as well as the pairs of Bēl – Bēlit and Nabû – Tašmētum.

The letters discussed here concern ordinary everyday matters – offerings, the transport of a statue of Nanāja or her robes, repairing a statue. The name of the goddess is attested usually next to that of Ištar, a fact that again confirms the close ties between the two divinities.

SUMMARY

The diverse texts presented in this study attest the presence of a cult of Nanāja starting from the Ur III period (specifically the 21st century BC) and terminating in Seleucid times. Despite a few-centuries gap in the sources (16th, 14th, 13th, 11th, 10th, 5th, 4th centuries), the continuity of this cult should be accepted.

In view of the minimal number of archaeological sources uncovered to date, the textual evidence provides the only grounds for a study of the goddess Nanāja.

The texts containing mentions of Nanāja form an essentially uniform picture of the goddess. The issue of her origins is of fundamental importance, but due to insufficient sources it cannot be resolved at this stage in the research. The hypothesis about Nanāja's cult being borrowed and introduced in Mesopotamia around the 21st century BC should be accepted as being just as likely as the theory about the cult developing locally in the city of Uruk at an earlier period. M. Hutter's idea about the cult being borrowed from the pre-Aramaic nomadic tribes (the Amorites whom Šulgi battled in the Kurdistan region) is based on Nanāja's assumed links with the planet Venus. This identification, however, should be recognized as false.

As for Nanāja's ties with the celestial planets, suggested by the statement that she is identified as a Venus deity, I have found only a list of stars of the god Enlil (V R 46), where it is written: MUL BAL.TEŠ$_2$.A ^{d}*Na-na-a* (l. 10).[481] The reading, however, seems incorrect, as CT 26, 42, col. II 13' gives: MUL BAL.TEŠ$_2$.A ^{d}MIN, and CT 33, 1, col. I 14: MU]L BAL.TEŠ$_2$.A *sukkal* ^{d}*Tišpak*(MUŠ$_2$).[482]

H. Sauren has proved[483] that offerings to Nanāja in the Neo-Sumerian period were performed according to a specific cycle — the appearance and disappearance of the planet Venus. During this

[481] So E. F. Weidner, *Handbuch der babylonischen Astronomie*, Leipzig 1915, p. 51. The star is identified with the *Corona Borealis*.
[482] In the translation by H. Hunger, D. Pingree, MUL.APIN, *An Astronomical Compendium in Cuneiform*, Horn 1989, tabl. I i 14: "the Star of Dignity, the messenger of Tišpak."
[483] H. Sauren, in: CRRAI 17, p. 24-25 ; see the opinion of H. Hunger, WZKM 65/66 (1973/74), p. 72-73.

cycle which lasts 584 days, Venus twice becomes invisible to the observer: when she is closest and farthest away from Earth. The offerings made to the goddess in Uruk fall exactly on the days when the planet "disappeared" and then "reappeared."

There are also texts that attest to offerings being made to Nanāja as part of feasts celebrating the new moon and the full moon, thus not only in the Venus planet cycle. Despite the rareness of these texts, they tend to disprove Sauren's theory to some extent.

According to the same author, the offerings made to Inanna attest to the goddess's connection with the lunar cycle. They were offered to the goddess every seven days, corresponding to the phases of the moon. The literary texts, however, relate Inanna to the planet Venus, representing the goddess as the planet personified.

The literary texts discussed in this study do not substantiate Nanāja's ties with Venus. It is true though that the epithets and designations bestowed on the goddess in these texts connect her with the heavens, imbuing her with the inherent attributes of beauty and light. The oldest among the hymns (from the turn of the 21st century BC) uses such descriptors as: "shining like the day" and "woman – celestial star of An." She was "created in beauty", "forever in real beauty chosen."

Sūmû-el who reigned in the 19th century BC erected a temple for Nanāja and called it e_2 - i t u / i t i - d a "House of the Month", confirming the goddess's ties with the phases of the moon rather than with the planet Venus.

An 18th-century hymn to Nanāja designates the goddess as the sun – the luminous Šamaš, and the moon. Consequently, the goddess robed in glow is compared to various heavenly bodies shining like she. She is also endowed with many feminine attributes: fertility, sweetness, allure, charm, and she is accompanied by laughter and joy.

Another hymn, this time from the 8th century BC, refers to the goddess with the less than clear title MUL GU.LA *melammētu* ("star – (of the goddess?) Gula (of the) terrifying glow"?) and *šākinat nūri* "bringing light."

The three mentioned hymns cannot be taken as evidence for describing Nanāja as a Venus deity. Modern scholars (perhaps even Bar Bahlul in AD 1000) have assigned her, however, to the Venus divinities in view of her identification with the goddess Inanna. On the other hand, accepting H. Sauren's results, one should recognize Nanāja as a Venus deity, while Inanna would be a moon goddess. Meanwhile, both are sisters of the god of the sun and are recognized on occasion as daughters of the god of the heavens or the moon god.

Returning to the issue of the origins of Nanāja, we may safely assume that her ties with the Venus deity of the pre-Aramaic nomads are minimal (not to mention that the Venus divinity of the nomads is male). It is highly likely, however, that her cult did actually originate with these Semitic nomads. I have written of the coincidental (with Nanāja's cult) appearance of the worship of two other goddesses from the Kirkuk region: Bēlat-suḫnir and Bēlat-tirraban. The names of these goddesses are indubitably of Semitic origin and they were local town deities. Nanāja's name is hardly Semitic. The three goddesses were venerated together with Inanna and aspects of Ištar (Anunītum and Ulmašītum). They are mentioned together in connection with the offerings made in the "place of disappearance", which could be indicative of ties with the vegetation cycle and burial customs.

Nanāja's assimilation with Inanna occurred quite quickly. Testifying to this are joint offerings, the appearance of their names close together on the god lists (starting from the Ur III period) and the connections between the goddesses emphasized in Išbi-Erra's hymn (21st century BC). In turn, the hymn to Nanāja from the reign of Samsuiluna (18th century BC) is in style and structure (and subject foremost) a copy of a hymn to Ištar from the times of Ammī-ditāna (17th century BC), although from the point of view of chronology it is rather Ammī-ditāna's hymn that is a copy of Samsu-iluna's. The epithets used for the two goddesses are the same.

What could have stood behind the two goddesses becoming so close or at least being so similarly perceived by the worshippers? Let us take the oldest text and try to isolate the attributes that were characteristic of Nanāja.

Rulers of the III Dynasty of Ur venerated Nanāja in connection with the sacred marriage rites. Both the hymn of Išbi-Erra and the love dialogue of Rīm-Sîn are proof of this. The goddess is identified with fertility rituals that are essential to the development of the city-state (this feature is also Inanna's attribute). The erection of new places of cult for Nanāja (both separate sanctuaries and chapels inside temple complexes) testifies to the growing number of worshippers. Inseparable from places of worship are priests who could have also been in the service of Inanna simultaneously, as some of our sources demonstrate. Should we then treat Nanāja as no more than a kind of duplicate of Inanna? While we accept Anunītum as a hypostasis of the warrior-like Ištar, what is emphasized in Nanāja is her beauty, charm and allure. Could she then be a hypostasis of Inanna as the quintessence of womanhood?

The texts appear to confirm this idea, the most explicit ones being the b a l b a l e songs and the love spells depicting the goddess as wielding sexual appeal. She is referred to both as "lady of love" and as "lady of charm/sexual attractiveness." This is also confirmed by the names of temples built in homage to her by kings ruling in Neo-Sumerian, Neo-Assyrian and Late Babylonian times.

Parallel to her role of goddess-mistress, Nanāja is also asked in all of the hymns dedicated to her to extend her protection to the person of the king. Thus, it would seem that her original nature could be described as goddess-mistress and goddess-guardian. This led her to be recognized as a daughter/ward of Inanna. This stage ended in her identification with Inanna (hence also with the Venus deity) and later also with Ištar. The latter process made her a warrior goddess, too, for the Assyrian rulers.

An analysis of the family connections between the two goddesses reveals similarities and differences. The two goddesses are described as daughters of An; Inanna was also honored with the title of spouse of the god of the heavens. According to another tradition, both goddesses were called daughters of the Moon god and sisters of the Sun god. In lamentation texts Nanāja is also referred to as the daughter of a local god of Dilbat, Uraš. To date, there are only three texts in which Nanāja is designated the daughter of Inanna/Ištar. Her consort is never Dumuzi, who is Inanna's partner, while Nabû has absolutely no links with Ištar.

The issue of the syncretism of the divinities of the Ancient Near East seems crucial in the case of the pair Nanāja and Inanna/Ištar. The identification of Nanāja first with Inanna, and then with Ištar meant that the name of Nanāja became a synonym for the names of successive goddesses. This is demonstrated most clearly in the b a l a g and e r š e m m a texts. Yet, as Th. Jacobsen has pointed out, the border-line between the epithets and names of deities was blurred in all periods. It may be assumed that the lengthy lists of names-epithets rendered different aspects of the venerated deity, which the worshipper was likely not even aware of. The name of Nanāja thus served to render yet another aspect of Inanna/Ištar.

Whether borrowed or existing in Uruk since times immemorial, the cult of Nanāja was connected with fertility, love and protection. In recognition of this the goddess was identified with Inanna, who also featured similar attributes. The identification took place already in the Ur III period (perhaps it is why theophoric names with the Nanāja element are so infrequent and why there probably existed joint temples of the two goddesses). Just as quickly, however, Nanāja was separated from Inanna/Ištar, having had the aspect of physical love and personification of sex appeal added to her characteristics. The b a l b a l e songs discussed here were composed for Inanna, even though it is Nanāja who plays the main role in them. The 8th-century hymn identifying Nanāja with eighteen goddesses venerated in Mesopotamia reveals how the role of this goddess had grown substantially over time. A text which is presumably from the same period (BM 34030) puts it in a straightforward manner — Ištar's place has been taken by Nanāja. Hence, it should be assumed that in the 1st millennium BC Nanāja had become the equal of Ištar, stimulating the development of her cult.

Thus, to put it briefly, Nanāja started out in Mesopotamia as an independent goddess of love, fertility and protection in the Ur III period. Upon identification with Inanna in that same period (the genealogy of the two goddesses is not without importance in this regard), she became separate again as a goddess of physical love. In the 1st millennium BC her cult developed due to the full (secondary) identification with Ištar. It was then that Nanāja gained a spouse, Nabû, recognized as the son of Marduk, the chief god of Babylonia. The strengthening of her position in the Neo-Babylonian and Persian periods was reflected by the rapid increase in the number of personal names evoking the Nanāja name as an element. In my opinion, this was what permitted the memory of the goddess to be sustained until as late as AD 1000.

APPENDIX
THE PERIPHERIES

The cult of Nanāja spread beyond the borders of Mesopotamia proper in topographical terms and from a chronological point of view existed in Mesopotamia not only after the Persians conquered Babylon in 539 BC and in the era of the Achaemenids (as confirmed by the discussed cuneiform sources), but also after the death of Alexander the Great. These "peripheries" of space and time are presented here briefly.

The territory of Mesopotamia's eastern neighbor Elam, the region of Susa specifically, opens a discussion of Nanāja's manifestations in the peripheries. At least since the early 5th millennium BC the two regions shared very close cultural relations. The Elamites adopted Inanna into their pantheon of gods along with the Semitic Ištar, Sîn and Adad. In turn, the Elamite divinities were known in Mesopotamia. In the period of Seleucid domination, coins found at Susa represented Greek deities (Artemis and Apollo foremost), and the texts – specifically documents enfranchising slaves from the 3rd and 2nd century BC – cited Nanāja and mentioned a sanctuary of this goddess. Consequently, it is safe to conclude that Nanāja retained an important position in the Susa pantheon despite the appearance of Greek divinities after the Macedonian and Greek conquest. This naturally assumes that Nanāja was present earlier in the pantheon of Susa. G. Le Rider fails to explain the situation when writing of the goddess:[484] "Arrivée à Suse au III millénaire, (...)." Neither does G. Azarpay do so (citing G. Le Rider):[485] "At Susa, where the cult of Nanâ had been introduced from Mesopotamia as early as the third millennium BC, Nanâ's worship continued into the Seleucid age when the goddess was named as the principal deity of that city." The Old Elamite texts do not mention the name of Nanāja, hence the above statements seem doubtful at best. Priests from Uruk must have had contacts with Susa in the 3rd millennium BC and these

---

484 G. Le Rider, MDP XXXVII, p. 292 at the bottom and p. 293.

485 G. Azarpay, *JAOS* 96 (1976), p. 537b.

must not have been always of a peaceful nature, considering that around 2300-2200 BC a statue of Nanāja was carried off to Elam as loot (Aššur-bāni-apli says in his inscription that 1637 or 1537 years had passed from this act). Was it this date that the above cited scholars had in mind?[486]

Next M. Boyce and F. Grenet wrote:[487] "Nevertheless the temple of Nanaia, continuously maintained — possibly on the same spot — since the cult of the goddess had been brought from Erech in the twelfth century BC, remained the most prestigious temple of Susa; (...)." The authors were presumably referring to the raid by the Elamite ruler Šutruk-naḫḫunte in 1160 BC. It was then that the stele of Naram-Sîn and the obelisk with Hammurabi's codex were carried off, and a few years later the statue of Marduk. A statue of Nanāja may have also gone to Susa at this time. In a footnote Boyce and Grenet refer the reader to the second volume of *The History of Zoroastrianism*, p. 31, where we learn: "In the middle of the second millennium a king of Elam had carried off Nanâ's statue from Erech and set it up in Susa, where it remained, the object of veneration, until Assurbanipal seized it in the seventh century and restored it to Erech. Nanâ's cult continued nevertheless to flourish in Susa, where reference is made to it in the Seleucid times." I am not aware of any reason for this author's indicating of the middle of the 2nd millennium BC.

Despite Nanāja's continued veneration in Seleucid times, her representations never appeared on the coins. On the other hand, there is absolutely no proof that the Greeks in this period distinguished between Nanāja and Artemis whose image on the coins was very frequent. The dichotomy between local and official worship lasted until the 1st century BC (under Parthian rule in the region) when coins from around 110 BC were decorated with an image of an Oriental divinity dressed in long robes and a *polos*. This divinity is commonly

---

486 See "A modest proposal", in the article of D. T. Potts, S.R.A.A. VII (2001), p. 28-31. In his opinion, Susa is "the obvious sources of diffusion for the cult of Nana to the societies of Central Asia."

487 M. Boyce, F. Grenet, *A History of Zoroastrianism* III, Leiden 1991, p. 37.

assumed to be Artemis-Nanāja and the fact that it appears on coins is construed as evidence for the official introduction of coexisting Oriental deities into the Greek pantheon of Susa and the acceptance of the existing syncretism between Nanāja and Artemis (by bestowing Oriental accents upon them).[488] After the fall of the Parthian dynasty in Susa (around AD 45), bronze coins struck by the rulers of Elymais continued to represent a goddess that is to be identified as Artemis-Nanāja.[489]

Elymais of the Classical authors existed in the southwestern parts of Iran from the 2nd century BC to the early 3rd century AD. Surviving evidence lets it to be viewed as a successor to the Elamites.[490] In 164 BC, the Seleucid king Antioch IV attempted to desecrate the temple in Elymais (I Book of the Maccabees 6, 1-4). In the II Book of the Maccabees (1, 13-15) this temple is attributed to Nanāja (Gr. *nanaîon*). Although as a historical source the latter book should be treated with caution, it does mention a sacred marriage rite: Antioch IV entered the temple under the pretence of consuming this act with Nanāja and was then murdered there along with his companions by the priests of the goddess.

Elymaeans worshipped a goddess who drew from the Semitic Ištar and Nanāja, as well as perhaps from the Old Persian cult of a Venus deity. The goddess was assimilated with a Zoroastrian deity, Aredvī Sūra Anāhitā,[491] a river goddess connected with a fertility cult who enjoyed great veneration under the Achaemenid ruler Artaxerxes II (404-359 BC). J. Hansman has suggested,[492] that "the Elymaeans possibly worshipped the Iranian Anāhitā, and not the Semit-

---

488 G. Le Rider, *op. cit.*, p. 296 adds that the designation Artemis-Nanāja could also be used in reference to a deity appearing on the reverse of bronze coins of Hyspaosin from Characenos, minted between 120 and 110 BC.

489 J. Hansman is of a different opinion, being convinced that these representations should be interpreted as images of Artemis-Ištar (J. Hansman, Acta Iranica X, p. 233).

490 E. Herzfeld, *The Persian Empire*, Wiesbaden 1968, p. 189.

491 *Encyclopedia Iranica*, vol. 1/2, *item*: Anāhīd, p. 1003-1011.

492 J. Hansman, Acta Iranica X, p. 234.

ic Ishtar-Nana, or an Elamite deity with whom Anāhitā may have been syncretized."

A well preserved rock carving from Tang-i Sarvak in Elymaean territory and the accompanying inscription dated to the 2nd century AD depict an armed female figure among others. According to H. Seyrig,[493] who tended to connect all the gods appearing here with Zoroastrian religion, this figure was an image of Anahita-Athena; W. B. Henning,[494] in turn, saw in this figure the local goddess Anahita, meaning Nanāja. In his opinion, Tang-i Sarvak was a sanctuary of Bēl (and Nanāja presumably as well), the sacred coronation site of Elymaean kings of the 2nd century. Assuming the Elymaeans had succeeded the Elamites, one cannot but assume as well that they took over the religion with all of its Semitic connotations.

The Greek inscriptions from Susa (more appropriately from Seleucia-on-the-Eulaios) from the 2nd century BC confirm the cult of Nanāja. As said earlier, these are acts documenting the enfranchisement of slaves, which led the first scholars (F. Cumont, B. Haussouiller and P. Koschaker) to surmise that the released slaves were sacred prostitutes from the temple of Nanāja. Yet this goddess is merely a guarantor of the slave girls' newly obtained freedom (what's more, the texts also concern male slaves). It should be added that contrary to the Neo-Babylonian period when a temple slave could not be released,[495] in the Hellenistic period temples participated in the practice of freeing their slaves. The said acts, written down in Greek, mention the goddess Nanāja,[496] but are drawn up according to Greek law. These persons were offered to the goddess Nanāja (as the chief deity of Susa) and hence were freed from their previous dependence.

The cult of a deity called Nana – Lady (nnδm'βn)[497] is confirmed in distant Sogdiana, situated on the northeastern borders of the Sas-

---

[493] H. Seyrig, *Syria* XLVII (1970), p. 115-116.
[494] W. B. Henning, *Asia Major* XI (1952), p. 160.
[495] G. Ch. Sarkisjan is of this opinion, cf. *Drevnij Vostok* 5, p. 47.
[496] In five documents preserving the names of deities (SEG VII 15; 17; 18; 22; 24), Nanāja occurs four times.
[497] W. B. Henning, *BSOAS* XXVIII (1965), p. 252 and note 67.

sanid empire. There is a letter written in the 4th century by a Sogdanian merchant of the name of Nanaj-vandak ("Worshipper of Nanāja").[498] Numerous personal names of the 7th-9th centuries AD were also constructed with the Nana element.[499] Also from the same period is a mural depicting a four-armed goddess, identified commonly with Nanāja,[500] sitting on the back of a lion.

The Iranian (Old Persian) Anāhitā also bears the name Nanā, which could be related to the Iranian word for "mother" (*nana*) as an epithet proper for a female divinity. She was venerated in connection with the cult rituals of Ištar-Dumuzi, possibly substantiating the conviction that she was a goddess of love and fertility.

Silver coins (*drachmae*) from Central Asia, dated to the late first century BC, bear on the reverse a standing lion figure and the lunar crescent, surrounded by the name of Nanaia (written in Greek).[501]

An armed goddess, believed to be Nanāja, was represented on Kushan coins of the 3rd and 4th century.[502] The identification is confirmed by inscriptions (Greek and Kushan), placed next to an anthropomorphic representation of the goddess.[503]

Silver vessels from the 7th-9th centuries discovered in the territories of Choresm bear images of a four-armed goddess, who is also identified with Nanāja. Buddhist art (from the region of Chinese Turkestan) depicts a personified earth shown as a four-armed goddess sitting on a throne – Saka Śśandramata. According to G. Azarpay,[504] "it testifies rather to a mutual relationship in the conception of the two groups of divine images."

---

498 S. Dalley, *JAC* 12 (1997), p. 34.
499 W. B. Henning, *BSOAS* XII (1948), p. 602-603.
500 K. Tanabe, *Orient* XXX-XXXI (1975), p. 309-334.
501 *Ibid.*, p. 326, fig. 2.
502 M. Boyce, *A History of Zoroastrianism* II, Leiden 1982, p. 224 and note 75.
503 K. Tanabe, *op. cit.*, p. 326, fig. 3; R. Göbl, *System und Chronologie der Münzprägung der Kušanreiches*, Wien 1984, p. 19, 43, 76, pl. 167-168; C. Ambos, *ZA* 93/2 (2004), p. 259-265.
504 G. Azarpay, *JAOS* 96 (1976), p. 541.

The cult of Nanāja is also confirmed in territories lying further to the west and southwest of Mesopotamia. J. G. Février,[505] J. Teixidor[506] and M. Gawlikowski[507] have discussed this goddess as a deity of Palmyra, where she appears as the spouse of Nabû and is also mentioned in the inscriptions on *tesserae*[508] (from the 1st to the 3rd century) beside other divinities, most frequently Herta. Three *tesserae* (nos 285, 286 and 310) also preserve her image. On the first *tesserae*, she is depicted as a young woman in a short double chiton, holding a bow in her left hand and with her right drawing an arrow from a quiver across her back. The inscription which accompanies the image on tessera no. 285 runs as follows: NNY ŠKNY ŠY'T BBL "Nanāja, Šaknāja, doing good from Babylon" (perhaps Šaknāja should be identified with Herta, who appears most frequently next to Nanāja in the inscriptions). Nanāja's cult was indubitably known in Palmyra even before the beginning of our era, as evinced by inscriptions of the 6th century BC. This inscription mentioned Herta, Nanāja and Rešef.[509] Even so, as M. Gawlikowski reports,[510] personal names with the NNY element have yet to come to light in Palmyra.

The town of Dura Europos, established by the Seleucids in the end of the 4th century BC on the Euphrates, had a temple dedicated to Artemis. F. Cumont[511] was the first to assume that the goddess

505 J. G. Février, *La Religion des Palmyréniens*, Paris 1931, p. 99-102 (Nanaï).
506 J. Teixidor, *The Pantheon of Palmyra*, Leiden 1979.
507 M. Gawlikowski, *Les dieux de Palmyre*, ANRW II, 18/4 (1990), p. 2645.
508 H. Ingholt, H. Seyrig, J. Stracky, *Recueil des tessères de Palmyre*, Paris 1955, p. 194, (no 134, 238-242, 285) and C. du Mesnil du Buisson, *Les Tessères et les Monnaies de Palmyre*, Paris 1962, p. 381-385; cf. also J. Cantineau, *Syria* XVII (1936), p. 268-271; C. Ambos, *ZA* 93/2 (2003), p. 245-246, indicating the possibility of there being a figure of Nanāja on a relief in the peristyle of the Temple of Bēl (goddess with a bow identified as Nanāja, Allat or Atargatis).
509 J. Cantineau, *op. cit.*
510 M. Gawlikowski, *Recueil d'inscriptions palmyréniennes provenant de fouilles syriennes et polonaises récentes à Palmyre*, Paris 1973, p. 99.
511 F. Cumont, *Fouilles de Doura Europos (1922-1923). Texte*, Paris 1926, p. 196.

worshipped there was Nanāja, a local "incarnation" of Artemis. Others followed his thinking which was based on the Oriental characteristics imparted on images of this Greek goddess. This theory is currently believed to be erroneous,[512] despite the fact that the name of Nanāja is a theophoric element of personal names.

In the opinion of F. Vattioni,[513] Syrian Hatra (1st century AD) also worshipped Nanāja, who appeared there in a triad of divinities (*mrn* "our Lord", *mrtn* "our Lady", *brmrjn* – "son of our Lady" or "son of a pair of deities"). This triad also appears in inscriptions and has been interpreted variously. According to W. Al-Salihi,[514] the deity *mrn* should be identified with the sun god Šamaš, *mrtn* with Ištar-Atargatis, and *brmrjn* with the moon god Sîn. B. Aggoula[515] suggested a different identification of the triad: *mrn* – Šamaš, *mrtn* – Nanāja, *brmrjn* – Dionysos. Coming from the middle of the 2nd century AD is a statue of the goddess Nanāja[516] bearing an inscription. It is a female figure in a long robe and a tall tiara on the head, holding a long staff in her hand, the name of the goddess occurs also as a theophoric element of the personal names evidenced for this city.

Aramaic texts recorded in Demotic writing, representing the New Year liturgy celebrated in the 1st millennium BC in the territory of what was formerly Syene (now Assuan) by exiles from the city of Raš,[517] is further proof of the spreading of the cult of Nanāja. The ceremony took place in the seventh month of the year, in the New Year chapel, and was connected with the sacred marriage ritual. A statue of the goddess Marah – Queen *rš*, identified with Nanāja, was carried to the assembly of the gods, who then rose and commanded the goddess to sit on a throne among them. Each deity was requested to utter a blessing for the king. This ceremony was accompanied by

512 Cf. M. Gawlikowski, LIMC VIII/2, s.v. NANAI, p. 865.
513 F. Vattioni, *Le Inscrizioni di Ḥatra*, Suppl. n. 28 agli *AION* 14 (1981), fasc. 3, Napoli 1981.
514 W. Al-Salihi, *Sumer* 31 (1975), p. 75-80.
515 B. Aggoula, *Archéologia* 102 (1977), p. 52.
516 C. Ambos, *ZA* 93/2 (2003), p. 240.
517 R. Steiner, *JAOS* 111 (1991), p. 362-363.

offerings and singing. The feast was combined with the sacred marriage rites between the king and Nanāja. The culmination point came when Nanāja exchanged blessings with Baal and the king uttered a promise to rebuild the destroyed capital of *rš*.

The ties with the sacred marriage rites of the Ur III and Isin-Larsa periods are self-evident, especially in the part where the king (in this text identified with the god Baal) was coupled with Nanāja (here represented by her statue).

A *pithos* sherd discovered at Aššur from the Parthian period depicts five persons and a text in Aramaic. Accepting the explanation of crossing captions under the representations proposed by J. T. Milik,[518] the second figure from the left, depicted resting on a bedstead, is Nanāja. She is dressed in a cloak decorated with crescents. Her caption runs as follows: "Figure of Nanāja, Queen, our Lady, daughter of Bēl, Lord of the Gods." Other captions mention the temple of Nanāja and her servants (presumably freed slaves), while the second, damaged line of the inscription reads: "and he is ... and victorious forever thanks to Nanāja."

For the Roman period we have an inscription from Pireus, in which the author approaches the goddess Artemis-Nanāja.[519]

In the Syrian acts of the saintly Mu'ain we read of king Shapur II commanding in year AD 379 that offerings be made to Zeus, the great god, Nanāja, the great goddess of the entire world and the powerful gods Bēl and Nebo.[520]

In their article on Late Babylonian divinities occurring in Mandeian texts[521] (recorded after the Arab conquest of Mesopotamia),

---

[518] J. T. Milik, *Dédicaces faites par des dieux (Palmyre, Hatra, Tyr) et des thiases sémitique à l'époque romaine*, Paris 1972, p. 344-352. See also C. Ambos, *ZA* 93/2 (2003), p. 238-240.

[519] C.I.A. III, 131; cf. G. Hoffmann, Abhandlungen für die Kunde des Morgenlandes 7, Leipzig 1880, p. 156.

[520] G. Hoffmann, *op. cit.*, p. 131 and note 1122.

[521] Ch. Müller-Kessler, K. Kessler, *ZA* 89 (1999), p. 65-87 (p. 75-77 are devoted to Nanāja). See also Ch. Müller-Kessler, in: J. Renger (ed.), *Babylon*, Saarbrücken 1999, p. 433-434 (BM 135794 Ia, l. 16-17).

Ch. Müller-Kessler and K. Kessler list also the goddess Nanāja from Borsippa (next to Bēl, Ištar and Nabû). She bears the title of "Lady of the World", but magic appears to be her main domain.

The Syrian lexicographer Bar Bahlul writing around AD 1000 mentioned Nanāja in his Syrian-Arabic dictionary, explaining that it was the name with which the "Arabs" designated the planet Venus.[522]

522 Cf. R. Duval (ed.), *Lexicon Syriacum Auctore Hassano, Bar Bahlule*, Paris 1888-1901, p. 244 (reprint Amsterdam 1970). The term "Arabs" in this case refers to the settled Arabs.

BIBLIOGRAPHY

1 and 2 Machabean Books, Bible in translation of Bp K. Romaniuk, Warszawa 1997.

Al-Salihi, W., "New Light on the Identity of the Triad of Hatra", *Sumer* 31 (1975), p. 75-80.

Alster, B., "Marriage and Love in the Sumerian Love Songs", in: M. E. Cohen, D. C. Snell, D. B. Weisberg (eds), *The Tablet and the Scroll, Studies Hallo*, Bethesda 1993, p. 15-27.

Ambos, C., "Nanaja – eine ikonographische Studie zur Darstellung einer altorientalischen Göttin in hellenistisch-partischer Zeit", *ZA* 93/2 (2003), p. 231-272.

Archi, A., Pomponio, F., *Testi cuneiformi neo-sumerici da Drehem*, Mailand 1980.

Arnaud, D., "Deux *kudurru* de Larsa, II: Ètude épigraphique", *RA* LXVI (1972), p. 163-176.

Arnaud, D., *Emar. Textes de bibliothèque, transcriptions et traductions*, Emar VI/4, Paris 1987.

Arnaud, D., "Un document juridique concernant les oblats", *RA* LXVII (1973), p. 147-156.

Assante, J., "Sex, Magic and the Liminal Body in the Erotic Art and Texts of the Old Babylonian Period", in: CRRAI 47/1, p. 25-52.

Azarpay, G., "Nanâ, the Sumero-Akkadian Goddess of Transoxiana", *JAOS* 96 (1976), p. 536-542.

Bauer, Th., *Das Inschriftenwerk Assurbanipals* II, Leipzig 1933.

Beaulieu, P.-A., *The Pantheon of Uruk during the Neo-Babylonian Period*, CM 23, Leiden 2003.

Beaulieu, P.-A., "Antiquarian Theology in Seleucid Uruk", *ASJ* 14 (1992), p. 47-75.

Beaulieu, P.-A., "Textes administratifs inédits d'époque hellenistique provenant des archives du Bīt Reš", *RA* LXXXIII (1989), p. 53-87.

Beaulieu, P.-A., *The Reign of Nabonidus, King of Babylon 556-539 B.C.*, YNER 10, New Haven – London 1989.

Beaulieu, P.-A., "Un inventaire de joaillerie sacrée de l'Eanna d'Uruk", *RA* 93 (1999), 141-155.

Behrens, H., Loding, D., Roth, M. T. (eds), DUMU-E$_2$-DUB-BA-A, *Studies in Honor of A. W. Sjöberg*, Occasional Publications of S. N. Kramer Fund 11, Philadelphia 1989.

Bezold, C., *Catalogue of the Cuneiform Tablets in the Kouyunjik Collection of the British Museum* I-V, London 1889-1899.

Biggs, R. D., ŠA$_3$.ZI.GA, *Ancient Mesopotamian Potency Incantations*, TCS II, New York 1967.

Black, J. A., "A-še-er Gi$_6$-ta, a balag of Inana", *ASJ* 7 (1985), p. 11-87.

Black, J. A., "Babylonian Ballads: A New Genre", *JAOS* 103/1 (1983), p. 25 ff.

Black, J. A., *Sumerian Grammar in Babylonian Theory*, Romae 1984.

Black, J. A., Green, A., *Gods, Demons and Symbols of Ancient Mesopotamia. An Illustrated Dictionary*, London 1992.

Bongenaar, A. C. V. M., *The Neo-Babylonian Ebabbar Temple at Sippar: Its Administration and its Prosopography*, Leiden 1997.

Borger, R., *Beiträge zum Inschriftenwerk Assurbanipals*, Wiesbaden 1996.

Borger, R., *Die Inschriften Asarhaddons Königs von Assyrien*, *AfO* Beiheft 9, Graz 1956.

Boyce, M., *A History of Zoroastrianism* III, Leiden 1991.

Boyce, M., Grenet, F., *A History of Zoroastranism* II, Leiden 1982.

Buisson, M. du, *Les Tesséres et les Monnaises de Palmyre*, Paris 1962.

Cantineau, J., "Tadmorea", *Syria* XVIII (1936), p. 268-271.

Cassin, E., Glassner, J. J., *Anthroponymie et Anthropologie de Nuzi* I, Malibu 1977.

Cavigneaux, A., *Texts from Babylon. Textes scolaires du Temple de Nabû ša ḫarê* I, Baghdad 1981.

Cavigneaux, A., Boehmer, R. M., *Uruk. Altbabylonische Texte aus dem Planquadrat PE XVI-4/5*, AUWE 23, Mainz 1996.

Charpin, D., *Le clergé d'Ur au siècle d'Hammurabi*, Genève – Paris 1986.

Charpin, D., "Nouveaux textes de la «Dynastie de Mananâ» III", *RA* LXXIV (1980), p. 111-128.

Chiera, E., *Old Babylonian Contracts*, PBS VIII/2, Philadelphia 1922.

Çig, M., Kızılyay, H., Salonen, A., *Die Puzriš-Dagan-Texte der Istanbuler Archäologischen Museen* I, Helsinki 1954/1956.

Civil, M., "A New Lipit-Eštar Inscription", *N.A.B.U.* 1997/3, no 98.

Civil, M., "Correction to N.A.B.U. 1997/98", *N.A.B.U.* 1998/2, no 57.

Clay, A. T., *Babylonian Business Transactions of the First Millennium B.C.*, BRM I, New York 1912.

Clay, A. T., *Business Documents of Murashû Sons of Nippur dated in the Reign of Darius II*, BE X, Philadelphia 1904.

Clay, A. T., *Business Documents of Murashû Sons of Nippur dated in the Reign of Darius II*, PBS II/1, Philadelphia 1912.

Clay, A. T., *Epics, Hymns, Omens and other Texts*, BRM IV, New Haven 1923.

Clay, A. T., *Legal and Commercial Transactions, dated in the Assyrian, Neo-Babylonian and Persian Periods, chiefly from Nippur*, BE VIII/1, Philadelphia 1908.

Clay, A. T., *Legal Documents from Erech dated in the Seleucid era (312-65 B.C.)*, BRM II, New York 1913.

Clay, A. T., *Neo-Babylonian Letters from Erech*, YOS 3, New Haven – London 1919.

Clay, A. T., *Personal Names from Cuneiform Inscriptions of the Cassite Period*, YOS 1, New Haven 1912.

Cogan, M., *Imperialism and Religion: Assyria, Judah and Israel in the Eight and Seventh Centuries B.C.E.*, Missoula 1974.

Cohen, M. E., *Sumerian Hymnology: The Eršemma*, Cincinnati 1981.

Cohen, M. E., *The Canonical Lamentations of Ancient Mesopotamia* I-II, Ann Arbor 1988.

Cohen, M., *The Cultic Calendars of the Ancient Near East*, Bethesda 1993.

Cohen, M. E., Snell, D. C., Weisberg D. B. (eds), *The Tablet and the Scroll. Near Eastern Studies in Honor of W. W. Hallo*, Bethesda 1993.

Cole, S. W., "The Crime and Sacrileges of Nabû-šuma-iškun", *ZA* 84/2 (1994), p. 220-252.

Collon, D., *Catalogue of the Western Asiatic Seals in the British Museum III. Isin-Larsa and Old Babylonian Periods*, London 1986.

Contenau, G., *Contrats néo-babyloniens* I-II, Paris 1927, 1929.

Cooper, J. S., "VAT 8411. A Sumerian šu-il$_2$-la from Nimrud with a prayer for Sin-šar-iškun", *Iraq* 32 (1950), p. 51-67.

Craig, J. A., *Assyrian and Babylonian Religious Texts* I, Leipzig 1895.

Cumont, F., *Fouilles de Doura-Europos (1922-1923)*, Paris 1926.

Dalley, S., "Babylonian Influence in the Far East throught the Buddha and Mani", *JAC* 12 (1997), p. 25-35.

Degraeve, A., "Mesopotamia and its Nothern Neighbours, Part I", *Akkadica* 99-100 (1996), p. 15-35.

Deimel, A., *Pantheon Babylonicum*, Romae 1914.

Deimel, A., *Šumerisches Lexikon*, Teil II, Roma 1928-1933

Delitzsch, F., *Assyrische Grammatik*, Berlin 1906.

Dhorme, E., "La fille de Nabonide", *RA* XI (1914), p. 105-117.

Dietrich, M., Loretz, O., dubsar an-ta men. *Studien zur Altorientalistik, Festschrift für W. H. Ph. Römer*, AOAT 253, Münster 1998.

Dijk, J. J. van, *Textes divers*, TLB II, Leiden 1957.

Dijk, J. J. van, Goetze, A., Hussey, M. I., *Early Mesopotamian Incantations and Rituals*, YBT XI, New Haven – London 1985.

Dossin, G., "Le panthéon de Mari", in: A. Parrot (ed.), *Studia Mariana*, Leiden 1950, p. 14-50.

Dossin, G., "Un 'panthéon' d'Ur III à Mari", *RA* LXI (1967), p. 97-104.

Doty, L. T., "Akkadian *bīt pirišti*", Studies Hallo, p. 87-89.

Dougherty, R. P., *Archives from Erech, Neo-Babylonian and Persian Period*, GCCI II, New Haven 1933.

Dougherty, R. P., *Archives from Erech, Time of Nebuchadrezzar and Nabonidus*, GCCI I, New Haven 1923.

Dougherty, R. P., *Records from Erech, Time of Nabonidus (555-538 B.C.)*, YOS 6, New Haven 1920.

Durand, J.-M., "A propos du 'Panthéon d'Ur III à Mari'", *RA* LXXIV (1980), p. 174-176.

Durand, J.-M., *Catalogue of the Babylonian Tablets in the British Museum*, vol. II, London 1996.

Durand, J.-M., *Documents cunéiformes de la IVe Séction de l'École Pratique de Hautes Études*, T. I: *Catalogue et copies cunéiformes*, Genève – Paris 1982.

Duval, R., *Lexicon Syriacum auctore Hassano, Bar Bahlule* I, Paris 1888-1901 (reprint Amsterdam 1970).

Dyckhoff, Ch. B., "Priester und Priesterinnen im altbabylonischen Larsa. Das Amtsarchiv als Grundlage für prosopographische Forschung", in: CRRAI 47/1, p. 123-127.

Ebeling, E., "Beiträge zur Kenntnis der Beschwörungsserie Namburbi", *RA* XLIX/4 (1955), p. 178-192.

Ebeling, E., "Ein Hymnen-Katalog aus Assur", Berliner Beiträge zur Keilschriftforschung 1/III, Berlin 1923, p. 1-23.

Ebeling, E., "Ein Preislied auf die Kultstadt Arba-ilu aus neuassyrischer Zeit", *JkF* II/3 (1953), p. 274-282.

Ebeling, E., *Keilschrifttexte aus Assur juristischen Inhalts*, Lepzig 1927.

Ebeling, E., *Keilschrifttexte aus Assur religiösen Inhalts* I-II, Leipzig 1919, 1923.

Ebeling, E., *Literarische Keilschrifttexte aus Assur*, Berlin 1953.

Ebeling, E., "Sammlungen von Beschwörungsformeln", *ArOr* XXI (1953), p. 357-423.

Edzard, D. O., *Altbabylonische Rechts- und Wirtschaftsurkunden aus Tell ed-Dēr im Iraq Museum*, TIM 7, Baghdad – Wiesbaden 1971.

Edzard, D. O., "Kanisurra", RlA V, p. 389.

Edzard, D. O., "Nanaja", in: H. W. Haussig (ed.), *Wörterbuch der Mythologie* 1, Stuttgart 1952, p. 108.

Edzard, D. O., "Pantheon und Kult in Mari", in: CRRAI 15, p. 51-71.

Ellis, M. de Jong (ed.), *Nippur at the Centennial. Papers Read at the 35e Rencontre Assyriologique Internationale, Philadelphia, 1988.* Occasional Publications of the Samuel Noah Kramer Fund 14, Philadelphia 1992.

Evetts, E. T. A., *Inscriptions of the Reign of Evil Merodach, Neriglissar and Laborosoarchod*, BT 6B, Leipzig 1892.

Fales, F. M., Postgate, J. N. (eds), *Imperial Administrative Records, Part I*, SAA VII, Helsinki 1992.

Falkenstein, A., "Ein sumerisches Lied auf König Anam", *BaghM* 2 (1963), p. 80-82.

Falkenstein, A., *Literarische Keilschrifttexte aus Uruk*, Berlin 1931.

Falkenstein, A., "Sumerische religiöse Texte", *ZA* 49/NF 15 (1949), p. 80-150.

Falkenstein, A., *Topographie von Uruk I*, Leipzig 1941.

Falkenstein, A., "Zu den Inschriftenfunden der Grabung in Uruk-Warka 1960-1961", *BaghM* 2 (1963), p. 1-79.

Falkenstein, A., Soden von, W., *Sumerische und akkadische Hymnen und Gebete*, Zürich – Stuttgart 1953.

Farber, W. *et al.*, *Religiöse Texte. Rituale und Beschwörungen* I. Texte aus der Umwelt des Alten Testaments II/2, Gütersloh 1987.

Faust, D. E., *Contracts from Larsa dated in the Reign of Rîm-Sin*, YOS 8, New Haven 1941.

Feigin, S. I., *Legal and Administrative Texts of the Reign of Samsu-iluna*, YOS 12, New Haven – London 1979.

Février, J. G., *La Réligion de Palmyréniens*, Paris 1931.

Figulla, H., *Business Documents of the New-Babylonian Period*, UET IV, London 1949.

Figulla, H. H., Martin W. J., *Lettres and Documents of the Old-Babylonian Period*, UET V, London 1953.

Finet, A. (ed.), *Actes de la XVII RAI*, Ham-sur-Heure 1970.

Finkel, I. L., Geller, M. J. (eds), *Sumerian Gods and their Representations*, CM 7, Groningen 1997.

Finkelstein, J. J., *Late Old-Babylonian Documents and Letters*, YOS 13, London – New Haven 1972.

Foster, B. R., *Before the Muses. An Anthology of Akkadian Literature*, Betheshda 1993.

Frame, G., "ABL 1274 and the Careers of Sîn-šarra-uṣur and Sîn-tabni-uṣur", *N.A.B.U.* 2004/3, no. 69.

Frame, G., "Nabonidus, Nabû-šarra-uṣur, and the Eanna Temple", *ZA* 81/1 (1991), p. 37-86.

Frame, G., *Rulers of Babylonia. From the Second Dynasty of Isin to the End of Assyrian Domination (1157-612 B.C.)*, RIMB 2, Toronto 1995.

Frankena, R., *Tākultu, de sacrale maaltijd in het Assyrische Ritueel*, Leiden 1954.

Frayne, D., *Old Babylonian Period (2003-1595 B.C.)*, RIME 4, Toronto 1990.

Freydank, H., *Spätbabylonische Wirtschaftstexte aus Uruk*, Deutsche Akademie der Wissenschaften zu Berlin, Institut für Orientforschung 71, Berlin 1971.

Friedrich, T., *Altbabylonischen Urkunden aus Sippara*, BA 5/4, Leipzig 1906, p. 413 ff.

Gadd, C. J., *Cuneiform Texts from Babylonian tablets*, vol. 36, London 1921.

Gadd, C. J., Kramer, S. N., *Literary and Religious Texts*, Part II, UET VI/2, London 1966.

Gautier, I. E., *Archives d'une famille de Dilbat au temps de la première dynastie de Babylone*, Mémoires publiés par les membres de l'Institut Français d'archéologie orientale du Caire, 26, Le Caire 1908.

Gawlikowski, M., "NANAI", in: LIMC VIII/2, p. 865.

Gawlikowski, M., *Recueil d'inscriptions palmyréniennes provenant de fouilles syriennes et polonais récentes à Palmyre*, Paris 1973.

Gehlken, E., *Uruk. Spätbabylonische Wirtschaftstexte aus dem Eanna-Archiv*, Teil I, AUWE 5, Mainz am Rhein 1990.

Gehlken, E., *Uruk. Spätbabylonische Wirtschaftstexte aus dem Eanna-Archiv*, Teil II, AUWE 11, Mainz am Rhein 1996.

Gelb, I. J., Purves, P. M., MacRae, A. A., *Nuzi Personal Names*, OIP 57, Chicago 1943.

Genouillac de, H., "Grande liste de noms divins sumériens", *RA* XX (1923), p. 89-106.

Genouillac de, H., *Tablettes de Dréhem publiées avec inventaire et tables*, TCL II, Paris 1911.

Genouillac de, H., *Textes économiques d'Oumma de l'époque d'Our*, TCL V, Paris 1922.

George, A. R., "A Neo-Assyrian Literary Text", *SAAB* 1 (1987), p. 30-41.

George, A. R., *Babylonian Topographical Texts*, Part I-II, OLA 40, Leuven 1992.

George, A. R., *House Most High. The Temples of Ancient Mesopotamia*, Winona Lake 1993.

Gessel van, B. H. L., *Onomasticon of the Hittite Pantheon*, HdO 33, Leiden 1998.

Göbl, R., *System und Chronologie der Münzprägung der Kušānreiches*, Wien 1984.

Goedicke, H., Roberts, J. J. M. (eds), *Unity and Diversity*, Baltimore – London 1975.

Goetze, A., *Old Babylonian Omen Texts*, YOS 10, New Haven – London 1947.

Goetze, A., "Reports on Acts of Extispicy from Old Babylonian and Kassite Times", *JCS* 11 (1957), p. 89-105.

Goetze, A., "Sin-idinnam of Larsa, New Tablets from his Reign", *JCS* 4 (1950), p. 83 ff.

Gomi, T., "Ur III Texts in the John Rylands University Library of Manchester", *BJRL* 64 (1981/1982), p. 87-116.

Gomi, T., Sato, S., *Selected Neo-Sumerian Administrative Texts from the British Museum*, Tokyo 1990.

Gomi, T., Yıldız, F., *Die Puzriš-Dagan-Texte der Istanbuler-Archäologischen Museen* II, Stuttgart 1988.

Grayson, A. Kirk, *Assyrian Rulers of the Early First Millennium BC II (858-745 BC)*, RIMA 3, Toronto 2002

Grégoire, J.-P., *Archives administratives sumériennes*, Paris 1970.

Greengus, S., *Old Babylonian Tablets from Ischiali and Vicinity*, Leiden 1979.

Grice, E. M., *Records from Ur and Larsa dated in the Larsa Dynasty*, YOS 5, New Haven 1919.

Groneberg, B., "Ein Ritual an Ištar", MARI 8 (1997), p. 291-303.

Groneberg, B., "Liebes- und Hundebeschwörungen im Kontext", in: M. T. Roth *et al.* (eds), *Studies Presented to R. D. Biggs, June 4, 2004*, AS 27, Chicago 2004, p. 91-107.

Gurney, O. R., "Texts from Dur-Kurigalzu", *Iraq* 11 (1949), p. 131-149.

Gurney, O. R., Finkelstein, J. J., *The Sultantepe Tablets*, Part I, London 1957.

Gurney, O. R., Hulin, P., *The Sultantepe Tablets*, Part II, London 1964.

Güterbock, H. G., Jacobsen Th. (eds), *Studies in Honor of B. Landsberger on his seventy-fifth Birthday, April 21, 1965*, AS 16, Chicago 1965.

Haas, V., *Geschichte der hethitischen Religion*, Leiden 1994.

Haayer, G., "The Cuneiform Texts of the Bijbels Museum, Amsterdam", *JEOL* 26 (1979-1980), p. 47-52.

Haider, P. W., Hutter, M., Kreuzer, S. (eds), *Religionsgeschichte Syriens. Von der Frühzeit bis zur Gegenwart*, Stuttgart – Berlin – Köln 1996.

Hall, M. G., *A Study of Sumerian Moon-God Nanna/Suen*, Diss. Univ. of Chicago, 1953.
Hallo, W. W., "A Sumerian Amphictyony", *JCS* 14/3 (1960), p. 88-114.
Hallo, W. W., "New Hymns to the Kings of Isin", *BiOr* 23 (1966), 5/6 (1966), p. 239-247.
Hansman, J., "The Great Gods of Elymais", Acta Iranica X, Deuxième série, Leiden 1985, p. 229-246.
Harper, R. F., *Assyrian and Babylonian Letters belonging to the Kouyunjik Collection of the British Museum* I-XIV, London – Chicago 1892-1914.
Heidelberger Studien zum Alten Orient. Adam Falkenstein zum 17. September 1966, Wiesbaden 1967.
Heimpel, W., *A Catalogue of Near Eastern Venus Deities*, SMS 4/3, Malibu 1982.
Held, M., "A Faitful Lover in an Old Babylonian Dialogue", *JCS* 15 (1961), p. 1-26.
Held, M., "A Faitful Lover in an Old Babylonian Dialogue. Addenda et Corrigenda", *JCS* 16 (1962), p. 37-39.
Henning, W. B., "A Sogdian Gods", *BSOAS* XXVIII (1965), p. 242-254.
Henning, W. B., "The Date of the Sogdian Ancient Letters", *BSOAS* XII (1948), p. 601-615.
Henning, W. B., "The Monuments and Inscriptions of Tang-i Sarvak", *Asia Major* XI (1952), p. 151-178.
Herzfeld, E., *The Persian Empire*, Wiesbaden 1968.
Hilprecht, H. V., Clay, A. T., *Business Documents of Murashû Sons of Nippur dated in the Reign of Atraxerxes I*, BE IX, Philadelphia 1898.
Hinz, W., Koch, H., *Elamisches Wörterbuch*, Berlin 1987.
Hoffmann, G., "Auszüge aus Syrischen Akten Persischer Märtyrer", Abhandlungen für die Kunde des Morgenlandes 7, Leipzig 1880, p. 130-161.
Hrouda, B. (ed.), ISIN-IŠAN BAḪRĪYĀT III, München 1987.
Hrouda, B. (ed.), ISIN-IŠAN BAḪRĪYĀT IV, München 1992.
Hunger, H., "Das Archiv des Nabû-ušallim", *BaghM* 5 (1970), p. 193-304.
Hunger, H., *Spätbabylonische Texte aus Uruk* I, Berlin 1976.

Hunger, H., Pingree, D., MUL.APIN. *An Astronomical Compendium in Cuneiform*, *AfO* Beiheft 24, Horn 1989.

Hutter, M., *Religionen in der Umwelt des Alten Testaments*, I. *Babylonier, Syrier, Perser*, Stuttgart – Berlin – Köln 1996.

Ingholt, H., Seyrig, H., Starcky, J., *Recueil des tessères de Palmyre*, Paris 1955.

Jacobsen, Th., *Cuneiform Texts in the National Museum Copenhagen, Chiefly of Economical Contents*, Leiden 1939.

Jacobsen, Th., *The "Gimilsin" Temple and the Palace of the Rulers at Tell Asmar*, OIP 43, Chicago 1940.

Jakob-Rost, L., Freydank, H., *Spätbabylonische Rechtsurkunden und Wirtschaftstexte aus Uruk*, VAS XX, Berlin 1978.

Jean, Ch.-F., *Contrats de Larsa*, TCL X-XI, Paris 1926.

Jean, Ch.-F., *Le milieu biblique avant Jésus-Christ*, Part II: *La littérature*, Paris 1923.

Jean, Ch.-F., "Noms divins sumériens. Listes des élèves-scribes de Nippur du 3e millénaire environs avant J.-C.", *RA* XXVIII (1931), p. 179-194.

Jensen, P., *Texte zur assyrisch-babylonischen Religion*, KB 6/2, Berlin 1915 (Amsterdam 1970).

Joannès, F., "Les temples de Sippar et leurs trésors à l'époque néo-babylonienne", *RA* LXXXVI/2 (1992), p. 159-184.

Jones T., Snyder J., *Sumerian Economic Texts from the Third Ur Dynasty, a Catalogue and Discussion of Documents from Various Collections*, Minneapolis 1961.

Jursa, M., "Neu- und Spätbabylonische Texte aus den Sammlungen der Birmingham Museums and Art Gallery", *Iraq* LIX (1997), p. 97-174.

Kang, Sh. T., *Sumerian Economic Texts from the Drehem Archive*, SACT 1, Urbana 1972.

Kärki, I., *Die sumerischen Königsinschriften der frühaltbabylonischen Zeit*, Helsinki 1968.

Kärki, I., *Die sumerischen und akkadischen Königsinschriften der Altbabylonischen Zeit*, I. *Isin, Larsa, Uruk*; II. *Babylon*, StOr 49 and 55, Helsinki 1980 and 1983.

Keiser, C. E., *Letters and Contracts from Erech written in the Neo-Babylonian Period*, BIN I, New Haven 1917.

Keiser, C. E., *Neo-Sumerian Account Texts from Drehem*, BIN III, New Haven – London 1971.
Keiser, C. E., *Selected Temple Documents of the Ur Dynasty*, YOS 4, New Haven – Yale 1919.
Keiser, C. E., Nies, J. B., *Historical, Religious and Economic Texts and Antiquities*, BIN II, New Haven 1920.
Kennedy, D. A., *Cuneiform Texts from Babylonian Tablets*, vol. 49, London 1968.
Kienast, B., *Die Altbabylonischen Briefe und Urkunden aus Kisurra*, Teil I-II, FAOS 2, Wiesbaden 1978.
King, L. W., *Babylonian Boundary Stones*, London 1912.
King, L. W., *Cuneiform Texts from Babylonian Tablets*, vol. 25, London 1909.
King, L. W., *Cuneiform Texts from Babylonian Tablets*, vol. 26, London 1909.
King, L. W., *Cuneiform Texts from Babylonian Tablets*, vol. 33, London 1912.
Kingsbury, E. C., "A Seven Day Ritual in the Old Babylonian Cult at Larsa", *HUCA* 34 (1963), p. 1-34.
Knudtzon, J. A., *Assyrische Gebete an den Sonnengott für Staat und Königlisches Haus aus der Zeit Asarhaddons und Asurbanipals*, I-II, Leipzig 1893.
Köcher, F., "Ein mittelassyrisches Ritualfragment zum Neujahrsfest", *ZA* 50 (1952), p. 192-202.
Kohler, J., Peiser, F. E., *Aus dem babylonischen Rechtsleben*, 1-4, Leipzig 1890, 1891, 1894, 1898.
Kohler, J., Ungnad, A., *Assyrische Rechtsurkunden*, Leipzig 1913.
Kramer, S. N., *Sumerian Literary Texts from Nippur in the Museum of the Ancient Orient at Istanbul*, New Haven 1944.
Kramer, S. N., "The Death of Ur-Nammu", in: Fs Mikasa, p. 193-214.
Kraus, F. R., *Briefe aus Kleineren Westeuropäischen Sammlungen*, AbB 10, Leiden 1985.
Krebernik, M., "Die Textfunde der 9. Kampagnie (1986)", in: ISIN-IŠAN BAḪRĪYĀT IV, München 1992, p. 102-144.
Krebernik, M., "Mondgott", RlA VIII, p. 360-369.
Kümmel, H. M., *Familie, Beruf und Amt im spätbabylonischen Uruk. Prosopographische Untersuchungen zu Berufsgruppen des*

6. Jahrhunderts v.Chr. in Uruk, Abhandlungen der Deutschen Orient-Gesellschaft 20, Berlin 1979.
Kutscher, R., "A Torchlight Festival in Lagaš", *ASJ* 5 (1983), p. 59-66.
Lackenbacher, S., "Un nouveau fragment de la «Fête d'Ištar»", *RA* LXXI (1977), p. 39-50.
Lafont, B., "Quelques nouvelles tablettes dans les collections américaines", *RA* LXXXVI (1992), p. 97-111.
Lagarde, P. de, "Armenische Studien", Abhandlungen der Königlichen Gesellschaft der Wissenschaften zu Göttingen 22 (1877), p. 110, nr 1592.
Lambert, W. G., "A Babylonian Prayer to Anūna", in: DUMU-E_2-DUB-BA-A. Studies Sjöberg, Philadelphia 1989, p. 321-336.
Lambert, W. G., *Babylonian Wisdom Literature*, Oxford 1960.
Lambert, W. G., "Divine Love Lyrics from the Reign of Abi-ešuḫ", *MIO* XII/2 (1966), p. 41-56.
Lambert, W. G., "Götterlisten", RlA III, p. 473-479.
Lambert, W. G., "Processions to the Akītu House", *RA* XCI (1997), p. 49-80.
Lambert, W. G., "Syncretism and Religious Controversy in Babylonia", *AoF* 24/1 (1997), p. 158-162.
Lambert, W. G., "The Pantheon of Mari", MARI 4 (1985), p. 525-539.
Landersdorfer, P. S., "Das assyrisch-babylonische Pantheon im vierten Jahrhundert n. Chr.", *MVAG* 21 (1916), p. 109 ff.
Landsberger, B., "Einige unerkannt gebliebene oder verkannte Nomina des Akkadischen", *WO* III (1964), p. 48 ff.
Landsberger, B., Falkenstein, A., Jacobsen Th., *Emesal-Vocabulary*, MSL 4, I, Roma 1937.
Langdon, S., *Babylonian Liturgies*, Paris 1913.
Langdon, S., *Babylonian Penitential Psalms*, OECT VI, Paris 1927.
Langdon, S., "Calendars of Liturgies and Prayers", *AJSL* 42/2 (1926), p. 110-122.
Langdon, S., *Die Neubabylonische Königsinschriften*, Leipzig 1912.
Langdon, S., *Sumerian and Semitic Religious and Historical Texts*, OECT I, Oxford 1923.
Lapinkivi, P., *The Sumerian Sacred Marriage in the Light of Comparative Evidence*, SAAS XV, Helsinki 2004.
Laroche, E., *Les Noms des Hittites*, Paris 1966.

Le Rider, G., *Suse sous les Seleucides et les Parthes. Les trouvailles monétaires et l'histoire de la ville*, MDP XXXVII, Paris 1965.

Leemans, W. F., *Legal and Economic Records from the Kingdom of Larsa*, SLB 1/2, Leiden 1954.

Leemans, W. F., *Old Babylonian Legal and Administrative Documents*, TLB 1, Leiden 1954-1964.

Leeper, A., *Cuneiform Texts from Babylonian Tablets*, vol. 35, London 1918.

Legrain, L., *Business Documents of the Third Dynasty of Ur*, UET III, London 1937.

Legrain, L., *Le temps de rois d'Ur*, Paris 1912.

Legrain, L., *Seal Cylinders*, UE X, London – Philadelphia 1951.

Lehmann, C. F., *Šamaššumukîn, König von Babylonien*, Leipzig 1892.

Leick, G., *A Dictionary of Ancient Near Eastern Mythology*, London 1991.

Leick, G., *Sex and Eroticism in Mesopotamian Literature*, London – New York 1994.

Lenzen, H. J. von, Haller, A. von, Dijk, J. J. van, Strommenger, E., *XVIII. vorläufiger Bericht über die von dem Deutschen Archäologischen Institut und der Deutschen Orient-Gesellschaft aus Mitteln der Deutschen Forschungsgemeinschaft unternommenen Ausgrabungen in Uruk-Warka XVIII. Winter 1959/1960*, Berlin 1962.

Lewis, B., Jewell, E. R., "Sumerian Economic Texts from the Robert Hull Fleming Museum of the University of Vermont", *ASJ* 4 (1982), p. 53-68.

Limet, H., *Le travail du métal au pays de Sumer au temps de la III Dynastie d'Ur*, Paris 1960.

Lipiński, E., *Studies in Aramaic Inscriptions and Onomastics*, Leuven 1975.

Livingstone, A., *Court Poetry and Literary Miscellanea*, SAA III, Helsinki 1989.

Livingstone, A., *Mystical and Mythological Explanatory Works of Assyrian and Babylonian Scholars*, Oxford 1986.

Loding, D., *Economic Texts from the Third Dynasty*, UET IX, London 1976

Luckenbill, D. D., *Ancient Records of Assyria and Babylonia* I-II, Chicago 1926-1927.
Luckenbill, D. D., *The Annals of Sennacherib*, OIP 2, Chicago 1924.
Lutz, H. F., *Early Babylonian Letters from Larsa*, YOS 2, New Haven 1917.
Lutz, H. F., *Sumerian Temple Records of the Late Ur Dynasty*, UCP IX/2, Berkeley 1928.
Macmillan, K. D., *Some Cuneiform Tablets Bearing on the Religion of Babylonia and Assyria*, BA 5/5, Leipzig 1906, p. 531-712.
Maidman, M. P., *Two Hundred Nuzi Texts from the Oriental Institute of the University of Chicago*, Part I, SCCNH 6, Bethesda 1994.
Marchant, A. J., *Old Babylonian Tablets from Larsa in the Lowie Museum of Anthropology*, Diss. Univ. of California, Berkeley 1990.
Margolis, E., *Sumerian Temple Documents*, New York 1915.
Marti, L., "Les papiers du père Scheil", *N.A.B.U.* 2002/1, no. 25.
Martin, F., *Textes religieux assyriens et babyloniens*, Paris 1903.
Matsushima, E., "Divine Statues in Ancient Mesopotamia: their Fashioning and Clothing and their Interaction with the Society", in: E. Matsushima (ed.), *Official Cult and Popular Religion in the Ancient Near East*, Heidelberg 1993, p. 209-219.
Matsushima, E., "Le Rituel Hiérogamique de Nabû", *ASJ* 9 (1987), p. 131-175.
Matsushima, E., "Les Rituels du Mariage Divin dans les Documents Accadiens", *ASJ* 10 (1988), p. 95-128.
Matsushima, E., "Problèmes des deésses Tašmētum et Nanaia", *Orient* XVI (1980), p. 133-148.
Matsushima E., "Quelques problèmes supplémentaire de l'*elippu ša kusīti*", *Orient* XXX-XXXI (1995), p. 171-181.
Matsushima, E., "Quelques textes relatifs à l'*elippu ša kusīti*", in: H.I.H. Prince T. Mikasa (ed.), *Cult and Ritual in the Ancient Near East*, Wiesbaden 1992, p. 7-21.
Matsushima, E., "Some Remarks on the Divine Garments: *kusīti* and *naḫlaptu*", *ASJ* 17 (1995), p. 233-249.
Maul, S. M., *'Herzberuhigungsklagen'. Die sumerisch-akkadischen Eršaḫunga-Gebete*, Wiesbaden 1988.

Maul, S. M., "Zwei neue «Herzberuhingungsklagen»", *RA* LXXXV (1991), p. 67-74.

McEwan, G. J. P., *Late Babylonian Texts in the Ashmolean Museum*, OECT X, Oxford 1984.

McEwan, G. J. P., *Priests and Temple in the Hellenistic Babylonia*, FAOS 4, Wiesbaden 1981.

McEwan, G. J. P., *Texts from Hellenistic Babylonia in the Ashmolean Museum*, OECT IX, Oxford 1982.

Meer, P. E. van der, *Syllabaries A, B[1] and B with Miscellaneous Lexicographical Texts from the Herbert Weld Collection*, OECT IV, Oxford – London 1938

Meier, G., *Die Assyrische Beschwörungssamlung Maqlû*, *AfO* Beiheft 2, Berlin 1937.

Messerschmidt, L., Ungnad, A., *Vorderasiatische Schriftdenkmäler* I, Leipzig 1907.

Milik, T., *Dédicaces faites par des dieux (Palmyre, Hatra, Tyr) et des thiases sémitiques à l'époque romaine*, Paris 1972.

Miller, D. B., Shipp, R. M., *An Akkadian Handbook*, Winona Lake 1996.

Montgomery, J., *Aramaic Incantation Texts from Nippur*, Philadelphia 1913.

Mori, M., Ogawa, H., Yoshikawa M. (eds), *Near Eastern Studies. Dedicated to H.I.H. Prince Takahito Mikasa on the Occasion of His Seventy-Fifth Birthday*, *BMECCJ* 5, Wiesbaden 1991.

Müller-Kessler, Ch., "Aramäische Beschwörungen und Astronomische Omina in nachbabylonischer Zeit. Das Fortleben mesopotamischen Kultur im Vorderen Orient", in: J. Renger (ed.), *Babylon: Focus Mesopotamicher Geschichte. Wiege früher Gelehrsamkeit, Mythos der Moderne, 2. Internationales Colloquium der Deutschen Orient-Gesellschaft, 24.–26. März 1998 in Berlin*, Saarbrücken 1999, p. 427-443.

Müller-Kessler, Ch., Kessler, K., "Spätbabylonische Gottheiten in spätantiken mandäischen Texten", *ZA* 89 (1999), p. 65-87.

Myhrman, D. W., "Die «Labartu»-Texte, babylonische Beschwörungsformeln gegen die Dämonin «Labartu»", *ZA* 15 (1902), p. 141 ff.

Nakata, I., *Deities in the Mari Texts: Complete Inventory of all the Information on the Deities found in the published Old Babylonian Cuneiform Texts from Mari and Analytical and Comparative Evaluation thereof with regard to the official and popular Pantheons of Mari*, Diss. Columbia Univ., 1974.

Nashef, Kh., *Die Orts- und Gewässernamen der mittelbabylonische Zeit*, RGTC 5, Wiesbaden 1992.

Nassouhi, E., "Textes divers relatifs à l'histoire de l'Assyrie", *MAOG* III/1-2 (1927).

Nesbit, W. M., *Sumerian Records from Drehem*, Columbia University Oriental Studies 8, New York 1914.

Nöldecke, A. von, Falkenstein, A., Haller, H., Heinrich, A. V., Lenzen, E., *Neuntern vorläufiger Bericht über die von der Deutschen Forschungsgemeinschaft in Uruk-Warka unternommen Ausgrabungen*, APAW XI, Berlin 1938.

Nougayrol, J., "Textes hépatoscopiques d'époque ancienne conservés au Musée du Louvre (III)", *RA* XLIV (1950), p. 1-44.

Nougayrol, J., "«Vocalises» et «Syllabes en liberté» à Ugarit", AS 16, Chicago 1965, p. 29-39.

Oppenheim, L., *Catalogue of the Cuneiform Tablets of the Wilberforce Eames Babylonian Collection in the New York Public Library*, New Haven 1948.

Oppenheim, L., "The Golden Garments of the God", *JNES* 8 (1949), p. 172-193.

Otten, H., *Texte aus Stadtplanquadrat L/18*, KBo XII, Berlin 1963.

Owen, D. I., Young, G. D., "Ur III Texts in the Zion Research Library, Boston", *JCS* 23 (1970), 95-115

Page, S., "A New Boundary Stone of Merodach-Baladan I", *Sumer* 23 (1967), p. 45-67, Pl. 1-6.

Parker, B., "The Nimrud Tablets", *Iraq* 16 (1954), p. 29-58.

Parker, B., "The Nimrud Tablets", *Iraq* 19 (1957), p. 125-138.

Parpola, S., *Assyrian Prophecies*, SAA IX, Helsinki 1992.

Parpola, S., *Letters from Assyrian and Babylonian Scholars*, SAA X, Helsinki 1993.

Parpola, S., *Letters from Assyrian Scholars to the Kings Esarhaddon and Assurbanipal*, AOAT 5/1, Neukirchen-Vluyn 1970.

Parpola, S., Watanabe, K. (eds), *Neo-Assyrian Treaties and Loyalty Oath*, SAA II, Helsinki 1988.

Parpola, S., Whiting, R. M. (eds), *Sex and Gender in the Ancient Near East. Proceedings of the 47th RAI, Helsinki, July 2-6, 2001*, Helsinki 2002.

Pettinato, G., "Lipit-Eštar e la dea Nanaja", AOAT 253, Münster 1998, p. 267-279.

Pinches, T. G., *Neo-Babylonian and Achaemenid Economic Texts*, CT 55-57, London 1982.

Pinches, T. G., Rawlinson, C. H., *A Selection from the Miscellaneous Inscriptions of Assyria* V, London 1875.

Poebel, A., *Babylonian Legal and Business Documents from the Time of the First Dynasty of Babylon, chiefly from Nippur*, BE VI/2, Philadelphia 1909.

Pomponio, F., *Nabû. Il culto e la figura di un dio del Pantheon babilonese ed assiro*, Studi Semitici 51, Roma 1978.

Pongratz-Leisten, B., *Ina šulmi īrub. Die Kulttopographische und ideologische Programmatik der* akitu-*Prozession in Babylonien und Assyrien im 1. Jahrtausend v.Chr.*, BaghForsch 16, Mainz 1994.

Pongratz-Leisten, B., Kühne, H., Xella, P., *Ana šadî Labnāni lū allik. Beiträge zur altorientalischen und mittelmeerischen Kulturen. Festschrift für Wolfgang Röllig*, AOAT 247, Neukirchen-Vluyn 1997.

Potts, D. T., "Nana in Bactria", S.R.A.A. VII (2001), p. 23-35.

Pritchard, J. B., *The Ancient Near East Supplementary Texts and Pictures relating to the Old Testament*, Princeton 1969.

Radner, K., *Die neusumerischen Texte aus Tell Šeḫ Hamad*, Berlin 2002.

Ranke, H., *Early Babylonian Personal Names*, Philadelphia 1905.

Reiner, E., "A Sumero-Akkadian Hymn of Nanâ", *JNES* 33/2 (1974), p. 221-236.

Reiner, E., *Šurpu. A Collection of Sumerian and Akkadian Incantations*, *AfO* Beiheft 11, Graz 1958.

Reisner, G., *Sumerisch-babylonische Hymne nach Thontafeln griechischer Zeit*, Berlin 1896.

Renger, J. (ed.), *Babylon: Focus Mesopotamischer Geschichte. Wiege früher Gelehrsamkeit, Mythos in der Moderne, 2. Internationale Colloquium der Deutschen Orient Gesellschaft, 24-26. März 1998 in Berlin*, Saarbrücken 1999.

Renger, J., "Götternamen in der Altbabylonischen Zeit", in: *Heidelberger Studien zum Alten Orient. Adam Falkenstein zum 17. September 1966*, Wiesbaden 1967, p. 137-172.

Renger, J., "Untersuchungen zum Priestertum in der altbabylonischen Zeit, 1. Teil", *ZA* 58 (1967), p. 110-188.

Renger, J., "Untersuchungen zum Priestertum in der altbabylonischen Zeit, 2. Teil", *ZA* 59 (1969), p. 104-230.

Richter, Th., *Untersuchungen zu den Lokalen Panthea Süd- und Mittelbabyloniens in altbabylonischer Zeit*, AOAT 257, Münster 1999.

Riva, R. da, *Der Ebabbar-Tempel von Sippar in frühneubabylonischen Zeit (640-580 v. Chr.)*, AOAT 291, Münster 2002.

Riva, R. da, "Pfründen in Eanna in der Zeit der Unruhe", *AfO* 50 (2003/2004), pp. 245-254.

Roberts, J. J. M., *The Earliest Semitic Pantheon. A Study of the Semitic Deities attested in Mesopotamia before Ur III*, Baltimore – London 1972.

Römer, W. H. Ph., Hecker, K., *Religiöse Texte. Lieder und Gebete* I, TUAT II/5, Gütersloh 1989

Rost, P., *Die Keilschrifttexte Tiglat-Pilesers III* II, Leipzig 1853.

Rost, P., "Untersuchungen zur altorientalischen Geschichte", *MVAG* 2/II (1897), p. 108 ff.

Roth, M., Farber, W., Stolper M. W., Bechtolsheim, P. von (eds), *Studies Presented to R. D. Biggs, June 4, 2004*, AS 27, Chicago 2007.

Rutten, M., *Contrats de l'époque séleucides conservés au Musée du Louvre*, Paris 1935.

Sack, R. H., *Cuneiform Documents from the Chaldean and Persian Periods*, London 1994.

Sack, R. H., "Some Remarks on Jewelry Inventories from Sixth Century B.C. Erech", *ZA* 69/1 (1979), p. 41-46.

Sallaberger, W., *Der Kultische Kalender der Ur III-Zeit*, Bd. 1-2, Berlin 1993.

Salonen A., Çig, M., Kızılyay, D., *Die Puzriš-Dagan Texte der Istanbuler Archäologischen Museen*, Teil I, Helsinki 1954.

Sanati-Müller, Sh., "Texte aus dem Sînkāšid-Palast. Erster Teil", *BaghM* 19 (1988), p. 513-515 (nr 30), p. 538 (nr 43).

Sanati-Müller, Sh., "Texte aus dem Sînkāšid-Palast. Zweiter Teil", *BaghM* 20 (1989), p. 290 (nr 71).

Sanati-Müller, Sh., "Texte aus dem Sînkāšid-Palast. Dritter Teil", *BaghM* 21 (1990), p. 138-140 (nr 89), p. 177 (nr 123), p. 180-181 (nr 126), p. 182 (nr 127), p. 186 (nr 131), p. 191-193 (nr 135), p. 202-203 (nr 142), p. 206 (nr 145), p. 209 (nr 148), p. 211 (nr 150).

Sanati-Müller, Sh., "Texte aus dem Sînkāšid-Palast. Viertel Teil", *BaghM* 22 (1991), p. 316-317, 320 (nr 154), p. 317-318, 320 (nr 155), p. 323-325 (nr 159), p. 328-329 (nr 162), p. 329-330 (nr 163).

Sanati-Müller, Sh., "Texte aus dem Sînkāšid-Palast. Fünfter Teil", *BaghM* 23 (1992), p. 126 (nr 166), p. 157 (nr 192), p. 160-161 (nr 195, 196, 197).

Саркисиян, Г. Х., "Манумиссии в селевкидско-аршакидском Уруке", Древний Восток 5, p. 41-56.

Sauren, H., "Les fêtes néo-sumériennes et leurs périodicité", in: CRRAI 17 (1969), p. 11-29.

Sauren, H., *Les tablettes cunéiformes de l'époque d'Ur des collections de la New York Public Library*, PIOL 19, Louvain-la-Neuve 1978.

Schaeffer, F. A., *Le palais royal d'Ugarit* IV, Paris 1956.

Scheil, V., "Contrat babylonien à légende araméenne", *RA* XI (1914), p. 183-187.

Scheil, V., *Textes élamites-sémitiques, troisième série*, MDP VI, Paris 1905.

Scheil, V., *Textes élamites-sémitiques, quatrième série*, MDP X, Paris 1908.

Schneider, N., *Die Drehem- und Djoḫatexte im Kloster Montserrat (Barcelona)*, AnOr 7, Roma 1932.

Schneider, N., *Die Götternamen von Ur III*, AnOr 19, Roma 1939.

Schroeder, O., "Ein neuer Götterlistentypus aus Assur", *ZA* 33 (1921), p. 123-147.

Schroeder, O., *Keilschrifttexte aus Assur verschiedenen Inhalts*, Leipzig 1920.

Schroeder, O., *Vorderasiatische Schriftdenkmäler XV*, Leipzig 1916.

Schwemer, D., "Ein akkadischer Liebeszauber aus Hattuša", *ZA* 94/1 (2004), p. 59-79.

Seidl, U., *Die babylonischen Kudurru-Reliefs*, Freiburg 1989.

Selz, G., *Untersuchungen zur Götterwelt des altsumerischen Stadtstaates von Lagaš*, Philadelphia 1995.

Seux, M.-J., *Hymnes et prières aux dieux de Babylonie et d'Assyrie*, Paris 1976.

Seux, M.-J., "Notes brèves 5", *RA* LXIII (1969), p. 95.

Seyrig, H., "Sur un bas-relief de Tang-i Sarvak", *Syria* XLVII (1970), p. 91-116.

Sigrist, M., *Drehem*, Bethesda 1992.

Sigrist, M., *Documents from Tablet Collections in Rochester*, New York – Bethesda 1991.

Sigrist, M., *Isin Year Names*, Berrien Springs 1988.

Sigrist, M., "Le deuil pour Šu-Sin", in: Studies Sjöberg, Philadelphia 1989, p. 499-505.

Sigrist, M., *Les* sattukku *dans l'Ešumeša durant la période d'Isin et Larsa*, Malibu 1984.

Sigrist, M., *Neo-Sumerian Account Texts in the Horn Archaeological Museum*, AUCT 1-3, Berrien Spring 1984-88.

Sigrist, M., *Tablettes du Princeton Theological Seminary. Epoque d'Ur III*, Philadelphia 1990

Sigrist, M., Owen, D. J., Young, G. D., *The John Frederick Lewis Collection*, Part II, MSL XIII, Roma 1984.

Simmons, S. B., *Early Old Babylonian Documents*, YOS 14, New Haven – London 1978.

Sjöberg, A. W., "Miscellaneous Sumerian Texts II", *JCS* 29/1 (1977), p. 16-27.

Smith, G., Rawlinson, H. C., *A Selection from the Miscellaneous Inscriptions of Assyria* III, London 1870.

Snell, D. C., "A Neo-Babylonian Colophon", *RA* LXXXVIII (1994), p. 59-63.

Soden, W. von, *Akkadisches Handwörterbuch*, Wiesbaden 1959-1981.

Soden, W. von, "Altbabylonische Dialektdichtungen", *ZA* 44 (1938), p. 26-44.
Soden, W. von, "Ein Zwiegespräch Hammurabis mit einer Frau", *ZA* 49/NF 15 (1949), p. 151-194.
Soden, W. von, *Grundriss des akkadischen Grammatik*, AnOr 33, Roma 1952.
Soldt, W. H. van, *Letters in the British Museum*, AbB 12, Leiden 1990.
Sollberger, E., "A Three-Column *Silbenvokabular A*", AS 16, Chicago 1965, p. 21-28.
Sollberger, E., Kupper, J.-R., *Inscriptions royales sumériennes et akkadiennes*, Paris 1971.
Speleers, L., *Catalogue des intailles et impreintes orientales des Musées Royaux du Cinquantenaire*, Bruxelles 1917.
Spycket, A., *Les statues de culte dans les textes mésopotamiens des origine à la Ire dynastie de Babylone*, Paris 1968.
Stamm, J. J., *Die akkadische Namengebung*, Leipzig 1939.
Starr, I. (ed.), *Queries to the Sungod. Divination and Politics in Sargonic Assyria*, SAA IV, Helsinki 1990.
Steiner, R., "The Aramaic Text in Demotic Script: The Liturgy of a New Year's Festival Imported from Bethel to Syene by Exiles from Rash", *JAOS* 11 (1991), p. 362-363.
Stol, M., "Nanaja", RlA IX, p. 146-151.
Stol, M., "Nanea", DDD, p. 1152-1155.
Stolarczyk, M., "Akadyjski liryk miłosny", *Przegląd Orientalistyczny* 1986/1-2, p. 69-73.
Strassmaier, J. N., *Inschriften von Nabonidus, König von Babylon*, BT 1-4, Leipzig 1889.
Strassmaier, J. N., *Inschriften von Nabuchodonosor, König von Babylon (609-561 v.Chr.)*, BT 5, BT 6A, Leipzig 1889.
Strassmaier, J. N., *Inschriften von Cambyses, König von Babylon*, BT 8-9, Leipzig 1890.
Strassmaier, J. N., *Inschriften von Cyrus, König von Babylon*, BT 7, Leipzig 1890.
Streck, M., *Assurbanipal und die letzten assyrischen Könige bis zum Untergang Niniveh's*, Teil I-III, Leipzig 1916.
Sweet, R. F. G., "Sumerian Tablets in the National Museum of Man, Ottawa", *ARRIM* 1 (1983), p. 25-26.

Szczepański, W., *Najstarsze cywilizacje Wschodu klasycznego. Babilon*, Warszawa – Lwów 1923.
Tallqvist, K., *Akkadische Götterepitheta*, Helsingorsiae 1938.
Tallqvist, K., *Neubabylonische Namenbuch*, Helsingfors 1905.
Tanabe, K., "NANA ON LION – East and West in Sogdian Art", *Orient* XXX-XXXI (1995), p. 309-334.
Teixidor, J., *The Pantheon of Palmyra*, Leiden 1979.
Thompson, R. C., *Cuneiform Texts from Babylonian Tablets*, vol. 22, London 1905.
Thureau-Dangin, F., "Un acte de donation de Marduk-zâkir-šumi", *RA* XVI (1919), p. 117-141.
Thureau-Dangin, F., "Un barillet d'Assarhaddon", *RA* XI (1914), p. 96-101.
Thureau-Dangin, F., *Lettres et contrats de l'époque de la première dynastie babylonienne*, TCL I, Paris 1910.
Thureau-Dangin, F., *Tablettes d' Uruk*, Paris 1921.
Toorn, K. van der, *Family Religion in Babylonia, Syria and Israel. Studies in the History and Culture of Ancient Near East*, Leiden 1996.
Toorn, K. van der *et al.* (eds), *The Dictionary of Deities and Demons in the Bible*, Leiden – Boston – Köln 1999.
Tremayne, A., *Records from Erech, Time of Cyrus and Cambyses (538-521 B.C.)*, YOS 7, New Haven 1925.
Unger, E., *Babylon*, Berlin 1970.
Ungnad, A., "Datenlisten", RlA II, p. 165ff
Ungnad, A., *Vorderasiatische Schriftdenkmäler* V, Leipzig 1908.
Ungnad, A., *Vorderasiatische Schritdenkmäler* VI, Leipzig 1908.
Vattioni, F., "Le Inscrizioni di Ḥatra", Suppl n. 28 agli *AION* 14 (1981), fasc. 3, Napoli 1981.
Volk, K., *Die Balağ-Komposition* URU$_2$ AM$_3$-MA-IR-RA-BI, FAOS 18, Stuttgart 1989.
Vollenweider, M.-L., *Catalogue raisonnée des sceaux cylindres et intailles I, Musée d'Art et d'Histoire de Genève*, Genève 1967.
Wasserman, N., "A New Reading in an Old Babylonian Literary Text", *N.A.B.U.* 1992/3, no. 80.

Waterman, L., *Royal Correspondence of the Assyrian Empire*, Ann Arbor 1936.

Watson, P. J., *Catalogue of Cuneiform Tablets in Birmingham City Museum, Neo-Sumerian Texts from Drehem*, vol. 1, Warminster 1986.

Weidner, E. F., "Altbabylonische Götterlisten", *AfK* 2 (1924-1925), p. 1 ff., 71 ff.

Weidner, E. F., "Gazbaba", RlA III, p. 153.

Weidner, E. F., *Handbuch der babylonischen Astronomie* I, Leipzig 1915.

Weiher, E. von, "Marduk-apla-uṣur und Nabû-šum-iškun in einem spätbabylonischen Fragment aus Uruk", *BaghM* 15 (1984), p. 197-224.

Weiher, E. von, *Spätbabylonische Texte aus Uruk* II, Berlin 1982.

Weiher, E. von, *Spätbabylonische Texte aus Uruk* III, Berlin 1988.

Weisberg, D. B., *Texts from the Time of Nebuchadnezzar*, YOS 17, New Haven – London 1980.

Weisberg, D. B., "The Late Babylonian Texts of the Oriental Institute Collection", Bib. Mes. 24, Malibu 1991.

West, D. R., *Some Cults of Greek Goddesses and Female Demons of Oriental Origin*, AOAT 233, Neukirchen-Vluyn 1995.

Westenholz, J. G., "Nanaya: Lady of Mystery", in: I. L. Finkel, M. J. Geller (eds), *Sumerian Gods and their Representations*, CM 7, Groningen 1997, p. 57-84.

Westenholz, J. G., "The Clergy of Nippur: The Priestess of Enlil", in: CRRAI 35, p. 297-310.

Westenholz, J. G., "The True Shepherd of Uruk", in: M. T. Roth *et al.* (eds), *Studies Presented to R. D. Biggs, June 4, 2004*, AS 27, Chicago 2004, p. 305-324.

Whiting, R. M., "An Old Babylonian Incantation from Tell Asmar", *ZA* 75/2 (1985), p. 179-183.

Wilcke, C., "Die Inschriftenfunde der 7. und 8. Kampagnen", in: B. Hrouda (ed.), ISIN-IŠĀN BAHRĪYĀT III, *Die Ergebnisse der Ausgrabungen 1983 -1984*, München 1987.

Wilcke, C., "Nanāja-šamḫats Rechtsstreit um ihre Freiheit", in: Fs Röllig, AOAT 247, Neukirchen-Vluyn 1997, p. 413-429.

Wilcke, Cl., "Liebesbeschwärungen aus Isin", *ZA* 75/2 (1985), p. 188-209.

Winckler, H., *Sammlung von Keilschrifttexten II*, Leipzig 1894.
Wiseman, D. J., Black, J. A., *Literary Texts from the Temple of Nabû*, London 1996.
Yarshater, E. (ed.), "Anāhīd", in: *Encyclopaedia Iranica*, vol. 1/2, p. 1003-1011.
Yıldız, F., Waetzoldt, H., Renner, H. (eds), *Die Umma-Texte aus den Archäologischen Museen zu Istanbul. Nr. 1-600*, MVN XIV, Romae 1988.
Zadok, R., "An Achaemenid queen", *N.A.B.U.* 2002/3, nr 65.
Zadok, R., *Geographical Names according to New- and Late-Babylonian Texts*, RGTC 8, Wiesbaden 1985.
Zadok, R., "West Semitic Material in Neo-Babylonian and Neo-Assyrian Sources", *N.A.B.U.* 1998/2, nr 56.
Zadok, R., *The Elamite Onomasticon*, Napoli 1984.
Zadok, R., "Updating the Apammu Dossier", *N.A.B.U.* 2003/2, nr 33.
Zeebari-Al, A., *Altbabylonische Briefe des Iraq Museums*, Münster 1964.
Zimmern, H. *Sumerische Kultlieder aus altbabylonischer Zeit*, VS X, Leipzig 1913.
Zimmern, H., "Zum babylonischen Neujahrsfest", *BSGW* 58 (1906), p. 126 ff.
Zólyomi, G., "Two newly identified fragments from ISET 1", *N.A.B.U.* 2003/4, no. 91.